Island Time

Island Time

Speed and the Archipelago from St. Kitts and Nevis

JESSICA SWANSTON BAKER

The University of Chicago Press

Chicago and London

The University of Chicago Press, Chicago 60637
The University of Chicago Press, Ltd., London
© 2024 by The University of Chicago
Published 2024

33 32 10 30 29 28 27 26 25 24   1 2 3 4 5

ISBN-13: 978-0-226-83728-4 (cloth)
ISBN-13: 978-0-226-83730-7 (paper)
ISBN-13: 978-0-226-83729-1 (e-book)
DOI: https://doi.org/10.7208/chicago/9780226837291.001.0001

Library of Congress Cataloging-in-Publication Data

Names: Baker, Jessica Swanston, author.
Title: Island time : speed and the archipelago from St. Kitts and Nevis /
    Jessica Swanston Baker.
Other titles: Chicago studies in ethnomusicology.
Description: Chicago : The University of Chicago Press, 2024. | Series: Chicago
    studies in ethnomusicology | Includes bibliographical references and index.
Identifiers: LCCN 2024022975 | ISBN 9780226837284 (cloth) | ISBN 9780226837307
    (paperback) | ISBN 9780226837291 (ebook)
Subjects: LCSH: Popular music—Social aspects—Saint Kitts and Nevis. | Popular
    music—Social aspects—Caribbean Area.
Classification: LCC ML3917.S25 B35 2024 | DDC 306.4/84240972973
LC record available at https://lccn.loc.gov/2024022975

Contents

Preface

I did not set out to write a book about fast music in St. Kitts and Nevis. This research began as an effort to learn more about my paternal grandfather, Simeon "Santoy" Swanston. After Santoy's untimely death in 1964, all his personal effects were lost and the pain surrounding his passing, and the subsequent upheaval it caused my grandmother and his nine remaining children cemented a silence around him and his short life. This changed significantly when, in 2007, my father received recordings of Santoy performing three calypsos from a family member in Nevis. The tracks, we would come to learn, were the result of ethnographic projects undertaken separately by the music and folklore researchers Alan Lomax and Roger Abrahams in the summer of 1962.

From April to August 1962, Alan Lomax traveled across twelve Caribbean islands, including Anguilla, St. Barthélemey, Carriacou, Dominica, Grenada, Guadeloupe, Martinique, St. Lucia, Trinidad and Tobago, and St. Kitts and Nevis, with the intention of capturing the array interrelated musical expressions across the region. Ultimately, Lomax believed that the recordings might have supported decolonial political desires to unite the islands of the Caribbean into an archipelagic national state. The folklorist Roger D. Abrahams, with funding from the University of Texas, spent one week of his longer fieldwork recording local musical and dramatic performances alongside Lomax in St. Kitts and Nevis. Abrahams's focus was on the gamut of expressive forms, including games, speeches, jokes, and riddles, as well as different types of functional and more popular songs that he saw as an interrelated part of the dispersed Afro-descendant people of the Americas. In the process of expanding his research on male performance traditions in Afro-America, Abrahams was largely interested in comparing forms and styles of performance with those he encountered in his hometown of Philadelphia.

Despite their complementary aims, there were problems in Lomax and Abrahams working together, especially with regard to their approaches to soliciting performances. As Abrahams described it: "The differences between Alan's technique of eliciting performances and mine also were unsettling. . . . I was used to bringing with me the kinds of provisions that Nevisians like but often could not afford: sardines and other canned goods, refined sugar and flour. After the Lomaxes left, however, field work became that much more difficult; each session had to involve a discussion of why I was not able to pay cash."[1] Despite their conflicts, Lomax's and Abrahams' combined efforts in St. Kitts and Nevis resulted in more than sixty hours of recorded sound and hundreds of photographs. Copies of the recordings, as well as relevant field notes, were both deposited in the University of the West Indies and brought back to New York City with Lomax. After he became the founding director of the University of Pennsylvania's Center for Folklore and Ethnography, Abrahams's field notes and some recordings were deposited into the archives of the University of Pennsylvania Museum.

In the spring of 2010, during my first year of graduate school, I spent several hours digging through the uncataloged piles of Abrahams's Caribbean field notes. In one of the clumsily packed boxes, in the upper-right-hand corner of the last page of one of his field journals from June 1962, was a note that read "Santoy-Sardines." I was exhilarated. I had known my grandfather only through brief mentions of his name and had heard of his exceptional musicality and artistic talent. This proof of his life gestured toward the possibility that there was more to know, not only for myself but also for my father, who had expressly asked me to find out more about him through my "research."

While copies of the field recordings made by Lomax and Abrahams were deposited into institutional libraries and archives, those recordings were available primarily to researchers and academics. And then, of course, the recordings were available only to those who knew they even existed. However, between 1999 and 2001, seventeen CDs of various performances from the twelve islands Lomax visited during his 1962 trip were curated as part of a world music series of ethnographic recordings through Rounder Records. *Caribbean Voyage: Nevis and St. Kitts Tea Meetings, Christmas Sports and the Moonlight Night* was one album from that collection. The CDs were compiled by the Association of Cultural Equity, founded by Alan Lomax in 1983 to "stimulate cultural equity through preservation, research, and dissemination of the world's traditional music, and to reconnect people and communities with their creative heritage."[2]

In 2005, after spending three years digitizing the complete collection of Lomax's Caribbean research, and in collaboration with the Center for Black

Music Research of Columbia College Chicago, the Association of Cultural Equity pioneered an effort to repatriate copies of the original recordings to preservation societies and archives on the eastern Caribbean islands from which they came.[3] Among the first of these efforts took place in St. Kitts and Nevis, where CDs and prints of supporting materials—which included the *Nevis and St. Kitts* CD and accompanying liner notes—were deposited in the public archives of the Nevis Historical and Conservation Society in Charlestown, Nevis.

My interest in the music of St. Kitts and Nevis is tied directly to Santoy, who was featured prominently on the *Caribbean Voyage* collection, singing three of the thirty-one tracks on the album. During my initial fieldwork trips to St. Kitts and Nevis in 2010, I spent time locating and interviewing musicians (most of whom were in their eighties) to learn more about my grandfather and the social context of his life. These musicians, like the Nevisian fifer David Freeman, were active during a pivotal moment in Caribbean performance. As Gage Averill has described, the early 1960s was "the last era in which a generation of superb performers carried on traditions that they had inherited from their parents and from their parents before them. These patterns of intergenerational transmission of expressive culture were radically disrupted in the 1960s by the migration of rural residents to the cities and from the cities to the colonial metropoles in search of work, by the passing on of performers, and by the explosion of mediated cultural consumption in the decades following Lomax's voyage."[4] Many of my octogenarian interlocutors, while invested in establishing a genealogy of folk tradition, were most vocal in their lamentation of the state of current music—"music of today." I pivoted my research questions to focus on contemporary music, like wylers and soca, and contemporary iterations of carnival, which were a more pressing site of discourse around experiences of intergenerational change.

My desire to write a book about St. Kitts and Nevis, especially the music of those islands, still stems from a desire—a familial obligation, really—to do some of the legitimizing work that would insert Santoy and the everyday creativity and performance of poor Black people from small places into a larger history of Caribbean music. This kind of legitimizing work, which comes especially through writing—committing oral histories and experiences to text—and contributing to a lasting archive is also a part of my generational inheritance as a daughter of the Leeward archipelago. What I know of my mother's side of the family came to me through the ritual retelling of stories, anecdotes, and musings and also through booklets and occasional essays written by uncles and cousins, emailed to the family list, or self-published and disseminated for commemorative purposes. My knowledge of my father's side of the family has come to me through a more ephemeral archive of sonic and gestural inheritances. This repository, comprising mostly of intangibles like my knack for improvised vocal harmony and the specific texture of my vibrato, also includes material fragments like the beginning of a calypso my dad scrawled on the back of a program booklet.

I have been traveling to St. Kitts and Nevis regularly since the 1990s, when I was a small child accompanying my parents and other family members on their sojourns home. Those early trips, though not exactly fieldwork, were not entirely uncritical vacations, either. My parents and extended family members have always been clear and direct about my generation's responsibility to uphold traditions of family cohesion, to know where we are from, and to write and speak (and achieve) ourselves into history. While the sentiments behind this praxis of generational inheritance are uplifting, the task of following through and utilizing my training as an ethnomusicologist to tell stories about who we are, were, and could be sits, at times quite uncomfortably, between intellectual and familial imperatives.

A Note on St. Kitts and Nevis: Two Islands under One Flag

Roger Abrahams, whose work is central to my understanding of the history of Kittitian and Nevisian artistic productions (not least because his handwritten note is among the few relics of my grandfather's life) has described the relationship between St. Kitts and Nevis as "a strange, antagonistic symbiosis."[5] Much of the character of the relationship can be traced to the earliest days of French and English colonization of those islands, which at their closest points sit just two and a half miles apart. In 1862, the governor of the Leeward Islands described the relationship between people of St. Kitts and Nevis by saying, "A gentleman of Nevis says it is his duty to abhor everything belonging to St. Kitts, which, he adds, is the faith of all true Nevisians."[6] In 1883, all the governing authority of St. Kitts, Nevis, and Anguilla was located in St. Kitts, which was one source of the ongoing friction between the two islands.[7] More recently, on August 10, 1998, tensions came to one of the most explosive heads in their history when a referendum was held in response to the government of Nevis's efforts to secede from St. Kitts and form its own independent country. While the attempt at secession failed, talk of it, and of the presumed inherent and distinct differences between Kittitians and Nevisians, is still as prevalent as ever, particularly as Nevis maintains relative governmental autonomy and its own separate board of tourism.

Academic attention to these islands has often embraced the idea that, despite being linked by a governmental agreement, the distinctive geographic boundaries of each one provide a more logical framework for intellectual exploration. Notably, Nevis has been the focal point for much ethnographic work, whereas St. Kitts has been subject to more biological, zoological, and archaeological investigations.[8] These closely laid islands share rich musical and performance traditions and are frequently inhabited in tandem. As the daughter of a Kittitian and a Nevisian, I take St. Kitts–Nevis as cohesive cultural unit. One of my aims is to support and buoy future research, facilitating more nuanced examinations of the diverse facets of these island locales as both individual spaces and a functional archipelago.

Introduction

Fortified by a few hours of sleep and buzzing with the energy of cousin kinship, I was guided with my cousin Darnel and my husband, Harrison, through the dark morning by wind-carried pulses of the buoyantly syncopated percussion and bubble-pop sounds of wylers—a style of sonic revelry emanating from bands, electronic producers, and their dancing publics in the small Leeward Islands of St. Kitts and Nevis. When we arrived at our destination, our crew of three grew as family and friends, schoolmates, and neighbors gathered among other kin and peer groups in the parking lot. The powerful speakers were already stacked and strapped onto the decorated float. Several men were mixing big handles of rum and vodka with much smaller containers of tropical fruit juices in fifty-five-gallon blue-plastic drums. Blaring riffs overlapped into a sonic maelstrom. Bursts of whistle, banjo, steel pan, and cowbell timbres—emblems of Kittitian-Nevisian carnival—were flying and twisting in and out of the gathered sound as the pitch and tempo climbed collectively and inexorably over the next forty or so minutes of the "warm-up." As the music chased intensity, we pursued levity; we gathered alongside the mobile stage and passed our opaque plastic bottles up to men who dunked them, two at a time, into the sweet concoction. The slow pep (a slowed-down wylers riddim, often played at the beginning of a party or jam session) emphasized a sense of anticipation. The mixture of sound and spirits primed jammers for the following eight consecutive hours of party and play in motion.

Starting up the Bay Road, the DJ began playing what would be that year's winning road march song, "Do the DCH"—drop, cover, hold on—by the Small Axe Band, as we traveled toward the official parade route. This song, which draws at least one layer of meaning from a public service announcement produced by the Caribbean Disaster Emergency Management Agency, also melodically quotes the 1988 pop song "Kokomo" by the Beach Boys. With syrupy lyrics about a vacation romance, the original song centers Kokomo, a fictional island off the shore of Key West, Florida. The playful and repetitive stepwise motion of the chorus was transferred into a bridgelike section in the Small Axe Band's version:

> Can you feel it? You feel it? Tell me can you feel it? (4×)
> Earthquake a come, do the DCH. (4×)
> Drop. Cover. Hold on! (4×)

The island imagery of Kokomo, a place where one can "get there fast" and then "take it slow" is mirrored and reversed by the undulating mass of jammers who sang and danced along with the hook, or "chant." The parade route is only about a mile long, but we traversed it over the course of five hours, moving fast but going virtually nowhere. The energy in the crowd was panoramic as the preprogrammed backing track of the riddim (and rum) took us higher.

The energetic road jams that are the most ubiquitous part of modern carnival in St. Kitts–Nevis begin with J'ouvert (*joo-vay*), the predawn, Boxing Day celebration prevalent in much of the Anglicized Caribbean.[1] Around 4 a.m. on December 26, people from around the island and across various expanses of the sea, gather in Basseterre to dance, sing, and parade slowly through the streets. Carnival, like most big events, is the product of year-round planning, both by government organizations like the National Carnival Committee and by networks of individual celebrants and participants who infuse the annual celebration with various acts of creative enterprise. J'ouvert is just one of the street activities that makes up Sugar Mas, the St. Kitts–Nevis National Carnival.[2] Others include Children's Carnival (December 31), the New Year's Day "Grand Parade" (January 1), and "last lap" (January 2), which is the final jam (i.e., dance) session parade that ends the carnival season. The various J'ouvert and New Year's parade troupes follow a particular float as it lurches down the road, following the prescribed parade route. On each float there is a DJ or a live band surrounded by an array of massive speakers, stacked each on top of the other, that play the popular tunes that have registered to be part of the road march competition for that year.[3]

Carnivalgoers who wish to participate in J'ouvert or the Grand Parade choose from several troupes, which are differentiated by their colorful and playfully themed costumes (fig. 0.1). Each preceding October or November, the troupes reveal that year's theme with a festive fashion show event. J'ouvert troupes are generally more informal than Grand Parade troupes and, unlike the feathered and bedazzled bikini and fishnet ensembles that have

FIGURE 0.1. J'ouvert 2016–2017, lurching float (*foreground*) and stacked speakers (*background*) surrounding the Tribal Devils troupe, December 26, 2016. Photo by the author.

characterized Grand Parade costumes since the 1990s, J'ouvert uniforms for paid troupe members include a T-shirt, shorts, a whistle, a water bottle, a bandanna, and other playful accoutrements relating to the year's theme, such as a set of plastic devil ears, a glowing toy light saber, and a drawstring backpack. These J'ouvert essentials were included in my corporate sponsored J'ouvert package, along with the promise of "unlimited premium liquor," for a fee of $85 (about US$32), when I joined the Glow Devils troupe for J'ouvert in 2012.[4]

The Glow Devils were just one of a handful of troupes that amassed hundreds of people into temporary communities in motion. Glowing in the dark with our devil ears and plastic sabers lighting the way through town, we jammed down the Bay Road, passing the tourist port, Port Zante, St. George's Anglican Church, and the Circus—a large clock and roundabout just like the one in Bath, England (one of many colonial remnants). Mostly younger people, from young teenagers to those in their early thirties, danced and jammed, "chooking," "shubbing back," and "wukin" down the road, bursting into momentary demonstrations of skill, flexibility, nonsense, stamina, and sexuality.[5] The chanting together anchored a wildly divergent set of improvisational responses. More than a set of dance moves, DCH, and wylers more broadly, gestures toward an "open specificity" of movements—gestures, interpretations—that proliferate within the crowd.[6] These individual acts demand that other revelers make space, literally and conceptually in order to interpret the act as a gesture in a sea of movement; listen, to the music, to the callings in their own body; and react in ways that both sustain and transfigure the energy powering the exchange.

We are all chanting, "Drop, cover, hold on!" A man wearing inside-out, mismatched pajamas and with a pair of boxer shorts on the outside "drops" into a plank position. Nearby, a young woman flings her leg up in the air and grips her heel to hold it in place. A companion crouches to take "cover" under the jiggling appendage, thrusting her hips back and bopping one leg to make the exposed flesh of her backside jiggle in double time. Initially acting in response, the crouching friend becomes the "call" when a man covered in lime-green paint comes up behind her to "hold on" to her waist. He quickly finds her rhythm and they "wuk up" together for a moment before dispersing into new positions, new relations in motion and sound, new possibilities for interpretation.

If J'ouvert starts in those first hours of Boxing Day, the anticipation begins months before. The wylers bands that have dominated the local St. Kitts and Nevis carnival music scene since the mid-1990s play dozens of live jams, or fetes that introduce the band's sound for that year. These events present a series of opportunities for showcasing and experimenting with a set of riddims and chants that might later be recorded into a song and potentially entered into the official road march competition. Even chants and performances that are never recorded in a studio become part of a small number of live recordings that are uploaded onto file-sharing sites or disseminated as YouTube videos, often with footage from that year's festivities. Sugar Mas, like most other carnival-style festivals in the Caribbean, is one of several "homecoming events for those from the community who have emigrated."[7] The circulation of the recorded sounds and stylings of wylers, and the inevitable discourse oriented around it, participate in processes of home-making for audiences across the diaspora.

For folks like me and Darnel, a generational attachment to the islands of St. Kitts and Nevis as "home" is constituted by what Stuart Hall calls "unstable points of identification, of suture." Our cultural identification with these islands is "constructed through memory, fantasy, narrative and myth," orbiting our ever-shifting relationships to legacies of enslavement, sugar cultivation, carnival, calypso, rum, and respectability, to name a few.[8] Wylers aestheticizes the instability of these attachments and their propensity for rearrangement over and in time. Nowhere is this more apparent than in a 2019 wylers song, "Area Code 869." The anthem was written by the front man of the Nu

Vybes Band, Gregory "Mention" Hobson, as a "culture shock" to "free" Kittitians and Nevisians from old narratives about the island and its people as simply inheritors and not generators of music and culture. Over a speedy riddim, speckled with sounds of a racecar whooshing from ear to ear and high-pitched timbres, articulating microrhythms with the bumpy texture of a pea rolling around in a whistle, Hobson sings:

> Anywhere that we go
> People watching and they asking what you know
> Why the hell we get on so?
> And I tell them, must be the place we born and grow
> Got me, got me hyperactive, we hyperactive
> We come from St. Kitts so sugar in we system

"Sugar in we system" might be an apt description for any part of St. Kitts and Nevis's history since its introduction to the islands in the 1640s (first in Barbados, then St. Kitts, followed by Nevis). Between 1675 and 1740, Nevis was the capital port for the Royal African Company, one of Britain's most prominent slave-trading enterprises that transported the West Africans who would become what the Antigua Legislature of 1788 referred to as "the Main Sinews of a Sugar Plantation" through chattel slavery.[9] Sugar continued to make up the largest portion of the St. Kitts–Nevis economy after emancipation in 1884. St. Kitts–Nevis's first national hero, Robert Llewellyn Bradshaw, began his political career as a sugar machine apprentice in the 1930s. When the following generation inherited the colonial state through independence in 1983, St. Kitts–Nevis was the last sugar monoculture in the eastern Caribbean to shutter its sugar industry, in 2005. During the nationalist lead-up to independence, the celebrated Kittitian calypsonian Ellie Matt coined "Sugar City" to refer to St. Kitts as an eastern Caribbean answer to the "Chocolate City" of Black America.[10] It tracks, then, that the national carnival is known as Sugar Mas, with headquarters each year at a site temporarily renamed the "Sugar Mill" for the season; that the Nu Vybes Band is called "Sugar Band," and the Small Axe Band is dubbed "the sweetest band in the world!"

"Area Code 869" goes a step further, engendering the kind of "nonrecognition" a musical "shock" requires, adding to the already-miraculous reinvention sugar has taken as an emblem of the islands and their people.[11] Casting local attachment to sugar as a source of perennial energy, stamina, and ultimately speed, the song stakes a historical relationship to forced labor on sugar plantations that carries through the high-energy performances and music associated with the islands:

> We full of stamina and energy now for days
> Two brothers on the plantation a cut through the cane
> A so it come along and so it runs in our veins
> In the 869 things, we real, it will never change.

"Area Code 869" wades into the music and cultural debates that circulate in its genre. That things do not change, especially with regard to wylers, is one position staked by wylers musicians and fans as they carve out a sense of legitimacy by appealing to discourses of tradition versus modernity that posit wylers as a continuation of older performance practices, such as the big drum ensembles, masquerade troupes, clowns, string bands, and roving plays that characterized the Christmas sports ("sport" here is a general term for entertainment and play). In contrast, critics of wylers, particularly the aspirational and upper middle classes of the islands with a vested interest in the music's relationship to its representation of the islands' national character, tend to cast the music as a sonic rupture, a deviation from a clearly projected course of musical development prescribed by what Sylvia Wynter called the "bourgeoisie hegemony" that "imposed the form of its expression on every other form in its vicinity."[12]

What conjunctures of history, sound, and experience make a claim as innocuous as "things will never change" so relevant, recurrent, and even controversial, for people in St. Kitts and Nevis? Through what means can the implied relationship of global geopolitics, musical acceleration, nationalist imaginaries, and the lived time of Black bodies be apprehended? And what structures of thought and feeling meaningfully draw these disparate registers of temporality and experience together? *Island Time* queries the popular music of the Leeward Islands, particularly through an examination of the Kittitian Nevisian carnival music, wylers, an energetic and accelerating style of popular music that emerged in the mid-1990s and proliferated throughout the first decades of the twenty-first century. Based on autoethnographic and archival research in St. Kitts and Nevis, this book explores historical anxieties about things and people that are "too fast" in the context of a larger intergenerational discourse that centers preoccupations with and attunement to development and decorum in the postcolonial Anglicized Caribbean.

Attestations to specific kinds of changes, like the speeding up of local music or the uptick in violent crime in the early 2000s, as compared to the political and decolonial concerns of the statehood generation of the mid-twentieth century, played an significant role in the public discourse around the small Leeward Islands of St. Kitts and Nevis in the first two decades of the 2000s. These islands as geographic formations have also been drawn into the discourse of change: the earlier claims of ecological purity and natural, unchanged wonder that have dominated local tourism advertisements since at least the 1980s have also been complicated by increased urbanization, tourism infrastructure, and foreign investment. Especially following the closure of the sugarcane industry in 2005, these changes have affected the landscape, agriculture, soil, and air quality.[13] More charged than the fact of change, a sense of deleterious acceleration pervades musical, epidemiological, social, and political discourses whose formulations insist on behavioral and temporal norms via the criticism of excessive and socially unacceptable behavior. These arguments and their ripples hinge on collective recognition and testament to change, especially as witnessed through the performance practices of West Indian youth, highlighting crucial tensions between imagined trajectories and their perceived deviations, social frictions that disclose the techniques and tactics "employed by people to mitigate the pace, quality, and intensity of change" in St. Kitts and Nevis.[14] Throughout, speed, as a subjective experience of deviation from a projected path, and the inherent island-to-island relationships of the archipelago become formal models bridging the literal and metaphorical. This book posits that these forms capture the intricate linkages and multiscale relations that define music and performance in St. Kitts–Nevis, with broader implications for how we might apprehend the complex time and space of contemporary musicking.[15]

Wylers, as a mobile set of sounds, practices, and aesthetic intentions, is the musical backbone where this book's literal is fused to the metaphorical. Speed, as an experience of change in motion, encapsulates the formal relationship between tempo, as measured by beats per minute; the pace of moving bodies and bodily movements over the course of a life; and the deep and expansive island times that structure musical and social worlds. As in "Area Code 869," a jubilant song about sugar's multiple parameters and their significance, wylers strengthens intergenerational and diasporic attachment to this small two-island nation because it lends phenomenal weight to an undulating set of circumstances specific to postcoloniality, islandness, Blackness, and smallness, unfolding from St. Kitts and Nevis on a global scale.

Unlike other discussions of Caribbean music that often focus on exceptional cases or influences on the US or European cultural landscape, *Island Time* spotlights wylers from a small archipelago in the broader Caribbean context. This perspective revitalizes the exploration of everyday Black aesthetics, such as joking, storytelling, and dancing, in relation to modernity, creativity, and neoliberalism. Ultimately, *Island Time* is not merely a study of St. Kitts and Nevis but an endeavor to map Caribbean music emanating from these islands and to offer a nuanced understanding of its diverse influences across space and time. *Island Time*, then, is not about St. Kitts and Nevis as much as it is an attempt to map Caribbean music, listening from these islands.

From Here

Experiences like the J'ouvert road march, of belonging through singing, dancing, joking, and shared corporeality, are central to my understanding of St. Kitts and Nevis as a place of origin. It was surprising to me, then, when the very terms on which I attempted to engage in conversation about music and performance as being from St. Kitts and Nevis were contested. In the early summer of 2010, I interviewed Creighton Pencheon, then director of the St. Kitts Ministry of Culture. Seated in his office, above the bustling Pelican Mall, where soca played from speakers below and a traveling string band serenaded ambling tourists, I was pleased with the choice, even as a first-year graduate student, to begin my investigation with someone in the know, like a minister of culture. Just as I was about to open my new Moleskine notebook, on which I had written "FIELD NOTES" in big black letters, before I could ask any questions, or describe what I understood my project to be, Mr. Pencheon prefaced our conversation with a simple caveat: "Nothing is really *from* here. Everything we have here is really from somewhere else."[16]

Betraying the sinking feeling growing in my stomach, I smiled and nodded politely as he described his research on the bull character in Jamaican folkloric performance and its role as a precursor to Kittitian and Nevisian iterations of the practice—a beloved feature of Christmas sports.[17] Mr. Pencheon's admission interfaced neatly with anxieties I had inherited. Born and raised in St. Kitts and Nevis, respectively, my mom and dad sat me down before this important trip to suggest that perhaps, if I wanted to research music in the Caribbean, I should go to Haiti, where the exceptionality of the first Black Republic would offer some starting legitimacy; or I could go to Trinidad, where the development of calypso into a world-class art form (not to mention a global pop-culture craze) had produced a whopping canon of research on which to base my own. "Plus," Mom added, "in Trinidad, they have a real university!"

My parents, who still casually check world maps to see that St. Kitts and Nevis have been included, are used to a kind of geographic invisibility that extends to historical absence. Mr. Pencheon's distinction highlighted the unspoken categorical chasm between big, important places we research, and thus know to be sites of origination, invention, and diffusion (Jamaica, Haiti, Trinidad), and smaller places we can safely assume we know because we researched the bigger places—sites of origin. In the intervening decade, I came to understand Mr. Pencheon's summary as background and signpost. His opinion backlit the particular histories of social and historical erasure in the Caribbean while signaling that I should reconsider my affinity toward a "being from" discourse as a powerful unifying conceptual feature in music scholarship.

To know where someone or something, some sound, some music, is from is to understand something foundational and integral to the full essence of the thing even while acknowledging the possibility of infinite iterations. Music and its clusters of objects, including instruments, sounds, and performance practices, to name a relatively small number of things, are no exceptions to the rule. Figuring out where something is from creates a funnel through which all accolades, legitimacy, and far-reaching ramifications can be poured back into their original container. My initial disbelief and impetus to disprove Mr. Pencheon's assertion stemmed from my misunderstanding of what the alternatives to "being from" could be. My emphasis on tracing origins made Mr. Pencheon's statement sound like an admission of inferiority—of St. Kitts and Nevis's historical tangentiality, at best, and Kittitians' and Nevisians' cultural irrelevance at worst. Beyond that, his remarks spurred deeper questions about the nature and scope of the "here" to which he referred.

Archipelagic Geography

The two-island nation of St. Kitts and Nevis is a tiny archipelago in the series of archipelagos that makes up the Caribbean (fig. 0.2). Curving from the tip of Florida, the Caribbean archipelago traces an S shape that alights on the coast of South America. The Greater Antilles, the larger islands of the Caribbean, are the most recognizable to the world at large. Cuba, the largest of the Greater Antilles islands (about 42,426 square miles), sits at the northern edge of the "sunken cordillera"—in the words of the Barbadian poet and philosopher Kamau Brathwaite—of the island chain, about 90 miles north of Jamaica (which is approximately 4,244 square miles). To the east of Cuba is the island of Hispaniola (about 29,418 square miles), shared by Haiti to the west and the Dominican Republic to the east. The main island of Puerto Rico (about 3,515 square miles), the smallest of the Greater Antilles, lies 100 miles east of the Dominican Republic, across the Mona Passage. The scattering of smaller islands that includes St. Kitts and Nevis (68 and 36 square miles, respectively), sweeping from the Virgin Islands in the north to Grenada in the south, make up the Lesser Antilles. Within this archipelago, and riding the boundary between the Caribbean Plate and the Atlantic Ocean floor, a string of volcanic and limestone islands make up the northern part of the Lesser Antilles known as the Leeward Islands.[18]

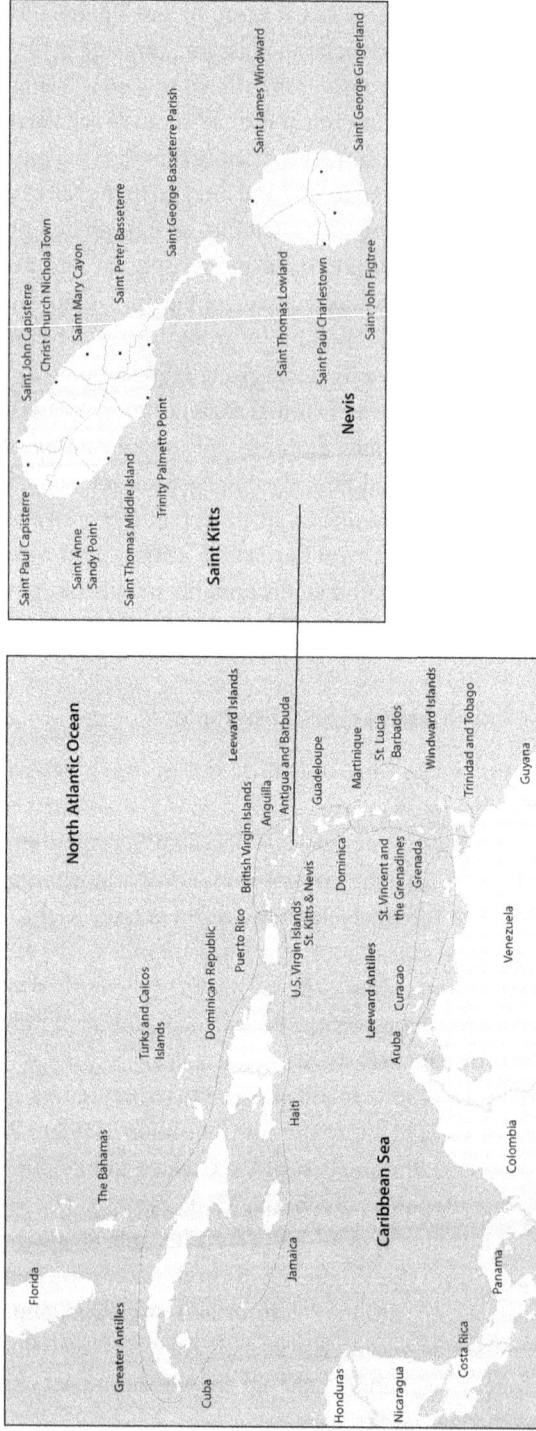

FIGURE 0.2. Maps illustrating "archipelagos of archipelagos," nested archipelagos held simultaneously in the local cartographic imaginary of island time. At left are the islands of the circum-Caribbean, including the small islands of the Leewards. At right is the two-island nation of St. Kitts–Nevis.

The Leeward Islands, which include small islands such as Montserrat (39 square miles), St. Kitts, Nevis, and Antigua (108 square miles), as well as smaller islets and cays, are distinctive in their experiential amplification of the main features of an archipelago. Some sense of proximity (physical or symbolic) is what qualifies a set or group of island entities as an archipelago. St. Kitts and Nevis are, at their closest points, two miles apart. Montserrat, whose namesake serrated peaks are visible from Nevis, is about thirty miles away. On a regular drive up the island's main road, the peaks of Saba and St. Eustatius appear close by. In the small Leeward Islands, this proximity has historically been experienced sensorially through the mutual intervisibility and intertraversability of the island spaces.

Geographically speaking, Mr. Pencheon was right. A lot of things in St. Kitts–Nevis, especially cultural practices, could be traced to other territorial locations.

All the Caribbean islands, Brathwaite's "sunken cordillera," are the product of repeated acts of fragmentation. At the site of its geological formation, more than three hundred million years ago (and over the course of millions of years), tectonic forces broke the Caribbean Plateau from Pangaea, "an ancient mountain range, once part of mainland America, which swung out catastrophically from that double continent's western spine."[19] Although archipelagos like the Caribbean may be understood as a product of a break from a contiguous whole, as Michelle Stephens and Yolanda Martinez-San Miguel remind us, "they are not immanent or natural categories existing independently of interpretation." In other words, "archipelagos happen, congeal, take place."[20] The interpretation overlaid onto the Atlantic world as a product of European colonialism and Western expansion has become the most prevalent episteme for apprehending the Caribbean islands. Nomenclature like "Leeward" and "Windward" refers to trade winds and currents that benefited European exploration and colonization. These islands "rest at an environmental nexus in the greater Atlantic." In particular, "year-round trade winds from Europe as well as a strong oceanic current that pushes northward . . . made the region a key hub for imperial power and regional trade."[21] The English established their first permanent settlement in the Caribbean on St. Kitts in 1623, making the island "ground zero for the spread of Western Imperialism."[22]

Archaeological research has suggested that in the case of the precolonial Amerindian inhabitants, the Leeward Islands were lived between as a unit with a "rhythm" that accounted for weather patterns, availability of food and resources, and political affiliations across the region.[23] The Caribbean Sea, more than a separator of individual islands, is a connector of landed spaces, and "the Lesser Antillean physical setting was conducive to main-taining both extensive and intensive contact across the region."[24] By the time the Leewards were largely inhabited by enslaved Africans (until 1834), the intervisibility and intertraversability of the islands offered some advantage to them, as they could use the steep volcanic mountains as lookouts to see beyond the immediate locality.[25] In an account of an enslaved man, called Frank, in the early eighteenth century, the historian James Dator describes how the close proximity of the British Leeward Islands (Antigua, Montser-rat, Nevis, St. Kitts, and many of the Virgin Islands), facilitated a context that necessitated "adapting to an archipelagic context."[26] These adaptations, forged in the colonial Caribbean "experience of living within the shadow of genocide and unfreedom," included important acts of self-fashioning, such as taking on names that allowed the enslaved to identify themselves as associated with and knowledgeable of regional island spaces. These articulations of island individuality attested to specific "islanded" knowledge that was useful and recognizable in contexts on other nearby islands.

Throughout the twentieth and twenty-first centuries, St. Kitts and Nevis have been included various kinds of archipelagic arrangements: St. Christo-pher, Nevis, and Anguilla were combined as a British colonial administra-tive unit until 1967. In the wake of the demise of the West Indies Federation in 1962, St. Kitts and Nevis were among eight islands—the "Little 8"—that sought regional cooperative agreements across various island polities. Social and familial connections across the Leeward Islands and the wider Caribbean region, including continental "Caribbeanized" locales in the larger Black At-lantic world, are shaped by geography, history, and policy in ways that com-bine and overlap national, linguistic, colonial, and racial distinctions.[27]

Soca: Hearing the Caribbean

While wylers is the genre at the center of this study, it is necessary to ground its idiom in the broader world of Caribbean popular music and Caribbeanist eth-nomusicology. The accepted history of soca treats it as a product of Trinida-dian multicultural nationalism. In the early 1970s, a Trinidadian calypsonian, Lord Shorty (known later as Ras Shorty I), combined the rhythmic patterns of Indian drumming, brought to Trinidad by indentured Indian workers in the early twentieth century, with elements of Afro-Creole calypso to create a new genre that he called "sokah," or the "soul of calypso." This new party- and dance-oriented genre appealed to a younger audience after the calypso craze of the previous decades had waned. In such varied forums as academic texts, online chat rooms, and corner cookshops, Caribbean people have expended a great deal of effort trying to distinguish calypso from soca. Peter Manuel and Michael Largey have suggested that "'soca' is best used specifically to distinguish dance music, as opposed to calypso proper, whose essence remains the text."[28] Offering a more subjective definition, Shannon Dudley has noted that the difference typically boils down to one of "kinetic quality."[29]

"Soca" has become an umbrella term for a swath of Afro-Caribbean party and carnival musics sung in English or a regional Creole language. Soca, and its regional inflections like Barbadian bashment soca, St. Lucian dennery segment, and Kittitian-Nevisian wylers, are examples of postcolonial Caribbean popular music styles that are sonically identifiable by "small and detailed musical gestures."[30] Sonically, wylers can be understood as drawing rhythmic patterns and timbral cues from traditional and folkloric Kittitian-Nevisian musical practices that date to the eighteenth century, with European military rudiments, and stretch through the mid-twentieth century, with the signature "ping-pong" sound of the steel pan.

Lyrically and discursively, soca's material and metaphorical reliance on modes and acts of travel—automobiles, walking, going, running, cycling, jumping, cooking, working, "shubbing," pushing, bending, giving, taking, calling a woman's butt a "bumper," and the importance of "de road"—highlights an implicit relationship to movement, in terms of both the genre's inextricable relationship to dance and larger scales of movement (e.g., migration) as an essential facet of Caribbeanness more broadly. Soca in the Caribbean and its diasporas is a sonic and bodily expression of presence, on de road, in de place, and anywhere else, predicated on mobility—another integral source of kinetic quality. Elaborating this point, and drawing on Heidegger's interpretation of Aristotle's description of place as process constituted by the potential for "proper presence," Michaeline Crichlow argues for an understanding of Caribbean people ("Creole subjects") as "located in, and moving through, ontologies of lived space" and not solely via the effects of the historical past. She brilliantly argues: "It is a banal observation, of course, that Caribbean or Atlantic creolization practices emerge in the context of power imposition of colonial and later the national and developmentalist state, now the instrument of a neoliberal globalization project. However, in all these complexly translated phases of power, we argue that Caribbean sociocultural productions which *present* themselves through cultural and biopolitical strategies and seek to create difference *or* newness . . . are pivotally about assertions of self, affirmations, or rather *a will to place*, inducing a journeying from place to place."[31] In this formulation, being-in-the-world is "engendered by the interaction between vertical demands . . . and the self's horizontal necessities . . . (the struggle for moving one's place-in-time by morphing cultures of power)."[32]

Caribbean bands such as Ellie Matt and the G.I.'s Brass, of St. Kitts, and Imaginations Brass, of St. Thomas, were experimenting freely with creolized genre labels that gestured in the general direction of referential sounds, ideas, and places—cadencelypso, kadans rampa, rocklypso, discolypso, and polcalypso, to name a few. Bands in the English-speaking "down islands" continued to utilize "calypso" as a general lexical marker of their music.[33] Small-island musicians with aspirations of off-island notoriety and professional musicianship benefited from being able to participate in international calypso competitions and hoped to be counted among the skilled and legitimized calypsonians of Trinidad.

By the mid-1970s, a new word, "sokah," had come to represent what was understood as a newly emergent body of sound, fed by streams from India and Afro-Creole traditions from all around the Caribbean. This novel music was marked first by the presence of Indian sonorities (instruments such as the tabla and Hindi vocalizations) sung by an Afro-Creole Trinidadian man, Garfield Blackman, who performed under the name Lord Shorty. The second most salient feature of sokah was the up-tempo feel and the lyrical focus on the body and movement; songs were explicitly about what listeners should feel and do in the moment, and they were less invested in what listeners should think outside of the song's immediate temporality. The emergence of soca was, in part, a response to the global appeal of what would later be called "world music" (in European markets and "world beat" in North America), as demonstrated by the widespread embrace of reggae music in the 1970s and 1980s. Critics of the time feared that soca was "a kind of fast food, mass-produced, slickly packaged and meant for rapid consumption and swift obsolescence."[34]

Despite these fears, in an Anglophone Caribbean landscape dominated sonically and representationally by calypso and reggae, soca indexed an alternative category of West Indian subjectivity. Since its invention, a large suite of West Indian genres of modern movement music (or party music) has found a broad listenership under the label "soca," despite a staggering array of sonic and linguistic difference among them. In this way, soca has been a device for market visibility. More broadly and crucially, the racial, ethnic, geographic, and political import of soca's emergence as a lexical marker can be understood via the "repressed realities" that this ontological category of anticolonial subjectivity buoyed.[35]

This book recognizes the term "soca" and its development not so much as indexing a new sound but as a device that accounts for the errant sonic hybridity of the archipelagic postcolonial West Indies. Following Jocelyne Guilbault's take on music-labeling practices in the Anglophone Caribbean, I regard the generic label "soca" as one of a constellation of "devices which are used . . . to produce statements through which other objects are constructed, and hence, other sets of issues are addressed."[36] The modes of quickly acquiring instruments and digital sound files, the sexually suggestive lyrics, the women who dance with and inspire them, the collapsing of spaces of practice with spaces of performance, the breakneck pace at which ideas are sampled, borrowed, localized, parodied, and recycled from everywhere and turned into material for wylers songs and performances—all these behaviors, these musicking practices on various scale—push up against boundaries of normative temporality in different registers. We might think of soca as Samuel Floyd wrote of all Caribbean music, as "a large and variegated complex of genres." Whereas Sylvia Wynter has argued that Blackness within the Western episteme amounts to the "non-norm," we might consider Black music like soca and its correlates as a temporal and sonic expression, a negotiation of this fundamental aspect of Black experience in the Caribbean.

Where dance is concerned, soca's most identifiable movement is the wine. A creolized pronunciation of "wind," "wining" is the skillful and rhythmic isolation and undulation of a dancer's behind and hips. While some form of hip thrusting and pelvic gyration have characterized many Caribbean dances (e.g., the vacunao of rumba, Garifuna punta dances), the particular manner in which a person wines can signal much about the places and sounds that have entrained the body. In emphasizing this point, the Caribbean dance scholar Adanna Jones quoted one of the "wine connoisseurs" in her research as confident in his ability to map points of origin for various wining bodies. He notes: "I can tell where West Indian women are from. I mean I know how Trini girls does wine, easy. Bajans do more of a wukkin' up, and Grenadian women have like a kinda jab-jab wine, like a jukkin' jukkin' kinda ting. Jamaican women wine a bit more . . . raunchy. And the smaller island countries, like Nevis or St. Kitts, can REL wine. Like di party could jus' start and dey already sweatin', yuh know."[37]

In St. Kitts and Nevis, wining is referred to most commonly as "wuking up," where the labor, or bodily exertion of wining, is referenced plainly as work, or "wuk." That "work" refers to labor, sex, and dancing in a constellation of Black diasporic milieus alludes to the Black body's ability—indeed, its propensity—to be "reclaimed from the world of work" as "a symbol of freedom from the constraints of the discipline of the wage."[38] Soca, in its encouragement of and sonic accompaniment to various forms of wining, participates in a labor of pleasure and self-identification for dancers. As an example of what Paul Gilroy has called the "politics of transfiguration," soca music, in its celebration of revelry, togetherness, and the wuk of pleasure, describes, entrains, and contextualizes "the new modes of friendship, happiness, and solidarity" that could be realized in some version of a subjunctive future or past freedom from the haunting vectors of colonial and postcolonial power.[39]

A Phenomenology of Speed

Island Time presents speed and the archipelago as the central organizing concepts from which a broad range of West Indian performance practices emerge. In so doing, it participates in a project of imagining horizontal alternatives for how we might know, plot, and contextualize Black island time in an archipelagic frame. Speed, as the subjective experience of "a deviation from a projected path," and the archipelago's inherent island-to-island relation offer formal models that inhabit the inlet between the literal and the metaphorical.[40] These forms account for the infinite linkages, connections, and irreducible relations that characterize music in St. Kitts–Nevis and, I suggest, other reverberating acts of creativity across scales of space and time.

But how is speed experienced? In the middle of summer 2010, I spoke with James Phipps, a former brass player who enjoyed the height of his music career amid the orchestral dance music scene of the 1940s and 1950s. Sitting on the cement steps outside his small, two-room home in Taylor's Village, in central Basseterre, I asked him if he had any opinions on the "music of today." With very little hesitation, he responded, "They play *too fast* now." He added, "The women dem, they got their skirts on their heads. Disgraceful. And if you go up to these guys and say, 'I don't like that, play something else,' they look to pull machete and chop you up!"[41]

In the twenty years before our conversation, a period that constituted the contemporary moment for Mr. Phipps, who at the time I interviewed him was in his late eighties, the landscape of local life and music had changed significantly. The prevalence of amplified bands on the carnival scene essentially had overtaken steel pans and smaller string band ensembles as equal participants in the street activities of carnival. The road march competition that had once been the arena of individual calypsonian contenders vying to create the most popular tune had morphed into a competition between youth bands one-upping each other with new sounds to control throngs of amped revelers. Bands that had been playing roots reggae covers began experimenting with drum machines and alternative performances spaces for local audiences who embraced the "jump-up" style of music that would come to be known as wylers.

The Small Axe Band, for example, which began in 1980 as a roots reggae band called Vibrational Roots, was a staple of the relatively small hotel entertainment scene. In the late 1980s, in search of their own sound and local audiences, the seven young men from the rural Old Road Town area, west of Basseterre, began to provide impromptu performances of their dance sound on basketball courts and empty lots around the island. As carnival became an increasingly nationalized and state-run event, neighborhood bands utilized relatively unregulated community gathering spaces to perform and make some cash by selling drinks and jamming through the night. These jam sessions, and the competition and sonic clash between bands on the annual J'ouvert parade route, were sites of social and sonic experiments in the increased tempo of Kittitian-Nevisian music. Convened at places like the basketball court in Newtown, one of the five parishes in the northern "sugar belt" of St. Kitts, an area that was mostly populated by sugar laborers and their descendants, jam sessions were often dismissed by upper- and aspirationally middle-class people (living closer to "town") as dangerous "country" or "ghetto" affairs of the poor and unruly.

Jam sessions, or "jams," are predicated on experiences of bending time that include jamming (playing and improvising music) at all hours of the night (or, as is the case for J'ouvert, deep into the morning), chanting, and dancing—what Vijay Iyer describes as "the participatory act of marking time with rhythmic bodily activity [that] physicalizes a sense of shared time."[42] In the late 1990s and into the new millennium, new technologies, especially the innovation, increasing accessibility, and incorporation of drum machines and MIDI (Musical Instrument Digital Interface) technology in St. Kitts and Nevis, as well as the wider Caribbean region, opened new avenues for sonic expression of local temporalities. Reactions to these sounds varied, with responses like Mr. Phipps's—that the music is "too fast"—being prominent among the older generation.

However, James Phipps's insistence on behavioral and temporal norms via the castigation of socially transgressive (though not unpredictable) behavior was not just a response to an increase in beats per minute in local popular music. It was also indicative of a relationship between overlapping experiences of change and difference as temporally defined in local discourse. Each description of that which is "too fast" that I explore throughout this book— fast music, fast women, fast lives—integrally charts a trajectory and a marked temporal deviation from it. This divergence is fundamental to the phenomenology of speed.

I use "speed" as a way of accounting for varied and interrelated experiences of (and references to) the "too fast" as revealing a structure of lived experience and "infrastructures of sociability" through which various scales and taxonomies of temporal relation are composed in St. Kitts and Nevis.[43]

Whether as aesthetic judgments or self-conscious performances of a kind of subjectivity, critiques of wylers refer to the music as problematically fast and therefore "stupidness" or "noise" (the product of unauthorized or illegitimate musicianship), as inciting violence, or as promoting deviant sexuality.

A main conceit of *Island Time* is that there is a structural relationship between temporal categorizations within local parlance. For example, Black girls and young women in St. Kitts and Nevis are often subjected to critiques about their bodies and behavior that characterize them as overly sexual and "fast." During the anthropologist Deborah Curtis's fieldwork in Nevis, one of her male interlocutors lamented that "the girls on Nevis were maturing at a faster rate than girls of previous generations as the result of the increase in the consumption of processed foods": "Dey come to you like dey big women and den you see dat dey just children . . . De hormones in de chicken, dis ma-kin' dem sick.' I, myself, made this mistake a number of times. At the beach I would be talking to girls who I assumed were at least eighteen given their developed breasts, their height, and their full hips, only to be informed that I was mistaken. On one occasion I mistook a twelve-year-old for a woman in her early twenties."[44] These descriptions of "fast" girls target both the speed of their bodily development and the manner in which their bodies move and are perceived. As Natasha Crooks and her colleagues noted in a US context, "cultural messages such as 'fast' or 'fast tailed girl,' synonymous with slutty or ho, have been employed by older Black women to warn Black girls to 'slow down.' "[45] In St. Kitts and Nevis, these messages are often heightened around carnival time in order to curtail excessive deviant sexual activity. As in Mr. Phipps's statement ("skirts on their heads"), these conceptions of fast girls and women are sometimes collapsed with other conceptions of "too fast" be-havior, especially as it pertains to wylers.

In my discussions with an older generation of musicians, another tempo-ral dimension emerged. Valentine Morris, for example, who served as leader of the St. Kitts–Nevis Defense Force Band throughout the 1980s, described the difference between older musicians and the younger crop of would-be instrumentalists:

> See I do a little teaching still . . . and we started with a good number of persons, maybe 20–25 and they gradually began to drop out because they come here and think, 'in two weeks' time I can play something.' They don't understand it takes time. That is it! hey don't have the patience. They don't love it enough. They just want to play something—it can't go so.[46]

During my fieldwork, many of the people who I recognized as revelers on J'ouvert morning, at fetes, and at emphatically more subdued, respectable religious Christmas concerts around the island were reluctant to use the term "musician" to refer to wylers band members and producers. When pressed, some noted that they failed to recognize any level of notable skill necessary to play wylers music. This assessment resonates with regional uses of the word "fass" (fast) to describe people who are inappropriately inquisitive or prematurely participate in conversations or social situations to which they are not entitled.[47] These judgments, temporal assessments of a deviation from a set of norms, like attestations to wylers music's rapid tempo, are responses to experiences of speed.

In developing a phenomenology of speed, the political theorist Simon Glezos tackles a central distinction between speed and movement in the work of Deleuze and Guattari, who wrote, "A movement may be very fast, but that does not give it speed; a speed may be very slow, or even immobile, yet it is still speed."[48] Recognizing that there is "no absolute point beyond which movement becomes speed," and rejecting velocity's measurement of a differential as sufficient for attributing speed to an object, Glezos appeals to the experiential: "the attribution of speed comes about as a result of a conscious experience. Something has speed when it 'feels' fast, when we experience it as speed. It produces particular corporeal and perceptual effects (the sense of acceleration, the drop in the pit of the stomach, the tingle of adrenaline). This is not to say that speed is only a psychological phenomenon. Rather, speed is a material phenomenon attested to by subjective insight."[49] As a feeling, a conscious experience of change, speed is a "relational phenomenon" in that it may be experienced similarly irrespective of an objective velocity (or beats per minute), or inversely, two identical velocities may be experienced differently. This may explain why a well-loved Kittitian calypso like Ellie Matt's 1978 classic "Shang Shang," despite its "fiery tempo," is not considered among the "too fast" local musical productions. The song's sense of movement is propelled forward by the rapid strumming of electric guitar and catchy brass riffs reverberating in the hopeful years of the Black Power movement and the long lead-up to national sovereignty. Speed's relationality also offers some explanation for why in 2013, during my fieldwork, a relatively slow song about peace and unity, "One Order," by Nu Vybes, was roped into the familiar "too fast" discourse when it was pinpointed as instigating gun violence. The indefinable timbre of synthesized metal against the deep bass drum that characterizes wylers' resonating during a period of heightened violent crime and unprecedented economic shift sounds and feels different. As Glezos notes, it "is in the duration of change that speed lives."[50]

Aestheticizing change is key to wylers. Ask the jammers—or their disapproving elders—to describe wylers, and they will tell you it's fast. A few hours after the sun had risen over our J'ouvert celebrations, the tempo of the music had accelerated from the 120 beats per minute (bpm) of the early-morning "slow riddim" warm-up to a breathless 170 bpm at its apex. The exuberant and unpredictable behaviors wylers elicits (the "going wild" after which it is named), and its explicit and irreverent lyrical content create an arena marked by the anticipation and expression of change as speed and fastness (social audacity, sexual flagrance, and palpable velocity). On St. Kitts or Nevis, these elements come together most spectacularly "on de road" or the carnival processional.

Speed in Relation

To better understand speed in relational terms, I turn to Édouard Glissant (1928–2011), the poet, novelist, and philosopher who is among the foremost thinkers of the intense relationality that describes the "experience of rapid social and cultural change" that "modernity" names.[51] Born in Le Lamentin, Martinique, Glissant's interconnected body of work draws on the spatiotemporal specificity of the Caribbean, especially the string of Lesser Antilles of which Martinique is a part. In texts like *Poetics of Relation* (1990), Glissant forwards a philosophy and model for imagining a world that is defined not by binaristic or hierarchical assumptions of Western reason, or static notions of space, place, or time, but through "relation." This relation (which is not so much a thing as it is an action between things), Glissant insists, constitutes the only totality or whole of our realized world. Comprising both the material world (as represented by world-as-Earth and all that is on it) and consciousness of it (attempts to conceptualize its whole), relation is "a dynamic totality of interacting communities, all aware of each other and all constantly changing."[52]

In addition to relation, Glissant "invent[s] a variety of more or less synonymous names for this phenomenon: *creolization, chaos-monde, Tout-monde.*"[53] In defining creolization, Glissant distinguishes it from creolité, or popular conceptions of mixture or hybridity that insist on a formula of thing + thing = new thing. To Glissant, "hybridity is the product of two purportedly pure and knowable origins, and . . . its outcomes can be easily foreseen." The creolization that Glissant proposes refers to a diversity of "ever-increasing interconnection, combination, and unpredictability."[54] In describing the characteristics of creolization, Glissant offers that the "lightning speed with which this creolization is being proposed to our consciences" is among the foremost.[55] Here, Glissant marks speed as a relation to relation—as a way that we might experience being in relation to the ongoing and highly mobile processes of relation. So, when Glissant repeats throughout his work that "the whole world is archipelagizing and creolizing," he affirms the "archetypal status" of the Caribbean archipelago and the creolization born of its historical and geo-material context. "Creolization and archipelagos," as Michael Wiedorn holds, "go hand in hand."[56] Small islands like St. Kitts and Nevis, then, become ideal sites for theorizing relation in general and speed in particular.

As a relation to relation, speed clarifies that the alternative to things not "being from" St. Kitts and Nevis was not that they were from any other singular locale. Indeed, as I argue in this book, the layered archipelagic relation of the interactive, intervisible, intertraversable cluster of small islands in the eastern Caribbean cannot be apprehended via the definitive, two-laned continental imaginary buoyed by a "going to" and "coming from" discourse. Instead, comprehension of the small-island inhabitance of Kittitians and Nevisians, a central focus of this book, is better served by the relationality and multiplicity inherent to the archipelago. The archipelago is a form that accounts for the infinitude of the "somewhere else"—something else, someone else, sometime else—from which "everything" comes. Crucially, it does that accounting without relying on contiguity. If, as Aliocha Wald Lasowski has offered, "every philosophy is a geography," the archipelago is conceptual terrain for apprehending Caribbean music's movements.[57]

The archipelago is a string of islands without order; they are inherently related but also definitionally singular as islands. Speed, more than a characteristic or a possession of one thing or another, is also the recognition of a relation in motion. In St. Kitts and Nevis, I understand speed and change to be related to experiences of the incommensurability of old forms, concepts, discourses, and metrics to apprehend realities[58] For Phipps, and those who share his proclivities, these incommensurabilities included the very speed with which wylers music is created and the fact that its reliance on digital instruments, preprogrammed riddims, and engagement with passing global trends is done by artists without formal training. If experiences of speed conjure a resentment, or at least healthy distrust of the future, fear of young people, and a change in the practices and norms that mediated experiences of other kinds of realities (unrespectable ones, ones where women are unashamedly displaying themselves sexually in public or where the youth feel entitled to and violently defend their behavior against impositions or propositions from respectable elders), then inferences that music or attendant behavior is too fast are invocations of speed's many affective referents.

Speed, experienced as a moment of change—an accented event of change, however small—is the subjective and intensive relationship between an expectation and its unpredictable deviation. This kind of speed as a form of relation is composed through the relationship of musical tempo, bodily pace, and the large-scale temporality of the island. These temporal layers contribute to an experience of speed that signals the drawing together of what Antonio Benitez-Rojo has described as the "polyrhythm of planes" that "gives pan-Caribbean cultures a way of being, a style that is repeated through time and space in all its differences and variants."[59] In *Island Time*, these planes are openly defined: "island time" refers to the temporality produced through the geomateriality of the island, the long history of Eurocentric island imaginaries that plot the island and its people as isolated and remote, and attempts to mitigate those effects on behalf of the island's Black inheritors. "Pace," referring to a temporal scale of moving (human) bodies, focuses on the temporalities of embodied movements recognized, as Kamau Brathwaite does in his description of "tidalectics" as a site of entrainment.[60] "Tempo" accounts for the shortest duration of temporal events, musical time, which is itself experienced at the intersection of a listener's "internal rhythm, beat, clave, timeline, melody, etc., that makes [musical] rhythm intelligible."[61]

Archipelagic Listening

The archipelago is a model that accounts for an infinitude of scopes mostly because it draws our attention to the island as an irreducible unit that is always in relation to other islands. I have tried to illustrate how two of my first "official" fieldwork experiences pointed me toward place (*here* on the island of St. Kitts—where the vast majority of my fieldwork took place—or St. Kitts–Nevis as an archipelago) and time (the *now* that marks a feeling of difference from a previous generation on the island). I understand the recurrence of these kinds of conversations, whether as part of my "official" ethnographic process or in the orbit of my family to amount to a revelation of forms that account for time and space as trajectories through, with, and against which we all flow. In her illuminating book *Forms: Whole, Rhythm, Hierarchy, Network*, Caroline Levine defines form as "all shapes and configurations, all ordering principals, all patterns as repetitions and difference."[62] *Island Time* regards the island and speed as two salient, relational forms through which Kittitian-Nevisian worlds are composed and performed. Crucially, colonial conceptions of those forms have played a significant role in making and sustaining hierarchies of nation, race, sexuality, and temporality that have come to shape the past and present of the mostly Black inhabitants of small islands that were once British colonial outposts in the Atlantic ocean. What we know about speed and the island as forms depends on from where and from when we know them.

The archipelago is a useful concept, one that can be creatively and criti-cally applied. For example, when Michelle Anne Stephens and Brian Rus-sell Roberts take up the mantle of the "anti-explorer," they do so in hopes of extending the vision of St. Lucian poet Derek Walcott, whose response to the question "What is the nature of the island?" stood as a productive prov-ocation.[63] They write, "[Walcott] answers less with an answer than with a hint toward a method for imagining a possible answer: '[This question] has stuck . . . [with me] for over thirty-five years. I do not know if I am ready to answer it. . . . Except by. . . . the opposite method to the explorer's.' "[64] For Ste-phens and Roberts, the anti-explorer method comes to represent processes, tools, and methods of knowledge production that are alternatives (apposite if not quite opposite) to the explorer's: "The explorer . . . is a figure who, traditionally speaking, sallies forth with confidence that if the world is as yet unknown, then it at least may be surveyed and hence known via the Euclid-ean geometry of a latitudinal and longitudinal grid superimposed upon an idealized sphere. In the explorer's world, space is mapped, before it is known, by a globe-enveloping set of bisecting lines that drive toward human efforts at discovering or knowing the portions of the grid that contain *terra incognita* and *mare incognitum*."[65]

The anti-explorer method finds resonances with the work of the math-ematician Benoit Mandelbrot, whose groundbreaking discovery of the Man-delbrot fractal provided a mathematics for the "forms" like the shoreline that "Euclid leaves aside as being 'formless.'" This "morphology of the amor-phous" was intended to counter the proliferation of "theories unrelated to anything we can see and feel" with "a new geometry of nature."[66] Two of the major insights Roberts and Stephens draw from fractal geometry include the concept of the infinite island as an affirmation of the "unknowability" of our world and the importance of scale to questions of measure and definition.[67]

In asking how long the coast of Britain is, Mandelbrot summarizes that where "a continent is a special kind of island with infinite diameter," because of its corrugation, any attempt to evaluate its length, will have "peculiar" re-sults: "coastline length turns out to be an elusive notion that slips between the fingers of one who wants to grasp it. All measurement methods ultimately lead to the conclusion that the typical coastline's length is very large and so ill determined that it is best considered infinite."[68] Illustrating this point, Man-delbrot deploys a menagerie of hypothetical beach walkers of decreasing scale (a man, a mouse, an ant), each of whom would find that, even as they are able to stay increasingly closer to the specific contours of the coastline, its ir-regularity, its folded, craggy surface, ensures that "the distance to be covered continues to increase with no limit."[69]

The anti-explorer, aware of this mathematical fact and unsure of how she might hitch a ride on a mouse, knows that the unknowability, the infinitude, of the coastline of an island—of thought, of sound—is true at any scale. Moving away from attempts to fill in a gridded map, she focuses her attention on the experience of locating herself in space and time at intermittent points on her metaphorical walk. This is where autoethnography (writing of myself in relation to others) helps. I think *with* music of the Caribbean region and its intersections with Black music practices in the United States as a Black woman with generational attachments to the Leeward archipelago and lived experience as someone born and raised on the East Coast of the United States. My anti-explorer field site was ultimately wherever I was, and it was focused on various scales of musicality, whether my pulse after jamming hard to a wylers song; the anxiety associated with navigating an overwhelmingly male-dominated music scene; the beat of riddims on the radio or playing out of speakers in corner shops or large, repurposed carnival spaces; the pace of everyday life as I followed my auntie, cousins, and other interlocutors around the island and performed dutiful womanhood for my grandmother; and the various island temporalities that mark the passage of time through their cyclical inevitability: mango season, hurricane season, Christmastime, departures from the island, return migrations. As these things stay the same, people, plants, and pets die; land erodes; new buildings are erected; new roads carved and paved; new generations take hold.

Despite the difference between the navigational strategies of the different generations and the specificity of their respective geopolitical and pop cultural situations, the importance of the archipelago as a meaningful, lived geophysical reality and conceptual model in the clusters of islands of the Leeward archipelago is a constant. Wylers musicians alongside other Caribbean genres like bouyon, jam band, and champeta artists recognize bands like the Burning Flames as playing music that influenced their understanding of the possibility of a local and intelligible sound and style. For folks in the small-island Caribbean, the interrelation between genres of island sounds is archipelagic in its recognition of repetition beyond replication. When we see the repeating island as not a cause for synthesis but the revelation of form, the archipelago, island-to-island, riddim-to-riddim relation becomes useful in its accounting for repetition and multiplicity. In this view, genres like bouyon, champeta, and wylers, and the funk, soul, soukous, and hip-hop to which they are archipelagically related, are expressions of enchained sonic geometries and geographies of power and creativity and not plots on a static grid defined by African and European influences or unidirectional, contiguously traceable flows.

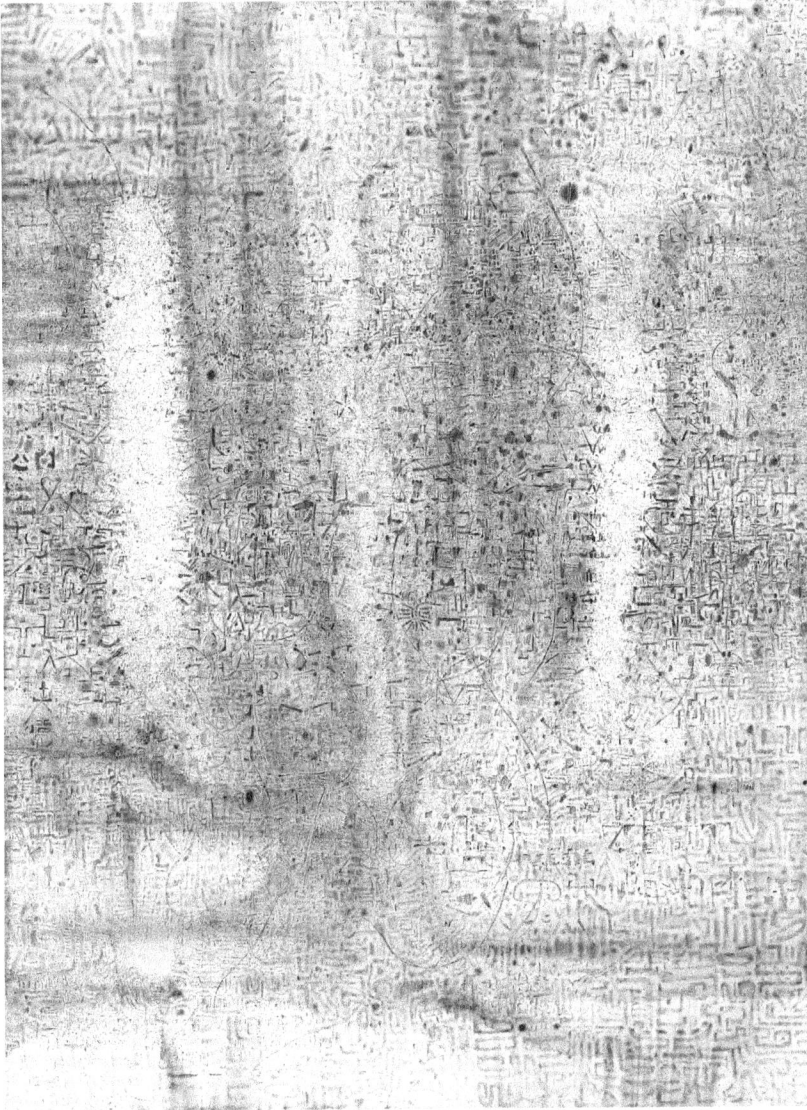

FIGURE 0.3. Tomm El-Saieh, *Cursive Grid*, acrylic on canvas, 2017–2018. © Tomm El-Saieh; Courtesy of the artist, CENTRAL FINE, Miami Beach, and Luhring Augustine, New York. Photo: Armando Vaquer.

In his painting *Cursive Grid* (2017–2018), the Haitian artist Tomm El-Saieh depicts what could be seen as three "islands" amid hieroglyphic-like markings that blur and sharpen in different areas of the piece (fig 0.3). Utilizing a method called frottage, El-Saieh rubs a "partially dried paintbrush across the canvas" such that "minute forms emerge, often leaving visible the canvas's white primer."[70] The painting conveys a sense of contradiction with its

title—the swirly, conjoining contiguity of cursive with the straight, discrete-
ness of a grid—and offers something like a map. In imagining this piece as
an alternative mapping of island-to-island relation, we might see the etchings
and doodles, at various depths of the canvas's surface, as depictions of the
stuff—perhaps air and sea—that connects these discrete island bodies. Up
close, what appeared to be random lines and curvatures begin to take shape
as recognizable patterns: a face, a heart, a star. Archipelagic listening is an
optimistic act of sonic relation based on a similar kind of paradoxical, counterintuitive mapping of the diminutive.[71]

Archipelagic listening is the kind of listening that draws the different parts
of a wylers song together to gather meaning and interest. I was first attuned to
the frictions and flows of tempo, pace, and island time when I participated in
the Caribbean online streaming-radio community Large Radio—a place where
those who imagine themselves as part of the small-island archipelago engage in
archipelagic listening. Hearing the relationships between music from around
the Caribbean archipelago, including continental regions such as Guyana and
mainland Colombia, and from various moments in time, including the to-the-
day most recent tracks from producers, artists, and DJs of Caribbean music,
habituated me to a geography of thought and listening modeled on the island-
to-island relations the archipelago represents. Materially, tracks on the site featured genres such as soca, calypso, reggae, dancehall, and all manner of carnival
music by artists from or "representing" every island in the Caribbean Sea. Often DJs would be located somewhere within the Caribbean diaspora but outside of the region circumscribed by the Caribbean Sea (such as Denmark), they
would still identify themselves as "representing" a particular island space (e.g.,
Aruba). Hearing the juxtaposition, melding, and interplay of these regional
sounds, some from the first half of the twentieth century and some produced
mere hours before broadcast, attuned me to an open unity constituted by relations in sound. The repetition inherent to listening to regional musics together,
songs with shared instruments, tracks that feature resemblant but divergent accents promoted an apprehension of Caribbean music's taken togetherness as
recognizably unified and yet comprising discrete sonic units.

The archipelago emerged as a useful model for apprehending the relationality across scales that governs the temporal and spatial logics that undergird
Caribbean performance and make it a meaningful medium for world making
in the present. The archipelago typically refers to a stretch, cluster, or recognized group of geographic islands that are taken together as a unit. While
the relationships between each individual island and another are subject
to changes of all kinds, the archipelago recognizes various permutations of
unity within diversity. Archipelagic listening is a tool of intelligibility across

the conjuncture of historical events, contemporary relations, sustained affinities, and processes of belonging that draw disparate but resonant experiences together under various banners of belonging. These banners, like "West Indian," "small islander," "Black," and "European," occupy the cultural-political space that Paul Gilroy describes as the Black Atlantic.

Gilroy's seminal text, *The Black Atlantic: Modernity and Double Consciousness* (1993) was an effort to write against nationalist, ethnically essentialist discourses that sought to position Blackness and Europeanness as mutually exclusive identities. Deploying W. E. B. Du Bois's term "double consciousness" to address manners of "occupying the space between" seemingly incongruous identities, Gilroy introduces the Atlantic as a singular "complex unit of analysis" that might "produce an explicitly transnational and intercultural perspective" .Within this project of moving beyond nationalist versus diasporic or essentialist versus vehemently nonessentialist discourses that position Blackness as an "entirely situational non-essence," Gilroy argues that Black expressive culture, particularly manifested as Black music, plays an especially important role:

> The histories of borrowing displacement, transformation, and continual reinscription that the musical culture encloses are a living legacy that should not be reified in the primary symbol of the diaspora and then employed as an alternative to the recurrent appeal of fixity and rootedness. Music and its rituals can be used to create a model whereby identity can be understood neither as a fixed essence nor as a vague and utterly contingent construction to be reinvented . . . Black identity is not simply a social and political category to be used or abandoned . . . it is lived as a coherent (if not always stable) experiential sense of self."[72]

Where the archipelago acts as a centerless set of islands that are taken, understood, lived, or known together, it stands as a useful metaphor and model for an understanding of Blackness (Caribbeanness and modernity, too) as experienced and produced through and within Black music. This relationship, Gilroy writes, "cannot be reduced to a fixed dialogue between a thinking racial self and a stable racial community" like a "diaspora." Instead, as Gilroy argues, "the original call" of Africa or shared enslavement "is becoming harder to locate," and our models should recognize that the "communicative gestures" inherent to Black musicality "are not expressive of an essence that exists outside of the acts which perform them."[73] The archipelago, then, as a model for not just the geographic Caribbean but also relation at any scale, accounts for wider audiences of Black music and the transmission of structures of racial feeling throughout the world (a bird's-eye tracing of the island) and the increasing specificity and localizing gestures that mark new genres and styles of music (measurement from the back of an ant).

How communities hear and are moved by particular sounds is the most reliably traceable aspect of regional music. Archipelagic listening takes all sound as functional wholes and recognizes the archipelago as a unit of understanding and a mode of relation between islands and island people. Archipelagic listening accounts for sonic vibrations, echoes, traces, and trends. It considers the archipelago a "field of sound" in the way that Josh Kun conceptualizes "the aural border."[74] As a concept and a mode of engagement with music and sound, archipelagic listening is both archaeological and genealogical in its function for members of groups like Large Radio and in its potential application in music studies, geography, and historians. Deploying "genealogy" as a mode of historical inquiry that is concerned not with origins but with revealing the multiple and often conflicting understandings of the past, which are signs of power's effect on truth, Michel Foucault's deployment of genealogy, in its archaeological vein, seeks to uncover hidden, lost, or missing links through processes of distributed archiving (largely online), sharing, storytelling, and discussion that elucidate possible pasts. Genealogical connections to various genres as resembling or countering—antiphonal to—other forms of Black music are recurrent and prevalent within the discourse.

What Mandelbrot's "new geometry of nature" offered to what already was—the natural world that continued to "play a joke" on mathematicians who tried to harness it with rigid, inadequate theories—was a different way of assessing what is knowable.[75] Archipelagic listening as a tool in the anti-explorer's toolbox is premised on the infinite, repeating, and highly mobile beat as a modern geometry of Black sound. Wylers, the mobile assemblage of sounds, techniques, and politics at the center of this study, demand an archipelagic mode of listening because they reveal the archipelagic thinking of the music's producers and audiences.

Archipelagic listening is predicated on a sense of archipelagic belonging as a genre of Caribbeanness that is both imaginary and moored to a geomaterial conception of the Caribbean region as an archipelago or a string of related islands. Even in its human-generated imaginativeness, its metaphoricity, the idea of the relation between Caribbean islands is beyond the timescale of humanity. That is, it is based on the prehuman movements of tectonic plates and mass-forming explosions as described by the Barbadian poet and philosopher Kamau Brathwaite: "The Caribbean, a survival archipelago—a curve of 3000 miles—is a sunken cordillera."[76] This deep image of an underwater mountain range is echoed in Brathwaite's insistence that amid the hypercreolization and across the expanse of multiplicity that is the Caribbean, the "unity is submarine."[77]

Caribbean thought and its geography is particularly useful for considering speed—fast sounds, collapsing space, fast girls, island time—alongside
music on a larger scale and with increasing specificity. Specifically, where Édouard Glissant describes continental thought as something that strives for
fixity and singularity, he characterizes archipelagos as connecting disparate
parts in relation. We may understand this relation as prescriptive, as the only
primordial given of the creolizing world as archipelago. In the same way that I
understood my own archipelagic listening via Large Radio as retrospectively
presenting a sonic model for understanding the specificity of small-island
music within a broader frame, I'm optimistic about the possibility of the archipelago as an imaginary to do similar work in connecting disparate parts—
impulses, incomplete considerations, fragments of ideas—in productive relation. Attempting to historically contextualize, to remap, the music of small
islands like St. Kitts and Nevis requires this kind of imaginary. Resources
are relatively scarce and incomplete. In addition to conversations, participant observation, and formal interviews, I have relied on abandoned online
forums, Facebook postings, much-uncataloged archival material, and family relics to corroborate the pieces of stories I have been told. As the former
St. Kitts national archivist Victoria O'Flaherty has argued, because colonial
records did not register the realities, thoughts, or experiences of the colonized, "For most Kittitians, real history started in the 20th century." This history "falls within memory or at least within that of elders who love to recount
how much things have changed."[78] In a small place like St. Kitts and Nevis,
gossip, hearsay, and scandal move quickly, and secrecy and withholding are
artful forms of self-protection. Kittitian and Nevisian musicians are leery of
being taken advantage of after spending years at the bottom of recording industry hierarchies that extract from small islands and deny them equal status
within a Caribbean music landscape. The effects of this arrangement became
clearer to me when I was put in contact with a prominent calypsonian who,
after our initial interview, made it clear that he could not allow others to capi-
talize on his story before he did. He stopped answering my calls, and within a
year, his self-published autobiography was available for purchase on Amazon.
This, too, is a kind of island time. If thinking with the archipelago "fits the
speed of our worlds," it is a furtive and capacious model for listening to and
with those who experience the world at its temporal limits.[79]

Chapter Summaries

Chapter 1, "Island Time: Waiting for Bradshaw on the Slow Island," grounds
this study in the narrative of nationalism in St. Kitts–Nevis. Historicizing the

era of the most significant political change, I invoke the image and legacy of St. Kitts and Nevis's first national leader, Robert Bradshaw, whose temporally tinged rhetoric was a keystone of mid-twentieth-century decolonial agitation. The negotiation of representations of local music have been closely aligned with the management of competing island times. This dance between local rhythm and global flows has been a central feature of decolonial nationalism.[80] "Island time," the product on the decades-long negotiations, is theorized in this chapter as a composite of slowness and the irregular fits and starts associated with the peculiar, and plural, temporalities held on the island—the colonial counter to the continent. I will argue that temporality is also geography: island space as a metageographic concept has generated alternate temporalities closely related to notions of isolation and vulnerability to various outside forces, which, in effect, defines "islandness."

Chapter 2, "Women and the Pedagogy of Pace," shows that Black women's bodies occupy the tension between musical tempo and discourse about larger scenes of historical unfolding. As such, representations of Black women's bodies have been central to colonial, neoliberal nationalist, and intergenerational discourses of proper temporality. The pace of women's bodies is a central gauge for moral health, and they are deployed as navigational devices for enforcing ideological parameters. Women, of course, are highly aware of this and teach young girls to quickly understand their place in the hierarchy so that they can effectively manipulate it. The pageant stage is one space where prevalent critiques of the pace of women's bodies are routinely dramatized. By analyzing a few performances, understood against the backdrop of middle-class aspiration, chapter 2 traces how passed-down pedagogies of survival and pleasure allow women to discern and occupy favorable positions across changing social landscapes. In the wake of colonial respectability's shape-shifting into neoliberal professionalism and entrepreneurialism, women leverage new platforms using time-worn navigational techniques.

Although the physical voices of Black Caribbean women are conspicuously absent from wylers records, the pace of their mobile bodies is a galvanizing feature of the music's production and consumption, which is taken up in chapter 3, "Wylers and the Tempo of Development." As St. Kitts and Nevis gained independence in 1983, a new generation of Kittitian and Nevisian politicians and a set of new concerns shifted national efforts toward preserving, affecting, and promoting an air of backwardness as islands like St. Kitts and Nevis were economically dependent on their image and function as a respite from US and British—continental—accelerations. These political movements, in addition to the musical innovations of bands like Ellie Matt and the G.I.'s Brass, constituted an interwoven backdrop for Black youth like the Burning Flames, 17 Plus, and their followers, who embraced speed and newness as their own, and not solely as the conceptual property or mark of foreign influence. Soca, as a categorical alternative to those sanctioned by a colonial nationalist imaginary provided this generation of Caribbean artists with a resource for recognition and, importantly, revenue.

In St. Kitts and Nevis, the argument against newer styles was enflamed by the political upheaval of the 1990s. While tempo can include a measurement like beats per minute, it might also refer to elections per decade or murders per year. In any event, tempo is the recurrence rate of events that constitutes a pattern. For Kittitians and Nevisians, the 1990s were indeed fast times. Speed, as the shock of the new, was shiny new resorts, new music festivals, and increased plane routes just as much as it was newly visible drugs, crime, and political corruption. Marking a protracted moment of intense change from an agricultural economy to one focused primarily on tourism and foreign investment, the sonic experiments of wylers coincided with—and oftentimes worked against—the societal restructuring that accompanied the final decline of the sugar industry, which officially shuttered in 2005. As fast music continued to be associated with criminal "fast" behavior, wylers was ahistoricized as a kind of foreign imposition on indigenized local culture. I argue that youth, in tension with this view of wylers, aestheticizes polysemic notions of speed—refusals of singularity—that locate young, Black Kittitians as Caribbean youth from an archipelago of archipelagos.

Musicians like Alphonsus "Arrow" Cassell from Montserrat represent bridging figures between an older generation of eastern Caribbeans who decried the ascendance of soca as the decline of calypso as a pure form and a newer generation who felt represented by the simplicity and wild malleability of its form. Even as small-island soca artists imagine this genre as central to their musical history, large histories of regional Caribbean music do not recognize their relevance. In chapter 4, I deploy archipelagic listening, to broaden the scale of historiographical analysis to consider the project of historians who work against a continentalized narrative of soca music. In this chapter, I chart one possible island-to-island historiography of small-island music that centers archipelagic listening as a product of small-island inhabitance that has been amplified through new media technologies. By remapping this discussion of the Caribbean archipelago to include the continental Caribbean (Cartagena de Indias) as another kind of "small island," this chapter presents the archipelago as a malleable model for the invention of useful cartographic imaginaries for apprehending Black Caribbean music like champeta and soca.

In the conclusion, I turn from soca and its constellation of islands and historical narratives to a dancehall musician. In 2023, Byron Messia, a young artist from St. Kitts, earned top spots on global music charts, an international record deal, and a stage at prime time at the 2023 St. Kitts Music Festival. Messia's global presence represents both a pivotal juncture—a surprising change for a historically unmapped people and place—and a predictable inevitability of the international music industry. Understood in the context of the almost "tenselessly digital" contemporary moment, Messia's insistence on a Kittitian-Nevisian multiplicity underscores the continued resonance of the archipelago for "connecting the dots" of the Caribbean islands and an expansive archipelago of archipelagos that is Black music.

Island Time hopes to participate in a project of imagining alternatives for how we might understand and map island music and islands of music in an archipelagic frame, and it offers speed and the archipelago as generative models though which the "relational entanglement" of broad range of West Indian performance practices may be understood in irreducible relation. Where speed comes about as a sense, an awareness, of deviation from a projection, speed comes to be a useful and highly subjective metric for measuring the productive relations and tensions of aspirations, optimistic forecasts, and material realities. Hovering in the space that the anthropologist John Jackson has referred to as the "murky middle ground fusing the literal to the metaphorical," this book amplifies sonic "imagination[s] against history" as heard and understood from a small place like St. Kitts and Nevis through fast music like wylers.

1

Island Time

Island Temporalities

Uncle Irving is what you might call a naturally musical person. This is how he describes himself. Any reasonable stretch of time in his presence offers examples of his musicality—a propensity to sound. For example, the hum of a generator may suddenly transform under his influence into a drone over which Uncle Irving might scat a few lines of an impromptu calypso horn line. He listens discerningly, a characteristic some musicians in St. Kitts and Nevis might describe as having "light ears." I saw how sensitive his musical sense was when he invited me to grab a beer at a bar in central Basseterre in August 2010. It was a dimly lit, open-air establishment where a local cover band was playing a set of early 1990s soca songs. Things were going perfectly well until the rhythm guitarist, who was also providing background harmony, was singing under the pitch during a cover of the Burning Flames band's "Swinging Engine." Uncle Irving found the whole thing so jarringly discordant; we left soon after. For better or worse, Uncle Irving understands his sonic sensitivity—his light ears and musical proclivity—as an inheritance.

One source of this inheritance is from his father, my grandfather Simeon "Santoy" Swanston (whom he refers to interchangeably as Daddy and Old Man Santoy). "Daddy was a genius," he says often and emphatically. Old Man Santoy was, by all accounts, a multi-instrumentalist, a Calypso King, a basket weaver, fisherman, composer, and teacher. However, he lost his life at thirty-eight years old in a fishing accident before Uncle Irving's fifth birthday in 1963. Some part of Uncle Irving's musical life is owed to very early memories of hearing his father play the fife and trombone. Another fraction is composed of accumulated stories his older brothers retell about their daddy's musical accolades. However, Uncle Irving primarily understands his musical gifts as passed-down across lifetimes, as a series of generational inheritances that cannot be explained through early formal training. He understands his musicality as a genetic and "spiritual" inheritance that can be traced to Old Man Santoy, and further back and *up* to his African ancestors.

A set of sonic and often mystical experiences and memories, Uncle Irving's story of his own life is primarily a musical one. The happiest day of his life, for example, was when, in the early 1960s, his brother Lindley negotiated with a local steel band to buy their old worn pans, which he set up in their family's yard in Charlestown, Nevis. Years later, after time in the Defense Force Band, he learned of himself as a descendant of Africa. He gained a sense of political consciousness through the musical teaching of Bob Marley, whom he met as a twenty-year-old in the St. Croix airport in the summer of 1978. After stints as a trombonist and arranger for Kittitian-Nevisian bands like Grand Ash II Express, Ellie Matt and the G.I.'s Brass, and the G.I. Brass International, he moved in the early 1980s to New York, where he worked as a studio musician for soca and calypso producers like Frankie McIntosh. "I had to play everything" he told me, "being a studio musician means I was playing everything: jazz, salsa, merengue, R&B."[1]

By the early 1990s, Uncle Irving was a trombonist for the Montserratian calypsonian and soca star the Mighty Arrow, whose high-energy style of soca was a staple of massive music festivals throughout the 1990s. It was during this time that Uncle Irving toured the world as part of Arrow's band, spending time in Japan, Brazil, various islands of the Caribbean, South America, and Morocco. He mentioned to me that it was after he declined an offer to join James Brown's band that he came to live with my family in the Bronx for a few years in the late 1990s.

Uncle Irving wore a dashiki everyday with big wooden jewelry in the shape of the African continent. He allowed his kinky hair to tangle into free-formed locs. He smelled like incense and amber. He taught me, in a round-about way, about Zion and Babylon, about loving broad noses and deep black skin. He ate a mostly ital diet of unprocessed foods, fruits and vegetables, no salt, no added sugar. He spoke of music as meditation and as connection to an ancestral Africa, and of our racial and familial responsibility to make music—to put good vibrations into the world.

He took the responsibility seriously, and by the early 2000s, Uncle Irving had moved back to Nevis out of a concern that traditional music, especially fife music, "had almost died, and nobody else was capable of reviving it." He created a curriculum for the public schools in Nevis and St. Kitts that included the history and music of folk forms like string bands and fife and drum (big drum) groups. He taught trumpet, trombone, saxophone, and fife to primary school students on both islands, and he often spoke on the national radio station, ZIZ, about the importance of local heritage. He notes: "It was ignorance that allowed the culture to die. They thought that music was just something we used to do to entertain *Massa*. But that's not it. The music is how we find our way back to ourselves."

Across generations, the people of St. Kitts and Nevis have expressed their political and racial consciousness, as well as a sense of responsibility to their islands, through a deep and evolving relationship with traditional music, especially the performance practices of Christmas sports. When Uncle Irving references the "ignorance" of the generation before him, he's talking about a time commonly understood as the most pivotal moment in the national history of those islands, the statehood through independence era of the 1950s through 1970s. The official status of the islands in relation to the British colony was one marker of significant change that altered the social and political landscape of the region. A less obvious change, but one that the dynamic relationship to traditional music exposes, is the shifting awareness of and investment in representations of time and temporality on the islands. We might best understand the dynamics of this pivotal era through one of its most influential figures, Robert Bradshaw.[2]

Waiting for Bradshaw

Robert Llewellyn Bradshaw (1916–1978) is often referred to as St. Kitts–Nevis's "first national hero" for instigating the most significant period of social and political change on the islands since emancipation in 1838. A sugar worker who became a union agitator and later the Associated State's first premier, in 1967, Bradshaw is recognized as a singular force in the push to independence from colonial Britain. He succumbed to cancer in 1978, five years before full independence was achieved, but internationally recognized sovereignty was an inevitability by the mid-1970s. It was through Bradshaw's political maneuvers of the 1970s that Kittitians and Nevisians moved toward being seen "less as trespassers and more as participants in the world scene."[3]

Primarily, it was his reportedly despotic handling of what has been called interchangeably the Anguilla Revolution or "the Confusion" that branded him to the outside world as a power-hungry dictator with a penchant for British flair and fine wines.[4] Still, "Bradshaw became synonymous with St. Kitts, Nevis, Anguilla—whether the reference was to good or evil."[5] By all accounts, Bradshaw was "particularly Anglophone in his deportment" even while he espoused adamant pro-Black politics.[6] As one of the most visible and outspoken people of the small Caribbean islands, Bradshaw was known to speak with a refined British accent—rolled *R*s and all. He even drove a

Rolls-Royce around the tiny island and at times donned the uniform of a British general.[7] He was a known collector of antiques and a connoisseur of fine wines in spite of his elementary school education and his work background as a sugar factory worker. And yet despite flaunting his adoration of British affects, politically and philosophically Bradshaw was a staunch pan-Africanist who believed strongly in Black self-governance. He championed intellect and thirst for knowledge as a means out of racial subjugation and the squalor endemic to Britain's out-of-sight colonial outposts like St. Kitts, Nevis, and Anguilla in the first half of the twentieth century.

Indeed, the Jamaica-born pan-Africanist Marcus Garvey had been an especially early influence on Bradshaw, starting with Garvey's November 1937 visit to St. Kitts. Bradshaw was a twenty-one-year-old shop steward in the sugar factory when Garvey's speech introducing "a new philosophy of life" galvanized Bradshaw: "some people are born into a system and never enquire about it . . . but those who understand the system boss it." Garvey emphasized the importance of racial uplift via intellect, social and political awareness, and land ownership—particularly for Black people in a "small place" like St. Kitts. He warned: "The first duty of man or woman is to find out about himself. You will find out that you are wasting time—that you are too lazy. The world was waiting on Edison and he came, on Marconi and he came, on Henry Ford, and he came, on Mussolini and he came, on Hitler and he came. The world is waiting on you—when will you come?"[8] Within seven years of Garvey's visit, and his suggestion that Kittitians and Nevisians were effectively behind, Bradshaw rose to be vice president of the St. Kitts–Nevis Trades and Labour Union, a position from which he would become an outspoken champion of the working class.

Two years into that tenure came an important union uprising in the wake of which Bradshaw first voiced his critical stance toward Christmas sports, a musical tradition practiced almost entirely by the Black working class to whom Bradshaw was most dedicated. During the Christmas season of 1947, in the midst of tense negotiations between the sugar workers' union and the planters, Bradshaw "admonished those who play Sports—mostly sugarcane workers—that they should not entertain 'bukra' any longer, because they were the same villains who were intractably refusing to agree to decent wages and working conditions for the laborers."[9] Bradshaw was referring to the Christmas sports, a set of music and dance practices that included roving serenading bands, salacious reenactments, and colorful and energetic masquerading troupes. These performances were often nominally compensated by white planter audiences, who might have offered a small donation of money or rum to especially energetic performers as they walked from one plantation to another. Glossed, by 1947, as a remnant of the same social order union efforts were working to overturn, the Christmas sports represented a much broader history of colonial domination in the West Indies.

Christmas Sports in the Colonies

St. Kitts, known as "The Mother Colony," was the first island in the Caribbean to be colonized by the British, in 1623, and in 1625, the French also established a colony there. The British settled in the island's center, while the French occupied the two ends. In 1627, the French founded the capital, Basseterre, which locals now often refer to simply as "town." By 1628, the British had also colonized Nevis. Both islands had large populations of enslaved Africans and European indentured servants, predominantly Irish and Scottish, who were part of the early colonial labor force. Many of these indentured servants were convicted criminals who worked for two to seven years in lieu of prison sentences in Britain.

Initially, both the indentured servants and the enslaved Africans were seen as belonging to the same social class, often working and suffering side by side. The Irish, many of whom were Irish Catholic, were an especially derided group. In 1673, Christopher Jefferson, a St. Kitts planter, offered a ranking of European laborers, suggesting that the Irish were "the worst, many of them being good for nothing but mischief."[10] However, the introduction of sugar cultivation, starting in Barbados and spreading to St. Kitts and Nevis, changed the agricultural and economic landscape from small family farms to large plantations. This also led to a social shift; by the 1640s, indentured servants were moving into more privileged roles as artisans and managers, while the enslaved Africans faced increasingly harsh conditions.

Enslaved Africans participated in some leisure activities, particularly on Sunday afternoons and holidays, in which, according to European travel accounts, music and dance was central. In 1657, for example Richard Lingon's account of life on Barbados features long descriptions of musical abilities of the enslaved in which he highlights complex rhythms and drumming (noting how they "vary their time" more than their "tune").[11] However, toward the end of the seventeenth century and throughout the eighteenth, colonists, fearing rebellion and social upheaval, enacted laws prohibiting the musical practices of the enslaved, especially drumming. A 1737 act specifically punished anyone caught beating "Negro-drums."[12]

The cultural exchange between Irish indentured servants, French, and English colonists, and enslaved Africans influenced the creation of music and dance forms in St. Kitts and Nevis that draw from British winter solstice

FIGURE 1.1. *Early Masquerades,* photo showing masquerade at the bottom of Church Street in Basse-terre, St. Kitts, ca. 1920. National Archives, St. Kitts & Nevis. https://www.nationalarchives.gov.kn/317. Courtesy of the National Archives, St. Kitts and Nevis.

celebrations, folk plays, mumming traditions, French square dances, Irish fifing, and a world of West African and Indigenous practices. Throughout the colonial period, the French and British competed for control of St. Kitts (while the British had a solid hold on Nevis), with the island changing hands several times until 1713, when the Treaty of Utrecht gave Britain full control of it. Despite the power struggles, the cultural influence of both colonizers left a lasting legacy on the island. Utilizing the Christmas season as a time for merriment and many forms of leisure and play was one among many enduring colonial practices. Creolized and vernacularized by generations of Kittitians and Nevisians, the Christmas sports (Christmastime entertainments and performances) are now understood as indigenous to St. Kitts and Nevis (fig. 1.1).

Two different types of ensembles have historically accompanied Christmas sports in St. Kitts and Nevis: the big drum ensemble and the string band ensemble. The big drum ensemble utilizes a bass drum, a kettledrum, and a fife.[13] This type of roving ensemble finds its roots in the instrumentation of British military and Irish fife and drum music. The big drum ensemble most commonly provides musical accompaniment for masquerades and clowns, two types of interrelated performance characters. During the masquerade, young boys and men typically wear colorful shirts and pants with long, multicolored ribbons sewn around the entire ensemble.[14] Each masquerader wears a mask with a tall hat with peacock feathers that accentuate each dance and movement. Over the course of a performance, which includes traveling through various neighborhoods and stopping occasionally to dance for gatherers, a masquerader performs many steps demonstrating footwork, jumping and laterally shaking his isolated head—making the feathers and ribbons move in syncopation. The masqueraders usually hold a wooden tomahawk in their left hand and perform dance moves that mimic striking a blow with the weapon. One particular dance, called the "wild dance," has the masqueraders "explod[ing] into a fierce display of body movements, their crown-like headgear of peacock feathers waving vigorously, as they . . . exhibit a typical African war dance" that occurs "when the music develops into a fiery tempo."[15]

Masqueraders generally perform as a group or in short, choreographed routines that include some couple and individual dancing. The origin of the prominent tunes is disputed, but descriptions of big drum music have emphasized the importance of intricate rhythms between the interplay of the fife, kettle, and bass drums contributing to the sound: "as the tempo of the drum beat develops, with the man on the fife—generally a virtuoso of class— fluting out the traditional 'balie' tune; tomahawks are hurled into the air, to be skillfully caught by the same hand that threw them" (fig. 1.2).[16]

Any typical big drum performance occurs in two parts: the quadrille and the "wild mas" (or dance). The quadrille begins at a steady and moderate

FIGURE 1.2. Masqueraders with wooden tomahawks on the ground, Port Zante, Basseterre, December 2010. Photo by the author.

Quadrille

FIGURE 1.3. Transcription of big drum quadrille.

pace, in the 12/8 time signature, counted in four downbeats, and it features fluid, melodic improvisation on fife of a basic tune (fig. 1.3). Accenting the triple eighth-note subdivisions played on the kettledrum, the big drum (which is sometimes locally referred to as the bull drum) plays on the four downbeats of each measure. During the quadrille, the masquerade dancers perform choreographed dances, sometimes in lines or in couples. The wild mas is a sped-up version of the quadrille in which the eighth notes are played increasingly faster on the kettledrum. The fife takes a background role to the percussion instruments during the wild mas and typically plays shorter, repetitive, and more rhythmic lines than during the quadrille. During the wild mas, the masqueraders perform larger, faster, and more individualized movements that accentuate the shaking of the ribbons and the feathers on their heads. Both the quadrille and wild mas feature rolls, flams, and other drum rudiments that add to the thick rhythmic texture.

Clowns can be understood as "a modern manifestation of the generic traditional masquerades that have appeared in the Eastern Caribbean throughout the years." These performers wear similarly colorful attire in a "loose, flabby style."[17] The main differences between clowns and masqueraders are that clowns fasten bells to their attire, carry a cattle-skin whip (locally referred to as a "hunter"), and wear just one tall feather on top of their conical clown mask (figs. 1.4 and 1.5).

FIGURE 1.4. *Clowns,* ca. 1976. Courtesy of the National Archives, St. Kitts and Nevis.

FIGURE 1.5. Masqueraders at Port Zante, with drum and fife, December 2010. Photo by the author.

The string band (or scratch band) makes up the other prong of Kittitian-Nevisian folk arts. The common understanding of this type of ensemble in the eastern Caribbean originates from European instrumentation and genres, such as quadrille, and African rhythmic styles.[18] The string band in its current form, and as it has been constituted since the late nineteenth century, makes use of at least one guitar, cuatro, four-stringed banjo, and mandolin. Additional percussion instruments include the triangle, guiro (or another form of scraper), shak-shak (or alternate shaker), and baha or baho—providing the bass for the ensemble.[19] Like the big drum ensemble, the bamboo fife (sometimes made of PVC) often provides the melody. The string band traditionally

accompanied several types of Christmas sports, especially those characterized by oratorical demonstrations. One particular Christmas sport, "Niega
Business," (also referred to as "Nega Business" and "Niega" or "Nyega Business"), was, as late as the 1950s, one of the first Christmas sports traditions to
mark the beginning of the season.[20] This type of play with string band inter-
lude is particularly indicative of the extremely localized and socially embedded nature of music, dance, and oratorical Christmas traditions. Mills and
Jones-Hendrickson provide a description:

> As the name implies, this group was concerned with the business of Nagos or
> "stupid vulgar blacks." The players . . . were accompanied by a small band of
> musicians with guitars, quatros, triangle and baha. Wire masks may or may
> not be worn, and occasionally on may have his entire face covered with soot
> and locomotive grease. The clothes were extraordinary: a derby on the head,
> long black scissors-type frock coats, rumpled tie or big bow tie, and trousers
> sometimes decorated with colored rags sewn thereon; and after a character or
> two who were men dressed like women, complete with wig, dress, and exag-
> gerated breasts and buttocks. . . . The pattern of Niega Business is to move
> through the streets, music at a tempo, the players leading the band as they
> dance, and children and adults following the procession till they stop tempo-
> rarily to play.[21]

Many Christmas troupes performed "ribald and scandalous inventions" that
focused on poking fun or staging an indirect critique of figures of power or
members of the community who had misbehaved. These groups, such as the
Saguas, the Schoolchildren, and the Buzzards, performed alternations of ad-
libbed speeches, rhymes, songs, and enactments of dramatized scenes from
everyday life: an overzealous preacher, a well-to-do lady with scandalous se-
crets, a pompous political leader.

After the fall of the Caribbean sugar empire in the early nineteenth century
and following full emancipation (after the four year "apprenticeship period")
in 1838, many Black people migrated to other islands to find work. Those who
stayed primarily found work on the same estates they and their ancestors
were once enslaved on, relegated to labor in the sugar fields or other parts
of its production and dissemination, and subject to demands and mistreat-
ment. Considering the relatively unchanging nature of the material, political,
and social conditions for Black people on St. Kitts and Nevis throughout the
previous three hundred years of colonial rule, Bradshaw's ultimate desires for
the working class of St. Kitts are captured in his speech after a sugar worker
strike in 1948: "We go back to work more dignified, more conscious of our

worth. Let us go forward together to the new St. Kitts, not looking back to the old St. Kitts with its degradation and shame which we are so anxious to leave behind. . . . Comrades, hold your heads high, look the world steadily in the face, move big!"[22]

To Bradshaw and those thinking similarly, Christmas sports, in all their variations, were both a container for and a symbol of the kind of contented ignorance through which the racial and class status quo had endured for centuries before. By the 1950s, the Labour Party–affiliated newspaper *Union Messenger* was regularly running editorials that lambasted the Christmas sports as having a "primitive appeal" from which the working class should be "elevated."[23] That the planter and merchant classes looked down on an almost entirely Black working class in a colonial society is not particularly novel. But when considered in conjunction with the distinctly temporal valance of the elevation project that characterized the period between the 1940s and the 1980s, Bradshaw's idea of shedding "the old St. Kitts" and Nevis emplaces the islands in a temporal middle space between the past, of which Christmas sports were a damning symbol, and the "new St. Kitts" to come.

What geographic temporalities emerge from these cultural and political debates? How does musical time participate in national history? In this chapter, I identify traces of an enduring relationality between conceptions of the slow time of the island and the nested temporalities of the traditional music practices of the Christmas sports. In the half-century preceding the 1983 full independence of St. Kitts and Nevis, Kittitians and Nevisians heavily mediated their relationships to various aspects of Christmastime performance practices and their biological and metageographic associations within a colonial schema. If a sense of anxious belatedness was a particularly present island temporality during the Bradshaw-era statehood-to-independence movement, then renewed national historicism in the accelerated 1980s staged a refiguration of island time's orbital referent, from colonial behindness (occupying a prohibitively distant position on a colonial timeline) to island time as a celebrated gravitational feature of the islands and their people. In both cases, Christmastime traditions resounded as especially mutable tools in processes of national self-determination for St. Kitts and Nevis as a "new" small-island state. After theorizing "island time," which in addition to slowness encompasses the irregular fits and starts associated with the peculiar and plural temporalities held on the island—the colonial counter to the continent—I show how the island space as a metageographic concept has generated alternate temporalities closely related to notions of isolation and vulnerability to various outside forces: this in effect defines "islandness."

Tourism and the Slow Island

In a 1982 *Boston Globe* article about Caribbean tourism, St. Kitts–Nevis's then minister of tourism Michael Powell said: "We have seen how other islands have spoiled themselves by over-building and rushing too headlong to get tourists. We want to sell St. Kitts and Nevis as the way the Caribbean used to be."[24] The title of the article was "The Relaxed Pace of St. Kitts Is Beginning to Pick Up," and it described St. Kitts as an "isle with an easy pace." Locals refer to St. Kitts and Nevis as the bat and ball because the shapes of the islands resemble those two essential pieces of cricket gear, so, with all the expected flourishes of travel writing and combining premonitions based on the fate of other Caribbean tourist destinations, the author encapsulates his brief time in St. Kitts: "after all, this is St. Kitts: and hurrying isn't cricket." Traveler, St. Kitts is a slow place.

More than slow, however, the reference to cricket points to the sport's historical role as a civilizing activity in the expansive British empire. Writing of the introduction of cricket in colonial India as an "affirmation of the superiority of controlled self-indulgence and controlled flair or style, combined with reaffirmation of a moral universe," Ashis Nandy notes: "The nineteenth century was also the period when the various post-Utilitarian theories of progress began to be applied to the new colonies of Britain. The emerging culture of cricket came in handy to those using these theories to hierarchize the cultures, faiths and societies which were, one by one, coming under colonial domination."[25] The multivalence of cricket within the British Caribbean colonies is made abundantly clear in the work of the Trinidadian Marxist writer C. L. R. James, who, writing in the late 1950s and early 1960s during the first wave of independence for West Indian states, recognized cricket as an art representing "the fundamental relationship between the One and the Many" in West Indian society. Describing the complex interplay of cricket, politics, and the racialized and classed stratification of colonial society, James describes how the phrase "it isn't cricket" was a product of mid-nineteenth-century English education reform that sought to consolidate power in an educated class of men. Organized sport, like cricket, was a space for "character training and the inculcation of moral excellence."[26] As James writes, "it isn't cricket" became watchwords of manners and virtue and the guardians of freedom and power." In that light, the travel writer's play on the geographic shape of St. Kitts as cricket bat, the slowness of a cricket game, and the colonial hegemonic sociality point to a larger constellation of interrelated features and histories at play.

What is most interesting about the article is its invocation of pace, or the tempo of things, to refer to the slow rhythm of daily life on St. Kitts and to the speed of development in the tourism industry. St. Kitts figures not as one among other slow Caribbean places but as a particularly slow place in relation to a set of developing states. The particular abundance of slowness in St. Kitts is what made the island unique in the Caribbean. This point is captured succinctly in another article, this one from a 1985 issue of the *New York Times* about Caribbean tourism in general: "There are islands for every taste: lively, quiet, rustic, glitzy. Even though the distance to most of the islands is not great, their atmosphere is distinctly foreign and they tend to feel far away. People seem to move at perhaps half to two-thirds the speed at which New Yorkers normally cruise and, unless you are trying to work in the Caribbean, that can have an enormously relaxing effect."[27]

Island Time and the Continent

Although attributing a slow pace of everyday life to island locations is a hallmark of tourist marketing in the region, it is a conceptual connection that predates the colonial Caribbean. The island studies scholar Elizabeth DeLoughrey points out that in Medieval and Renaissance texts, ideal sites for colonization are described using "repetition of the words remote and isolated, presumed synonyms for island space," which suggests that island spaces "are central to the ideological process of colonisation." She argues that in the Western imagination, "'island' and 'islandness' have metaphorical nuances that are highly contingent upon the repercussions of European colonialism and continental migration towards island spaces."[28] Ideas surrounding the isolated and distant island have functioned as the opposite of the continent which "has been regarded as the systemic building block of world history" through a series of naturalizing processes.[29] Colonization, particularly European colonization of the Americas, was central to the very conceptualization of the continent as a way of breaking up the earth's landmasses. "By going off shore," invading the islands of the Americas, Europe discovered itself "as a continent in its own right."[30] In an exploration of a later point in colonial history, Sidney Mintz's landmark exposition *Sweetness and Power: The Place of Sugar in Modern History*, locates the Caribbean and the plantation as distinctive loci of modernity. He considers that even as the slow island space would be configured as the antidote to modern acceleration taking place in (continental elsewhere), the island space and plantation are likewise the essential locations where industry and industrial capitalism would develop. The paradox is that the island space gestated the very capitalism from which islandness, that is, the island's slow insularity, was later imagined to provide respite.[31]

Island time, in its most popular formulation, accrues potency as an escape from the "real world" through its instance on time's inherent relationality. Business owners who are invested in tourist experiences evoke island time to encourage tourists to stay longer, suspend their other temporal realities, indulge, and spend more. Take, for example, Turtle Time bar on Pinney's Beach in Charlestown, Nevis, where, as it says on the menu, the drinks and atmosphere "will make you want to permanently change your watch to Turtle Time!" Or Reggae Beach Bar and Grill on the southeastern peninsula of St. Kitts, where a huge banner reminds patrons to rush *slowly* (fig. 1.6). Or consider a picture often reposted on the St. Kitts Tourism's social media pages that features massive clouds atop Mt. Liamuiga with the crystal-blue ocean in the foreground. The caption reads: "Island time, all the time #gonelimin" (fig. 1.7). In 2018, "Gone limin'" was the official slogan of the St. Kitts tourist board, along with "My St. Kitts." The economic invitation of island time encourages leisure, to be sure, but it captures more than that. It forges a relation between the geomateriality of the island itself and experiences of time.

In linking the primacy of continental theory to the creation and assertion of geographic continental "projects that rely on specific notions of spatiality" tethered to "Eurocentric conceptions of space and time," Nelson Maldonado-Torres advocates for the broadening of theoretical referents through "postcontinental" philosophy.[32] Deploying cultural geographers Martin Lewis and Kären Wigen's notion of metageography, as "the set of spatial structures through which people order their knowledge of the world" through "often unconscious frameworks" Maldonado-Torres marks continentality as a genre of metageographic bias.[33] If continentality is predicated on usually unconscious frameworks, island time, especially as practiced and demonstrated by Kittitians and Nevisians, encompasses an awareness of continentality's framing temporality.

Island time encompasses the precariousness of islandness itself and the economic and environmental isolation and dependence, and vulnerability, of the state of being a former British colony. These insecurities are especially amplified by the smallness of both islands. Small islandness in St. Kitts and Nevis can be experienced as waiting: for shipments of goods; for bureaucratic procedure to follow its course; for a ferry to move between the two island spaces. In my case, much of my fieldwork was spent waiting for musicians who religiously stood me up. It is very likely that some of our missed connections could be blamed on a distinctly Caribbean sense of time and place that made "Meet me up by the hotel in the morning" count as an appointment and allowed my insistence on further specification to appear excessive— "nagging." Surely, my being a young woman did not lend much to the urgency

FIGURE 1.6. Reggae Beach Bar and Grill sign advising "Rush slowly," on the southeastern peninsula of St. Kitts, June 2021. Photo by the author.

or gravity of my research or the value of my time. While the majority of my time in St. Kitts was spent in "Town" (Basseterre in St. Kitts and Charlestown in Nevis), about 75 percent of the country's inhabitants live in rural parishes that line the periphery of the island (with Mt. Liamuiga and Nevis Peak taking up much of the center of St. Kitts and Nevis, respectively). For people

FIGURE 1.7. Photo uploaded to My St. Kitts Facebook page with the caption "Island time, all the time. #GoneLimin | photo: @liilu.l." https://www.facebook.com/StKittsTourism/photos/a.80363322721/1015 6979878652722.

living on the northern part of St. Kitts, for example, daily life may revolve around waiting for transportation and services, for electricity to come back on, for the weekly produce markets. During the wet season between July and December, a wash of heavy rain may come out of nowhere, soaking only one side of a street until the bright sun returns. These flashes of rain force people to wait, too.

Bradshaw's legacy is linked to galvanizing labor consciousness in sugar workers on various plantations and estates, and "just as the plantation was foundational to modern production and labor organization, it was this phenomenon that also shaped the infrastructures, practices and processes of politics within post-colonial New World nationstates."[34] As Deborah Thomas notes, "In these plantation contexts, a nexus of customary rights related to long-standing patterns of land use and heritability, as well as forms of patronage and clientelistic loyalty, forged the ground on which and mechanisms through which nationalist citizenship claims developed in the 20th century."[35] Within the context of St. Kitts and Nevis, this has resulted in historically ingrained feeling that one group of citizens is always waiting for their preferred party to be back in power so that they may receive benefits like jobs, housing, acknowledgment, and other forms of party-based reward for their loyalty.

There is an immediacy to the time of the island, too. One summer evening in 2013, the national TV station, ZIZ, was playing old calypso show recordings when the image scrambled and became stuck on a distorted image with loud static. After looking the number up in her paper phone book, my Auntie P called the station and told whoever answered the phone: "Aye, we are trying to have some nice family time. Please fix it up." By the time she had put the cordless phone back on the dock, the image had cleared and a new program was beginning. The immediacy, human error, and potential relation felt incongruously intimate, relative to the distance I imagine between myself and the inner workings of mass technological mediation in the major US cities I have otherwise lived in.

The subjectivity of these experiences of slowness, waiting, immediacy, and speed are shaped, as Sarah Sharma notes, by "a differential economy," meaning that our senses of time are "limited or expanded by the ways and means" that we find ourselves and others "in and out of time."[36] Where Sharma maps these temporal differences as a matter of "power chronography," I understand the taken-for-granted temporal-ordering structures that are rooted in geographic and ultimately racialized, sexualized, and class-based conceptions of the relationship between space and time (as with continentality) as "metachronography." While power chronography uncovers the inherent unevenness of temporal relations, metachronography refers to the already-apparent pluralities of temporality that characterize interactions such as those in tourist spaces in island locales. Metageography, the way people order their worlds on the basis of geographic hierarchies, gives way to island time as a metachronographic concept that ascribes temporal conditions to metageographic sites.

What's key here is that continentality ascribes the primacy of a continent to different kinds of geographic sites. This makes island time an even more precarious fiction that is not dependent exclusively on the presence of an island. That is to say, all islands are not on island time. Island time, as a metachronographic concept, depends on islandness, however, which includes characteristics such as isolation and vulnerability to a host of outside factors both natural and man-made. And so islands like St. Kitts and Nevis come to represent the vagaries of islandness even in relation to other islands. This would become an important feature of the island nation's tourism product after more than forty years of political and social agitation against the stigma of being a small island and perpetually "behind." Island time, understood in a dialectical relationship to modernity's accelerations is necessarily about slowness, unmodernness, and a backwardness that is always relative to a standardized continental time. But island time, in its encompassing of the deep time of the island, and the far horizons of future national and personal development, is an irregular rhythm of fits and starts.

We might think of island time as something like what the ethnomusicologist Gerhard Kubik described as the "acoustic image" of East and Central African music. He describes the discrepancy between what instrumentalists play (their motor actions and individual rhythmic lines) and the salient resulting rhythm as perceived by a listener. More than just an accrual of patterns, the combination of rhythms is heard as a "conflict of other rhythms, which are not played as such but arise in [one's] imagination."[37] Kubik notes that for a drummer, for example, the motor image (what a drummer's individual hands are doing) and the acoustic image (the perceived rhythmic pattern) "stand in an inaudible but mentally very effective cross rhythm against each other."[38] Kubik's multimodal formulation (an acoustic image as a heard picture) offers another way of understanding island time as a multimodal temporality. More than just the opposite of power-laden vectors of hegemonic time (expediency, punctuality, linearity), and beyond invocations of island indolence or ritualistic cyclicity, I want to think of island time as something closer to an inaudible cross rhythm. If the perceived slowness of St. Kitts and Nevis signals a lack of modernity and development relative to the rest of the world, it is also as a critical component in Kittitian-Nevisian modernity, and the contemporaneity of Kittitians and Nevisians, as a deliberately cultivated characteristic.

Filling in the Gaps: Selling St. Kitts–Nevis through Sound

The 1950s and 1960s saw the largest era of Caribbean tourism expansion since the nineteenth century as the result of a series of overlapping advances, including "the advent of jet travel, the US embargo of Cuba, rising affluence in North America and Europe, aid-financed air and sea transport infrastructure, and the expansion of foreign hotel investment lured by tax incentives."[39] During the two decades, "the Bahamas, Puerto Rico and Virgin Islands in the north, and Aruba and Barbados in the south became established popular international resort destinations."[40] Musicians from islands in the Lesser Antilles for whom the tourist industry had not yet become a viable option often took up temporary residence in the other islands—particularly the British Virgin Islands—where their semicolonial status under Britain made their citizenship useful for travel.

Although St. Kitts was the first Caribbean island to be colonized by the British, it was among the last to begin developing a tourist product. It was not until the early 1980s, when independence was a sure deal, that St. Kitts and Nevis began to invest significant governmental resources in tourism as the way of diversifying the fledgling economy. Because of the islands' late status, St. Kitts, from the beginning, marketed itself as "unspoiled." This is a particularly remarkable marketing schema given that three hundred years of sugar cultivation had effectively depleted much of the once-fertile land. Within the Caribbean tourism industry, however, the notion of unspoiled referred less to the land and more practically to the inhabitants. By the 1980s, there was a growing sense among American vacationers that people on islands characterized by mass tourism, especially places like the Bahamas, had become jaded by the incessant presence of tourists and outsiders, which forever changed the landscape and social milieu of those islands. Meanwhile, Kittitians and Nevisians, especially those who backed the newly elected People's Action Movement government in 1980, were cautious with the heady potentialities of tourism after independence.

Since they were wary of falling into the same traps of mass tourism, St. Kitts–Nevis tourism planners were insistent on a slow approach to development. In an interview in 1987, Lee Moore, the premier of St. Kitts–Nevis and the leader of the Labour Party from 1979 to 1981, described the nation's tourism strategy: "Instead of going after the mass market, [we] targeted specific groups in the upper income brackets. In other words, Labour opted for 'class' tourism over 'mass' tourism."[41] There was even a TV show on the local station ZIZ called *Be My Guest* that taught Kittitians and Nevisians how to be polite and hospitable to visitors. Bradshaw's vision of abandoning Christmas sports because of their perceived subservience to white planters would be transformed into targeted education, via one of the media mechanisms he feared most, geared toward cultivating the most hospitable attitudes toward wealthy visitors.[42] If in 1937 Marcus Garvey was right that the world had already been "waiting on" St. Kitts to join the collective present, its eventual arrival, to be manifested in political independence, was the product of the efforts of successive eras of politicians, diplomats, and other leaders who met the economic challenges of that independence by embracing the island's slowness, farawayness, and behindness. Indeed, "those who understand the system, boss it."[43]

Infectious Music

In late December 2012 I met with Robert Kelly to discuss the trajectory of tourism in St. Kitts–Nevis since the 1980s. He had spent the better part of the previous thirty years working for the St. Kitts Board of Tourism in the United States, which was initially a one- and then two-man post from which he had recently retired. Kelly, who had also worked as a journalist and a radio host on the national radio station, ZIZ, had received official residence papers for Canada in 1985 when a member of Prime Minister Kennedy Simmons's government offered him a job as promotional officer in New York City. In that position he would be a liaison to the entirety of the United States and its three hundred million people. He said:

> When we got there [to New York] we realized that nobody knew what or where St. Kitts and Nevis were. If I said, "St. Kitts and Nevis!" they'd say, "Where in Jamaica is that?" Jamaica had been promoting their island for almost forty years before us. Jamaica, Bermuda, Barbados, Puerto Rico all had a head start.

As a comparatively underfunded operation, they focused exclusively on the states and major cities surrounding New York—New Jersey, Connecticut, and Philadelphia:

> St. Kitts still felt really far away at that time, too. Because in those days you still had to stop over in St. Maarten. But we realized that for the rich older people in Manhattan, in Greenwich [Connecticut], Westchester [New York] right? They liked that because they would say, "I want to go someplace where nobody has heard of." They didn't want to go to mass-tourism destinations. Rich people and celebrities want smaller, unheard-of places. That's where the masquerade came in.[44]

Kelly told me that he thought St. Kitts and Nevis were among the first of the smaller, former British colonial islands to recognize the importance of their traditional music to tourism. He speculated that other islands were ashamed of their traditions that seemed backward compared to big-island musical offerings. But while other islands were taking on the cosmopolitanism that could be manufactured in all-inclusive enclaves, St. Kitts and Nevis tourism took a different route. Ultimately, it courted the old wealthy demographic instead of the dinkies and yuppies of the mass-tourism counterparts. What that meant, however, was that its niche was the past. When Minister of Tourism Michael Powell said that St. Kitts and Nevis wanted to offer the Caribbean "as it used to be," it was the masquerade that became essential to selling that version of the Caribbean to American tourists.[45] Kelly explained:

> Masquerade was the kind of culture they hadn't seen before in real life. Television didn't cover music of the islands, really. They knew pan, they knew reggae, they knew calypso. They were looking for something else and different. Plus the [drum and fife] music has this kind of rhythmic influence. Once you listen to that music, instantaneously the body moves. They saw that as friendliness. That opened some doors for us. Mid-1980s, very early 1990s, clowns, masquerades, big drum, and fife was the infectious music that made those white people get out of their seats and dance in the aisle. That music was very different from anything anyone had heard from the Caribbean before at that time. One of the things that is good about it being late is that you learn from their mistakes, and you fill in the gaps the other islands leave.[46]

In the 1980s, during the boom of new tourism, trade shows and travel agent demonstrations along with "fam," or familiarization, visits were the lifeblood of the tourist industry. Tourist boards were tasked with giving an expansive impression of their destination via pictures, videos, and sometimes live performances. At that time, the sounds and sights of the bodies of the tourist board employees, too, were part of the entire pitch. Kelly continued:

In St. Kitts we talk fast. You've been here talking about Brad-Shaaaww. Here we say Bratchah. But they love that. Everything from us was fast. For them in that setting, in an office, in the Jacob Javits Center with the loud drums and the tall feathers, they're jingling as they walk and it's intense from the start. They love that. That's different for them because they know Caribbean music and people to be kind of mellow. Jamaica had Bob [Marley] doing a laid back thing. Trinidad is calypso and pan.

It is quite likely that the fife and drum was regarded as particularly intense by audiences in the 1980s. The general listener from the United States had long been initiated into many of the rhythms and forms of the Caribbean, including the twentieth-century sounds of calypso, roots reggae, salsa, and merengue, as well as nineteenth-century circulating rhythms from Cuba, such as danzón and habanera. However, to unfamiliar audiences, the folk form presented by the St. Kitts and Nevis tourist board was notably different. The masqueraders—in their feathered caps and hopping on one leg—represented an authentic folk tradition that had not yet been put through the tourism machine that refines, glosses, and smooths.[47] While there are mumming traditions in other parts of the Caribbean that closely resemble those in St. Kitts–Nevis, they were not prevalent parts of the tourist market or even parts of those islands' marketing.

Over the course of developing tourist economies on various Caribbean islands, music has played a key role in substantiating ideas of isolation as related to the notion of a timeless and unchanging local sound.[48] In Jamaica, by the 1940s, musicians who primarily played for tourists were experimenting with magic, mysticism, and stereotypes of Vodou, Obeah, and Africanity in drum shows that included fire swallowing, almost-naked people, and percussion exaggerated with performances of fatigue, trancelike states, and visibly aged and handmade drums. A similar focus on happy primitives was at the crux of Bahamian touristic nightlife until the 1970s, when musicians playing in tourist venues turned primarily to American popular genres such as R&B and soul. As Timothy Rommen notes, "The Bahamas were, at the close of the 1970s, being marketed as a destination, but not as a place with truly distinctive arts and cultural possibilities."[49] The St. Kitts and Nevis Tourism Authority (which would later be separated into two different entities) seized on the opportunity to present the islands through music as novel and unspoiled in a way that had been abandoned on larger islands that could infrastructurally and politically accommodate the all-inclusive model.[50] For the burgeoning tourist industry in St. Kitts and Nevis of the 1980s, the goal was to sell the islands as an antidote to the mass tourism of previous decades, as a playground for older tourists who have surplus time and money, and particular ideas about what the Caribbean used to be and how it used to sound.

However, even as big drum music and the masquerade came to represent the oldest and most authentic of Kittitian-Nevisian cultural practices, distinct changes in the performance sound helped them to become prominent attractions for visitors. Descriptions of Christmas sports from the late nineteenth and early twentieth centuries noted that significant portions involved recitation of lines from various British plays, biblical scenes, and other folkloric stories. However, with migration and the association of Christmas sports with the manual labor of the sugar factory, much of the oratory has been lost or, at the very least, transformed so as to have lost any obvious relation to older forms. By the 1980s, lamentations over the loss of these traditions (themselves a form of public rhetoric that were present even as early as the 1950s) were at an all-time high, particularly in the years immediately following independence.

According to the former principal archivist at the St. Kitts National archives, Victoria O'Flaherty, the publication of the only existing book describing, historicizing, and promoting the Christmas sports within the federation, *Christmas Sports in St. Kitts–Nevis: Our Neglected Cultural Tradition* (1984), spurred renewed nationalist energy surrounding the practices. However, the uptick in masquerade performances, as O'Flaherty notes, took on a more "commodified" form at the same time. In particular, in the 1980s, masqueraders and big drum bands were popular entertainment for children's birthday parties and later became spectacles in hotel lobbies.[51] Practically speaking, where earlier iterations of the performances were almost thirty minutes long and included many points of recitation and acting, "the birthday party version" was pared down to only the most exciting and celebratory parts of the tradition.[52] Roving bands that in the early twentieth century would have gone from village to village and performed for hours were instead performing in fifteen-minute spurts at cultural presentations. The version that resonates with today's youth, who experienced these performances, is ostensibly a significantly faster, more condensed version than earlier in the century. These intensified iterations of masquerade and fife and drum music remain a hallmark of Kittitian-Nevisian historical legitimacy today.

Intangible Heritage and Creating a Past

When I was looking for rare photographs from the 1960s, I met Winston "Zack" Nisbett, unofficial "doctor of culture." Nisbett had been the caretaker of Edgar Challenger, an early member of the St. Kitts Workers' League, which was integral in organizing the labor union and, finally, the Labour Party. During his life, Challenger was known to have been a collector of things and papers, which was unusual during his time. Various floods, fires, and political arguments had disastrous effects on the preservation of historical materials on the islands. Apart from that, the material conditions of the working class made it almost impossible to keep papers or pictures, as it was often necessary to move one's entire one-room wooden home to a different open field in the event of rent disputes and other economic or natural events throughout the 1950s. Victoria O'Flaherty, the national archivist, has speculated that such conditions created a general ethos wherein Kittitians and Nevisians were disinterested in the idea of a physical archive.

Moreover, local lore suggests that when the People's Action Movement political party won the election in 1980, one of its first moves was to "clean out" all the documents in the government house pertaining to what it deemed was a "corrupt" government. Edgar Challenger salvaged many of the documents, keeping them in his home for twenty years, until his death in 2000. Thus did Nisbett come into possession of Challenger's belongings, including many rare documents such as birth and death certificates, deeds, and papers pertaining to the sale and purchase of the enslaved. Nisbett has since converted his small home in central Basseterre into a museum, archive, and library to allow access to these valuable relics.

When I visited Nisbett in July 2010, he greeted me at the front gate and invited me into the front room of the library (I learned much later that this space was officially called the Edgar Challenger International House Museum and Library). Upon stepping inside the dimly lit house, I was shocked by the sheer amount of stuff packed into every possible space. Stacks of paper filled cupboards and tabletops. Piles of documents and books lined a very narrow path between the three rooms of the house. Nineteenth-century undergarments and early twentieth-century household items, like irons and washing boards, hung on the wall above almanacs and leather-bound journals filled with Edgar Challenger's personal notes. By the end of my tour, which included a short pass through Nisbett's side yard, home to a few chickens and an ancient iguana, and a ground-level space dedicated to the display of carnival memorabilia, I had seen an incredible array of historical treasures.

As doctor of culture, Nisbett has had his hands in several projects to preserve local ways on St. Kitts. He held classes on fife making and playing and described to me a guitar and string band class and recital he had held a few weeks earlier. Nisbett had become aware of UNESCO's intangible heritage project that at the time was providing training and some technological supplies to cultural workers in St. Kitts to document and "preserve" the folklore and oral history that was vanishing as those born in the early twentieth century passed away. That generation was the last to participate in traditions such as the Christmas sports before they were changed by the emergence of the labor union and political efforts. Nisbett was supportive of preservation efforts and appreciated support from agencies and individuals off the island. He spoke at length about a digital camera gifted to him by the Taiwanese government to aid his preservationist efforts.

UNESCO, as a subsidiary of the United Nations, worked through the official Kittitian-Nevisian government and not through the efforts of individuals such as Nisbett. That was cause for concern for him, and he was protective of the lot. He would not allow me to work with his materials if I was also speaking with government officials.

"Is dem or is me."

He was weary of official governmental efforts to document cultural practices because, he said, "what deh see is what deh want."[53] I asked Nisbett whether he meant that the government is guilty of hoarding historical relics away from the public or whether he was critical of what he saw as cherry-picking and misrepresentation of history.

"Hmm. So you know," he responded.

I did not know.

Fearing that governmental preservation would offer a skewed version of the past or that the collected materials would not be cared for properly, Nisbett did his best to maintain distance between himself and any official (national) archives. The tenacity with which he held that conviction led Nisbett, and some others who were dubious about national politics, to believe that the damp, crowded building on Central Street was a safer location than any air-conditioned government building. What Nisbett's belief points to is the many levels on which the creation of *a* history is a contested and contingent process of assemblage. Pressing, though, is the ever-present awareness that in St. Kitts and Nevis, various forces (volcanic eruption, overzealous political leader, hurricane, global pandemic, fire, or flood) at any time can precipitate the physical destruction of, the taking, suppression, subversion, or intentionally misremembering of what constitutes a past in those islands, in contrast to the understanding of a transatlantic slavery history that originates in Africa.

In September 2018, during celebrations leading up to the national celebration of independence on September 19, the Nisbett unveiled a new exhibit from his one-man archive. Called Zack's Historical-Cultural Library Museum, the freshly painted and organized space had been moved to Buckley's Estate, on the western outskirts of Basseterre, where the first labor riots in the 1930s that were so crucial to the fight for independence had occurred. In an interview with the *Labour Spokesman*, Nisbett commented that the move was significant because Buckley's Estate is "one [of] the more established places for tourism . . . tourists as well as locals can see what we once went through, where we came from and where we're going because it's always important to reflect. . . . It will be really good. It is something important for St. Kitts and Nevis. I am taking my time with it. This is a serious thing. I'm not making any joke."[54]

Nisbett's collecting and preserving was less about saving "history" and more about guarding these minutiae—material specificities—*against* History as a big, sweeping, summarizing effort.[55] The youth string band summer institute and material relics of bygone eras are to Nisbett, and the many who generously support his myriad efforts, the kinds of things that often get lost or thrown out in the transition from the "old St. Kitts" to the new. They are also the kinds of artifacts that take on different meaning when collective efforts shift from a push to sovereignty as a means out of colonial degradation, to a different kind of fight for economic viability in a global tourist economy.

Caribbean tourism is an unpredictable machine that can destroy and distort music and other forms of cultural heritage. For Kittitians and Nevisians, however, it has become a necessary and integral feature of cultural preservation and a unified understanding of heritage. But creating a past—imagining something happening now, even if relatively unchanged, as being related to the present is not the same as creating a musical history. Christmas sports, particularly the masquerade and the big drum, have been deployed time and again as a representation of something that proves St. Kitts and Nevis have history as a legitimizing possession and are not simply stuck in a particular moment. But where rejections of the practices of the 1940s and 1950s saw the sports as tethering the working class to a state of "primitivity," contemporary efforts to historicize the nation through the sports do similar work: they divorce the musical practices from the sounds considered wholly "modern" in the national context. In the long transition from a colonial sugar monoculture to an economy supported largely by tourism, Kittitian-Nevisian Christmas sports, particularly the masquerade and big drum, as they represent the changes in working-class society and the growing pains of a sovereign nation, have been integral to individual and government-backed efforts to stake claim to a particular relationship to the slow, unchanging island and its sonic iterations of heritage.

The Pedagogy of Pace

As a child, I loved it when my mom told the story of the time she "wuked up" in front of the Queen. Most of her stories about home, and her childhood and early adolescence in the 1950s and 1960s were about feeling stuck, unseen, and generally stifled by the narrowness of the lane she was expected to occupy as a poor Black girl. Respectability, as the "moral force behind the coercive power of colonialism and neo-colonialism," permeated everything.[1] She said: "Everybody was Black, you know. So it wasn't like I'm saying there's a big white man telling me I'm bad. It was other Black people telling me I'm chewing wrong, I'm laughing like a 'commoner,' I'm too loud, me hair too coarse, me nose too broad."[2] In the Queen story, though, there is a crack in the mask that coloniality crafted for her, and her retelling of it chips at mine, too.

It is 1966, and schoolchildren have lined the street as Queen Elizabeth II passes in a car, waving affectionately as they shout, "Hello, Dear One!" The girls are all dressed in white, wearing the finest shoes, frilly socks, and starched bows. Later, in Warner Park, the same girls are standing together, and watching the various demonstrations and performances presented in the Queen's honor (fig 2.1). A steel-pan orchestra played, followed by the big drum. During the latter, teachers instruct the children—especially the young girls—to "sway gently" to the music.

In our North Bronx kitchen, Mom dramatically recounts her confusion: "I was fourteen years old at the time and thought to myself, 'Sway? Gently? To this?'" She tilts her head to one side, the way she always does when she wants to emphasize the irony of a particularly juicy story. "The teacher is telling me to sway, and I'm hearing that riddim." Bending her knees slightly, she bounces to the memory of the booming bass drum while chanting its rhythm: *bum badumbum, bum badumbum.*

FIGURE 2.1. *Queen Elizabeth II, February 22, 1966.* The Queen and the Duke of Edinburgh's February 1966 tour of the West Indies was filmed by the British Film Institute and produced into a twenty-nine-minute newsreel, which can be viewed at the BFI's YouTube channel. Image courtesy of the National Archives, St. Kitts and Nevis.

"I did it for a little while," she says, clenching the seams of an imaginary skirt and swaying in a slow, wistful two-step. "But then I just couldn't take it anymore. It got me! I went crazy!" *Bum badumbum bum badumbum.* Wrapping her arms around herself, she pretends to be captured by the sound, struggling to get free. "I said 'to hell with this' and started goin' on and wukin up, shakin' my bum and ting." At this point, Mom throws her head back and winds her backside wildly, looking back at it occasionally like a hapless bystander, powerless against her batty's will.

"People around me pointed and laughed; they were shocked." I am especially tickled by her impersonations of scandalized onlookers—some with mouths agape, others using their puckered lips to point in her direction. "I was known for weeks after as 'the girl who was wukin up in front of the Queen.'" Eventually, she relaxes and shrugs her shoulders: "I was young and crazy. I didn't care. I think they wrote about me in the newspaper."[3]

News of the Queen's first visit to the British West Indies was reported around the world, but the experiences of individual people—especially schoolgirls—were not of particular interest to journalists at the time (fig. 2.1). To my mother, more important than any official account was her own recognition of the poorly timed, impulsive, and indecorously Black-girl behavior she exposed in the presence of the Queen. If, as it had been throughout Britain's colonial rule, the Queen was the ultimate symbol of feminine respectability in the British colonies, then my mother's behavior was gossip-worthy scandal.[4]

What mediates the tempo of music and the temporality of islands? What can the musical intensity of one Black girl's body reveal about the relationship between her small-island home and the broader colonial world? This chapter discusses the centrality of representations of Black women's bodies to colonial and neoliberal nationalist discourses of proper temporality. After a description of what I call "rituals of Black womanhood," I draw on the explicit history of anti-Black misogyny as manifested in the Sugar Islands to contextualize social aspirations after emancipation in 1834 toward middle-classness via the route of feminine respectability. While Caribbeanist scholars have argued that conversations about Caribbean femininities should move beyond discussions of respectability, the intensity of the prevailing discourses of respectability (often subsumed into other critiques about how women move and what they desire) continues to make respectability a relevant category, even if largely through humor and satire.

Respectability is also the most salient context of my own upbringing. As a millennial Black woman, notions of feminine respectability provided the boundaries of my existence, the content of my inner voice, as a good, worthy, and ultimately productive member of society. I was raised to desire heterosexual marriage, to make myself small, quiet, and useful. While "Caribbean sexuality is characterized by diversity, in which multiple partnering relationships by both men and women, serial monogamy, informal polygamy, and same-gender and bisexual relations are commonplace," the discursive norm still emphatically centers heterosexual monogamy as a key tenet of respectable womanhood.[5]

Or, as island spaces like St. Kitts and Nevis are always inclusive of the diasporic and other off-island locales (part of what Rosamond S. King calls the "Caribglobal"), my entrainment into normative sexuality by a certain generation of Kittitian-Nevisians inextricably tethers this era of sexual norms to contemporary understandings of the national and social boundaries of St. Kitts and Nevis.[6] In 2022, the Kittitian writer and researcher Xavienne-Roma Richardson, who hosted a radio show on sexuality on the national radio station ZIZ, described the regional context of sexuality and its expression as follows: "In a region where almost one-third of girls' first sexual encounter is forced . . . and where rape rates surpass the world average . . . , it is important that researchers, policymakers, parents and partners consider how limited sexual agency results in potentially permanent negative physical and psychological consequences."[7] In her work on expressions of sexual agency in St. Kitts, she emphasizes that the compulsory heterosexuality of the region, specifically in St. Kitts and Nevis, is shaped socially by myriad competing and coproducing vectors, including religion, media, and socialization. This chapter moves between performance, history, visual representation, storytelling, and ethnography to better elucidate the relationship between the island temporalities of colonization, the tempo and beat-based developments of the following chapters, and my own experiences of gender as a taught practice. This chapter posits that these experiences and histories, and the vantages they share, are rituals of intergenerational teaching about the implicit St. Kitts rules of Black womanhood.

Oomanship and Rituals of Black Womanhood

I grew up on soca music that described scenarios of women being "taken away," "caught," "infected," or "lured" by the rhythm and sound of the music— especially during carnival time—which apparently explained the fantasy protagonist's (usually a young woman) indecorous or impassioned behavior. These lyrics deployed the regular tropes of calypso and soca, including instructive lyrics, sexual innuendo, double entendre, and the exceptionality of carnival time. My mother's story captures the relationship between the music and the public, energized body of a dancing or performing Black womanhood beyond the scope of a stylistic metaphor espoused by men. In my mother's story, the "gentle sway" requested by the authority figure was a respectable stand-in for whatever kinds of movement the girls might have come up with on their own had they allowed the music to get hold of them, or had their bodies been allowed to tell the truth about the extent of their relationship to the kettledrum's syncopation.

In colonial St. Kitts and Nevis (which lasted from 1628 to 1983), the recognition of the infectiousness of music—infectious for its repetitiveness, drive, tempo, rhythm—was just one facet of the colonial discourses of respectability and elevation that rendered some forms of Black music as "contagions" and a threat to educated, decorous, and "civilized" white subjectivity. Local Black children dancing for the Queen is one example of the ways that moving Black bodies—particularly as objects of attention for a temporary, white gaze—are sites of uneven relationship to colonial respectability as a mode of national inclusion. The felt incongruence between the fast, intricate big drum rhythm and "gentle swaying" is demonstrative of the ways that Black girls' embodiment of familiar rhythms is a public performance disciplined through the moralization of temporality and the discourse of speed. The gently-swaying girls were expressly asked to represent the 4/4 big drum rhythm in 2, such that the fluid motion of their flouncy skirts stood in for the staccato eighth- and sixteenth-note motions that typically accompanied this music. The legiti-macy of the fife and drum band—which, by the 1960s, was used to represent the distinctive culture of St. Kitts—was dependent on Black girls' bodies to do the work of concealing the contemporary reality of the form and its bodily corollaries. The dainty two-step was meant to convey an air of bodily distance and disinterest in the music as a facet of a performance of learned European subjectivity.

Within the dense rhythm of the drum rolls and syncopation of the kettle-drum, each beat represented the threat of exposure, laying bare the connec-tion between local sounds and local behavior. This example of the tempo of a woman's body being the barrier between the missteps of the past and aspirational, sovereign futures is emblematic of the tradition of decoloniza-tion through nationalism in the Caribbean. These representations and the discourse surrounding Black girls' and women's bodies is as integral to the imagined community of the nation within St. Kitts and Nevis as the big drum is. What made my mother "go crazy" in front of the Queen can be understood in the context of a general discourse of deterioration and decline related to the themes of degeneracy that characterized transatlantic discourse.[8]

Since the inception of the plantation system, Black women in the Carib-bean have been portrayed and understood in relation to forms of degrada-tion that are inherent to European understandings of colonial outposts. As an augmentation of their Blackness—"the physical deformity so necessary to the invention of the servile soul"—poor Black women's bodies, "real and symbolic," were seen as carriers of physical pathogens and as harboring ill-ness and symptoms of contagion such as overflow (as caused by unexpressed breastmilk) and odor (especially that caused by menstruation or sweat on laboring bodies).[9] Using illness as an excuse to avoid some work in the sugar fields contributed to the association of Black women with notions of sickness and disease and with Black women's bodies as "unhygienic."[10]

A domino effect of uprisings among sugar workers in the 1930s cascaded across the string of islands in the Caribbean Sea and beyond to the Bahamas. These post-emancipation political insurrections—in St. Kitts, Trinidad, Ja-maica, British Guiana, St. Vincent, St. Lucia, and Barbados—were responses to low wages, poor working conditions, political disenfranchisement, and deleterious health conditions. In 1920, the infant mortality rate was 408 in-fant deaths per 1,000 live births, and life expectancy was less than fifty years. As Hermia Morton Anthony notes, Afro-Kittitian women were subject to especially severe hardship. In the 1930s, even as she worked alongside men on a sugar plantation, a Black Kittitian woman would be expected to have a fire burning and meal cooked well before the sun rose, and she would be responsible for the general management and survival of her household and any associated children. Plantation managers would sometimes refuse to pay women with money, offering only food or other household supplies, instead. White plantation managers, invested in upholding notions of respectability and patrilinear nuclear family, argued that if a woman wanted money, she should find a husband or turn to prostitution. On the other hand, as one plantation worker put it, Black women were still expected to perform arduous manual labor and were regarded, as one sugar plantation worker noted, like "men who could breed."[11]

In the face of these conditions, and, lest it go without saying, the effects of the previous four hundred years of enslavement, this collection of uprisings is significant because they led to voting rights for Black workers and ultimately some form of political independence on many of the islands. By the 1950s, the work of labor unions and a Black-led group of local political elites had deepened Kittitian-Nevisian investment in emerging notions of nationalism via various programs of social elevation. For some Black women, aspirational culture was enacted largely through forms of embodied respectability, such as modest dress and performances of piety. These acts were intended to distance upwardly mobile Black women from the ideas and discourses attached to poor Black women, who were regarded as particularly susceptible to (and as carriers of) certain kinds of contagion, especially in the form of sexual corruption (e.g., pregnancy—a girl or woman in St. Kitts and Nevis is often described as "getting children" as one might "get sick") or music (that may "take" or "overcome" her body).

These dominant sexualized and racialized colonial frames created the social and material context that Black women have historically navigated. One other example of an alternate category that accounts for this context and the realities of Black womanhood is in Hermia Morton Anthony's 1990s ethnography of Afro-Kittitian women who participated in the labor uprisings of the 1930s. She identifies "oomanship" as "a negotiated, fluid, gender category" that "defines the relations of women in Kittitian society, [and] their contributions to its development and transformation." Oomanship highlights womanhood as both imposed identity and a form of labor. That "ooman" is a Kittitian-Nevisian pronunciation of "woman" accounts for the structures of oppression, modes of transcendence, subversion, and experiences of hardship inherent to the inherited positionality of Blackness and womanness in colonial St. Kitts–Nevis. One of the most important aspects of oomanship includes preparing girl children physically, mentally, and economically for the realities of Black womanhood to ensure that they are not duped by the gendered fantasies of being taken care of by a man. Oomanship does not just articulate the conditions of hardship, it also articulates an inherited subjectivity; it is a technique for navigating the world with a body marked by the contradictions that Blackness and womanness pose to colonial categories.

For poor Black Kittitian women of the 1930s, significant vulnerability to physical violence perpetrated by any man and the nonrecognition of women's labor were significant sources of myriad hardships. As material conditions improved, the choreography of Black womanhood morphed to navigate new currents and conditions. As the performative demands of a burgeoning nationalism met the ascendance of beauty pageants as a facet of carnival celebrations in St. Kitts–Nevis, the National Queen Pageant stage provided a public space for another kind of articulation of Black femininity. Staging a counter to ideas of the vulnerable and contagious Black woman's body, the beauty pageant stage—especially during the talent portion of a typical "Queen Show"—presented opportunities for feminine displays of respectable and impervious bodily control.

The festivity surrounding the Queen's 1966 visit is an example of what Belinda Edmondson calls "popular culture rituals," which include recurrent, indigenized events such as carnival and calypso competitions. The enactment of these rituals constitutes arenas for public performances. In colonial society, Black and other nonwhite women were regarded as "the antiwoman, pathological and lascivious viragos who undermine the nationalist project."[12] In colonial society, which discursively relegated women's bodies to the domestic sphere of the home, public performance of these popular culture rituals was understood to be unrespectable and indecorous. Historically, representations of Black women in carnival have included exaggerated stereotypes of bodies and behavior. The occasion of the Queen's visit outside of carnival was another popular culture ritual that required decorous feminine behavior especially from the poorest and Blackest of its citizens.

Public arenas, which are coded as masculine in the colonial framework, function as the opposite of the "respectable" and feminine private space of the home and yard. Historically, then, Black women's performances in these public spaces—which we may understand as a woman's agential doing, being seen or heard—have served since the mid-twentieth century to restrict access to the social, economic, and political benefits reserved for "respectable" citizens. Where postcolonial nationalism is predicated on patrilineal, monogamous heterosexuality, the standing of Black women—whose Blackness and womanness present an exponential threat—functions as a gauge of the moral health of the nation. That is, Black women's bodies have served as the site on and through which discourse about the nation takes place. As Edmondson notes regarding Black women's public performances at venues surrounding

carnival in the postcolonial period of the mid-twentieth century, "the traditional attitude of the respectable and aspiring-respectable classes toward
(usually Black) women in the public sphere has been to perceive these performances as indices of Black women's innate degeneracy."[13]

Respectability from Post-Emancipation to Post-Colony, 1834–1983

Living between seemingly incompatible or incongruous cultural and social
structures is an integral feature of St. Kitts and Nevis. Karen Fog Olwig has
made evident in her discussion of post-emancipation Nevis the existence of
contradictory cultural traditions associated with essential aspects of life in
Caribbean societies.[14] The Nevisian traditions did not constitute bounded,
autonomous, and independent cultural units; instead, they were associated
with limited spheres of life, each of central importance to the African Caribbean population.[15] Olwig identifies three key "cultural traditions" in post-
emancipation Afro-Nevisian society: the implementation of a hierarchical
plantation system, the importance of African kinship relationships, and the
influence of Methodist missionaries in promoting an ideology of respectability. She notes how in the wake of emancipation, "as the plantocracy lost its
power during the last part of the nineteenth century, the ideology of respectability and its associated social institutions gradually attained a dominant position in colonial society."[16]

    In post-emancipation St. Kitts and Nevis, the Methodist Church and its
set of respectable morals came to represent a secondary channel to respectability that did not require wealth. Denouncing material extravagance, the
Methodist Church promoted a sexual modesty that included monogamy and
marriage and prohibited out-of-wedlock childbearing, which was often considered the result of premarital cohabitation. However, the ideology of Methodist respectability was not always implemented in practice. Even while respectability ideology dictated a particular approach to sexuality, especially for
women, a reliance on a much wider array of kinship relationships and alternative (woman-centered) approaches to land ownership were necessary for
women's survival. These familial and sexual arrangements, and the multiplicity of alternatives to respectable femininity they acknowledge, represent the
local navigational techniques of Black womanhood or oomanship. While the
implementation of the Methodist ideology signaled the growth of a culture
of competing discourses surrounding female sexual behavior, Black female
sexuality was solidified as one of the "organizing principle[s] for a new moral
order," as anthropologist Debra Curtis put it, "prompted and institutionalized
by the Methodist society."[17]

Discourse surrounding women's sexuality in the twenty-first century is still historically tied to and justified by religious mores and is augmented by the acknowledgment of outside—foreign—forces that compete with Christian ideology. As Curtis writes of Nevisian girls in 2003:

> Staying off the streets at night, abstaining from sexual activity, heading home after school and avoiding loitering in town, doing well in school, earning high scores on exams, avoiding the negative effects of US culture, specifically BET and soap operas, avoiding boys and older men, and attending church and church-sponsored youth group activities are conditions and activities that make a girl virtuous in the eyes of the religious community. When focusing on youth, community leaders often use US culture as a gauge by which to measure Nevisian morality. Interestingly, the more closely Nevisian youth appear to mirror the customs and lifestyles of US youth, the greater the perceived threat that Nevisian youth pose to Nevisian morality.[18]

Within the formulation of Caribbean nationalism's contentious relationship with foreign media, Samantha Pinto notes that "Black women's bodies come to stand in for the west—like a contagion—which has written its corruption onto their bodies."[19] In nationalist discourse, talk about Black female sexuality in relation to popular music and dance provides a measurement for the level of restraint and moral health of local society.

Going Wild: Tishima Browne and the National Carnival Queen Pageant

The proof of wylers' dark side is the "disgraceful" behavior of young Black women and the perceived and anticipated violence of young Black men who hear it. This correlation between the speed of the music and what it makes bodies do is so tightly woven that it constitutes a recognizable local logic that animates various kinds of public discourse.

One particularly salient example of this logic in motion occurred at the 2014–2015 St. Kitts and Nevis National Carnival Queen Pageant. Tishima Browne placed first in the talent segment and ultimately won the crown (fig. 2.2). Her talent was a dramatic monologue in which she played the role of an opinionated Kittitian woman participating in a version of exuberant exchange that Hermia Morton Anthony has described as "pung toary" or "pung melee."[20] This is best understood as a kind of storytelling gossip during which the storyteller may "happily talk about anyone, everyone, anything and everything."[21] Pung toary style, flying seamlessly between scales, referents, tenses, moods, and modes, is a decolonizing, subversive "method of discussing the minutiae, the fine details of an issue."[22] In this instance,

FIGURE 2.2. AND 2.3. Tishima Browne performing in the talent portion of the 2014–2015 St. Kitts and Nevis National Carnival Queen Pageant, as posted on the event's official Facebook page. The caption to the two photos read "Miss National Bank, Tishima Browne: Drama—Depicted a mas maker who is determined to enjoy herself but is frustrated at the music and dress codes in modern Carnival." Photo courtesy of the St. Kitts and Nevis National Carnival Facebook, December 28, 2014. https://m.facebook .com/SKNCarnival/photos/a.795993107104947.1073741929.144056438965287/796038507100407/.

Browne's performance was an impassioned and humorous take on generational changes in Kittitian-Nevisian society that, deploying a regional West
Indian logic, mapped to relations between the tempo of contemporary soca
and the comportment of Black women during carnival as proof of a changed
and changing society. Browne's monologue opened:

Things really change, you know? Everybody talk about how things ain' change.
Yes, things change.
Starting with we music.[23]

The practice of performatively marking and highlighting experiences of
difference or change—the shock, distortion, danger, awe—is what Tishima
Browne's character performed as a through line between two generations of
Kittitians and Nevisians. The older generation would have been youth during
or before the 1960s and 1970s: well before St. Kitts–Nevis's independence in
1983 and shortly before or during its statehood in 1967. The younger generation experienced their youthful freedom in the sovereign, federated, and in-
surgent 1980s and 1990s. To Browne, "we music" meant the music belonging
to the nation but reflecting the sounds of the former generation.

Whether or not things had, in fact, changed seems like a cheesy rhetori-
cal setup, but in St. Kitts and Nevis, it is an issue at the crux of political debates about the fate of the two-island federation. The notion that things had
not changed constitutes a significant feature of historical treatments of the
islands and saturates tourism advertisements. And yet, things like the materials people use to build houses, the western shoreline of St. Kitts, the cost of
a ferry ticket across the two-mile strait between Basseterre in St. Kitts and
Charlestown in Nevis had changed.

Browne's monologue continued:

Long time, you could have take a li'l chip. [*She subtly sways her hips and walks
     stage left.*]
Back then, the music didn't have to come with no warning label and instructions.
De music these days could *kill* you.
How you mean?
Long time you ain't hear, "De Lay Lay Shang Shang, De Lay Lay Shang Shang."
     [*She sings the chorus of a popular 1977 Ellie Matt calypso.*]
But you know, your heart ain't beating too fast, you taking you li'l chip and
     you eyeing somebody husband—"Hey, goodnight" [*She smiles at some-
     one's imaginary husband.*]
Nowadays . . . [*A snippet of a soca song begins to play from the speakers*].[24]

As if possessed, Browne shook her body violently, arms jerking wildly around her. She punched and kicked the air while her head flailed behind in every direction. The music stopped, and she stopped, too. Bent over, exhausted, she placed her hands on her knees and panted with quick, deliberate breaths. The percussive sound of the stuttering voice that ravished the common woman's body was from Trinidadian soca singer Iwer George's 2001 song "Let Me See Yuh Hand."[25] As Curwen Best notes, this song, which was both a critique and a parody, "reflected the newer directions that [soca] music was taking in the first decade of the new century."[26] At a speedy 166 beats per minute, "Let Me See Yuh Hand" begins with Iwer George yelling into a microphone: "Selecta! Gimme the wicked Iwer George tune dey, so fast!" By evoking the selecta, or DJ, a staple of dancehall music, George placed the song within a lineage that veered away from the musical heritage three decades of calypso and soca purists were seeking to preserve. Recognized as overly technologically reliant, insincere in its capitalist aspirations and obvious foreign influence, the reputation of "Let Me See" is a distillation of the parameters of early 2000s soca music. Calling further attention to the separation of the singer and the "tune" or "riddim," the entire song sounds like George is not so much singing with the track as singing over it—riding on top of it. With small tonal and rhythmic discrepancies between a riddim and a voice, characterizing what Peter Manuel and Wayne Marshall call the "riddim method," George's vocals sound more like talking than singing, and they do not adhere closely to anything we might call a melody or rhythm.[27] The riddim also samples from the light classical waltz "Chopsticks," an excerpt that is synonymous with easy, nonserious, classical music.[28]

Watching the pageant video from my home in Chicago, more than half a decade later, I can hear only the crowd's laughter in the background. I feel deprived of the small details in movement and sound that I am familiar with as key features of pageant attendance. The camera angle admits into view a few men watching from the wings, and their spontaneous smiles are a small consolation. Browne's character takes on a significant degree of humor and resonance because she draws on three irreducibly contradictory features of Kittitian-Nevisian sociality. First, she does this in a nested vortex of Black womanhood: a young Black woman playing an old Black woman critiquing other young Black women. Second, her vortex centralizes Black womanhood in modern notions of the nation within the St. Kitts–Nevis Federation, and in the importance of allowing space for representing Black womanhood and critiquing that same womanhood within the local community. Third, she identifies that it is specifically Black women's bottoms that are often invoked as markers for the limits of society, both in St. Kitts and Nevis and throughout the broader West Indies. Through dance, women can exhibit control over their bottoms by either concealing them entirely or displaying them as very controlled in intricate motion in dance. Black women's backsides delimit the boundary lines of sociality. To conceal a certain body (or body parts) was to defend that body's rightful place in the public sphere. In counterpoint, to exhibit, flash, or otherwise show the same body (or parts) could be effective offense against various incursions into public decorum.

The national beauty pageant sits on the flip side of these displays of the excess of the Black female bumsee as the first space of rituals of performance for women to showcase respectability. In my experience, Black women's butts are not significantly less visible at these pageants than at other times; the swimsuit segment is a regular fan favorite. However, their visibility is part of a performance of restraint that is understood as the product of concerted development under the direction of a team of handlers. As a counterweight to the overexposed and defiantly sexual Black woman, the pageant woman reaffirms the importance of women's sounding, moving bodies as gauges of the health and trajectory of the nation. In other words, it is not that Black women are meant to be hidden as caretakers of private spaces and family life. Instead, Black women's bodies are necessarily highly visible in their societal function as performers and promoters of bodily mastery (restraint and abandon), a duty that is referenced and performed onstage or among friends in speech acts like Browne's monologue:

Dat dey enough to give you a double heart attack and chikungunya.
Tings not the same.
Nowadays, everybody wants to play Simon Says for the carnival.
If the song say "clothes off" with that, nobody stops to think
Brap! Everybody naked! Tings just not de same.[79]

If the typical pageant woman should symbolize restraint, then Browne's performance identifies fast music as an impediment to that restraint, making it harder for the woman to control herself, her body, and her bottom in particular. When she names a series of scenarios that might temporarily trick, dupe, or otherwise force her character to relinquish autonomy over her body (including Simon Says, schizophrenia, viral infection, and heart attack), Browne's character frames speed as a categorically similar plane of experience as crying or screaming. The speed of unbridled, oversexualized, and uncivilized deviance (exemplified in exhibitionist-style, sexually suggestive dancing and lyrics) is the same "fast-fast" speed recognized later in the monologue in the brisk-walking, distanced professionalism of a banker at work, even as the deviant dancer and the professional banker are foils to each other. These articulations of and attestations *to* speed draw our attention to a conceptual constellation of social, ethical, aesthetic, physical, and metaphorical boundaries and the actions that constitute their transgression. Speed represents both the unproductive and the unthinkable, the physical, the dangerous and uncontrollable, the new, and the dubious professionalism of modern women and men who seek to participate in the best of many worlds. Speed represents the fear and trepidation of the new, of change, and of the unmeasured. The monologue goes on (fig 2.3):

Well eh eh, it's only thong they do sell in St. Kitts? [*Turning her body around so that her backside faces the audience, she squats deeply, cocking her bum back.*]
Everybody want dey bottom in de road!
[*In the background, the winning road march song for that year, the Small Axe Band's "Bottom in de Road" begins to play.*]
Look! Lock it off!
[*The music stops. With the left side of her body facing the audience, she bends over and strains her bum toward the crowd.*][30]

If "Bottom in de Road" was the anthem of that year's carnival, the phrase, coined by Iwer George in his 1997 song of the same name, is definitional for carnival across the Caribbean archipelago. Originally banned from the radio by the Trinidadian government for its lewd lyrics, the titular phrase is emblematic of two defining features of West Indian sociality: women's, especially Black women's, bums and the road, as constituted by the public spaces where mobile carnival activities are enacted. The version of the song that harassed her character at the monologue's opening and again toward the middle was by a Kittitian wylers band, the Small Axe Band International. The speedy riddim and buoyant chromaticism came blasting through the speakers as front man Mr. World, in his expressively monotone fashion, sang "plenty bottoms in de road." Browne's character yelled for it to be "locked off," before the end of the chorus, "what a bam bam! Shake it up, shake it up." She said:

Imagine me a go put my good bottom in de government road.
You could imagine dat?
Look, you see me good bum? I have no desire to hang my bottom.
Neither hang it, floss it, nor park it in de road. 'Tall.[31]

Soca, Sense, and Decorum in St. Vincent and Grenada

Friday, I was on Fort Street watching the parade and I see a slim ting
Up and dung in she tong [thong] [*Embodying the slim ting, she straightens her
    back and swivels her head side to side, affecting an air of confidence*]
[*Bending toward the audience*] She feel-say she look good, you see?
[*She takes a beat and squarely faces the crowd*]
She bottom mark up like an atlas!
She got the Caribbean on the left and Europe on the right [*She points to her
    left and right buttocks respectively.*]
I hear a little boy say, "Mommy, Mommy! Look, look! . . .
[*Beat*]
St. Vincent and the Grenadines."
[*Imitating the little boy, she bends low, extends her hand, and points her finger
    eagerly toward the imaginary butt*].

Spread across multiple inset layers of imagining, the moment the little
boy sees a map of St. Vincent and the Grenadines in the blemished skin of a
woman's exposed bottom at carnival is also the moment when the imaginary
woman's body, led by her butt, is revealed to have always been a navigational
tool for triangulating the changing status of "things"—of local society, the nation, the Caribbean, and the larger world. Attendees of the National Carnival
Queen Pageant tend to be Kittitian-Nevisian residents or visitors from neighboring eastern Caribbean islands. Their familiarity with the silhouette of
St. Vincent and the Grenadines, or at least its archipelagic shape, registered in
the howling laughter that followed the joke (fig. 2.4). Other island imaginaries, such as those reflected in images from 1992 associated with Colombian
champeta music, make similar connections with women's behinds and the
mapping of units—islands—of sound in relation (fig. 2.5).

Research from St. Vincent and the Grenadines underscores the conceptual junction formed by the atlas-assed woman in the story, Browne's use of
the verb "feel-say," and the political stakes of the pageant.[32] Roger Abrahams's
ethnography of St. Vincent discusses sense and nonsense in terms of their
relativity to time, place, and audience, noting how prevalent a subject speech
and decorum were in daily exchange: "the amount of talk one hears about
talk on the island . . . [is] truly striking."[33] He concluded that for Black peas-
ant West Indian societies, performances of decorous and indecorous speech
acts were a central conduit for the dramatized interplay of establishing flu-
ency and logic and for performatively and creatively departing from them.
If sense is an ideal, then nonsense juxtaposes sense by departing from it in

FIGURE 2.4. Silhouette of St. Vincent and Grenadines. © Creat Art | dreamstime.com. https://www
.dreamstime.com/saint-vincent-s-grenadines-map-silhouette-vector-illustration-isolated-white-back
ground-saint-vincent-s-grenadines-map-image125896118.

"perceptible" ways. "Being totally out of control of the language," he believed, was not speech at all but "making noise."[34]

Abrahams's consideration of speech in St. Vincent and Nevis as perfor-mance buoys my argument that the performance and appraisal of manners of speech and conventional acts of music making are governed by similar logics recognized in the social economies of these Caribbean islands. It is equally likely that a Kittitian or Nevisian comment on a skilled demonstration of col-loquial speech or a particularly good musical performance as "sweet." When the riddim emanating from a drum machine creates an especially driving groove, knowledgeable listeners might remark that the producer or key-boardist is "making de box talk." Abrahams argues: "Everyday communica-tive behavior is judged on the same terms as more stylized performances.

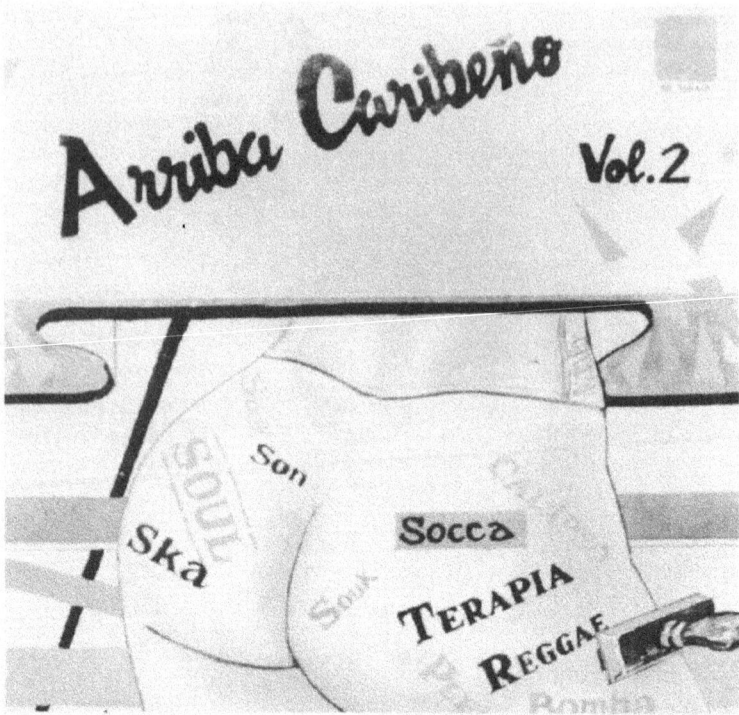

FIGURE 2.5. *Arriba Caribeño Vol. 2*, compilation album cover inscribing dance music styles from across the Caribbean on a woman's bottom using an ink-stamp. Reprinted in Deborah Pacini Hernandez, "A View from the South: Spanish Caribbean Perspectives on World Beat," *World of Music* 35, no. 2 (1993): 66.

Little distinction is made between formally and obviously structured expressive performances—such as singing a song, dancing, or telling a folk tale and ordinary expressive interactions. Thus while there would be no confusion in the community between a Carnival song and an everyday argument, they would be recognized as being related to each other as controlled contest forms and evaluated as performances."[35]

More than being judged by the same evaluative terms, everyday communicative behavior often occurs as stylized as events that are understood as performances. Browne's performance of an animated "giving word" ("gee wuhd," as my grandmother might have said) was not any more expressive than an offstage version shared between friends. Expressive components of her monologue—like bringing in language from currently circulating songs; making associative linkages between topics, sounds, concepts, and tenses; demonstrating kinetic energy; singing, dancing, and embodying various characters—are all characteristics of everyday communication in St. Kitts and Nevis. The stage magic of rehearsed musical cues and impeccable hair and makeup are the biggest things differentiating Browne's performance from others, just like it, happening elsewhere. It is exactly her performance of familiarity, with its different forms and logics of speech and relation that are meaningful in St. Kitts and Nevis, that marks Browne's presentation as masterful in the pageant. Her ability to affect a Kittitian accent and use it to critique the behavior of Black women marks her performance as authentic, decorous, and funny in its focus and metaperformance of (mis)behavior that is inauthentic, indecorous, and illogical.

Tings Change, Part 1: Women's Contagion

Tishima Browne's dramatic monologue on the threatened respectability of women during carnival time delighted the crowd. Prancing back and forth on the stage, she conjured an elder who was exasperated with the behavioral norms of today's young women. Browne weaves this thread throughout her monologue:

Tings really change, you know? Everybody talk about how things ain' change.
Yes, tings change.
Starting with we music.
Long time, you could have take a li'l chip. [*She subtly sways her hips and walks stage left.*]
Back then, the music didn't have to come with no warning label and instructions.
De music these days could kill you.
How you mean?
Long time you ain't hear, "De Lay Lay Shang Shang, De Lay Lay Shang Shang." [*She sings the chorus of a popular 1977 Ellie Matt calypso.*]
But you know, your heart ain't beating too fast, you taking you li'l chip and you eyeing somebody husband—"Hey, goodnight."
Nowadays . . .
[*A snippet of a soca song begins to play from the speakers. As if possessed, she shakes her body violently, with her arms jerking wildly around her. She punches the air and flails her head. The music stops and she stops, too. Bent over as if exhausted, she places her hands on her knees and pants.*]
Dat dey enough to give you a double heart attack and chikungunya.
Tings not the same.
Nowadays, everybody want to play Simon Says for the Carnival.
If the song say "clothes off" with that, nobody stops to think

Brap! Everybody naked! Tings just not de same. . . .

To me we schizophrenic. You hear me?

To me, we schizophrenic.

Because one day you could see a man and a woman unashamedly wukin it
   and chookin' it half naked through the streets in Carnival.

Then the next day, they well decent decent in de bank a walk and give me
   attitude. . . .

Ain't my fault the man behind me watchin' you bad because he can't believe
   you own clothes. . . .

Schizophrenic, I tell you.

You forget! You forget when your forehead was on the ground and your bumper was in the air?

You want decent man? You want to get married?

You catch fish based on the bait you set out. If you set a rat trap, what you
   expect to catch? A rat![36]

Browne's bikini top was somewhat obscured under the colorful, oversized
cowl of her folkloric quadrille masquerade costume—another performative
regional approximation of local heritage. The slit in her long and colorful,
plaid wraparound skirt revealed the short shorts she wore underneath. The
suggestiveness of her costume bolstered the claims of her character, who ex-
claimed at the end of her speech, "You see me? I am going to dance and have
fun, but not at the expense of my dignity."

In an effort to describe how women's behavior has become radically different since the mid-twentieth century, when national carnival began, Browne's
character compared Ellie Matt's "Shang Shang" (1977) to Iwer George's "Let
Me See Yuh Hand" (2001) as an example of down-tempo, easy music that accompanied innocuous flirting and was conducive to a woman's living a fun
but productive and otherwise meaningful life.[37] Browne's ability to use her
body to represent the wild, uncontrolled, and deleterious effects of the fast
music—the pace of which could cause a "double heart attack"—comically
stood in direct contrast to her performances of an earlier time and music.

Most striking to me was her character's assertion that dancing to that music could also give a listener chikungunya, a viral disease transmitted by mos-
quitoes that first appeared in the Caribbean islands in 2014. The collapsing
of a contemporary ailment with the timeless degeneracy of Black women—
and the injection of the notion of contagion and disease—is a true constant
of carnival celebration and the recurrent discourse surrounding women's
participation in the annual national event. The crowd howled with delight
when Browne mimicked the fast-walking and stone-faced bank employees

on Monday morning after having spent the previous weekend participating heartily in carnival activities. She was affecting a commonly understood persona: the professional woman.

While public performances of respectable Black womanhood have become a marker of modernity and cultural progress in the Caribbean, regional notions of respectability have broadened—or at least shifted and melded—with what Carla Freeman has described as a "discourse of professionalism" that, by the early 2000s, superseded respectability as the new form of aspirational culture for women in the Caribbean.[38] In the wake of neoliberal economic policies and significant changes in the labor landscape across the Caribbean, professionalism—as displayed by what Freeman has called "pink collar workers" in Barbados—is characterized in part by ideas and objects like punctuality, productivity, high heels, makeup, and most importantly, "the promise represented by the computer."[39] Essentially, an embrace of some aspects of US corporate culture has come to coexist with (if not replace) aspects of traditional respectability such that, as Edmondson argues, the upper middle class of the Caribbean "does not see its women 'wining' in the streets at Carnival as incompatible with the professional discourses of the office and the upwardly mobile home."[40] This may be the case comparatively speaking—that is, a professional, middle-class woman can now be seen enjoying herself at carnival in a way that would have been disastrously disreputable for her fifty years ago—however, even as respectability has shifted to professionalism and the good news of gender equality has reached the shores of postcolonial nations like St. Kitts and Nevis, the resistive pleasure of Black women's wining is best enjoyed as a counter to an otherwise fully realized middle-class existence. Feminist campaigns to promote wining as a normal part of Black Caribbean women's sociality rely heavily on images of Black women doctors, lawyers, and politicians who also wine.

While the vision of the Black woman wining in the street may not be incompatible with contemporary notions of professionalism, Browne's performance suggests that the performance of an older prevailing logic is still relevant. In referring to the switching between carnival behavior and professionalism as "schizophrenic," she points to an incongruence in women's social behavior that is indicative of other kinds of social ills of the nation. Other parts of the five-minute monologue elaborate: bad men are chosen by disrespectful, sick, schizophrenic women who believe that their bodies are attractive enough—despite dark, marked skin—to be paraded and unclothed in the streets; women who wear thongs in the street are schizophrenic to believe that they should have any say in the type of attention they receive as a result.[41] Women who desire marriage and family will be unable to catch a good man.

Evidenced by the following examples—and, as noted by M. Jacqui Alexander, standing as a challenge to colonial ideology of the nuclear heterosexual and patriarchal family—female sexuality and erotic autonomy have historically been problematic for the state. This is particularly true because adherence to colonial notions of citizenship "perpetuate[s] the fiction that the family is the cornerstone of society," while erotic autonomy "signals danger to the heterosexual family and to the nation." In this way, citizenship is "perennially colonized with reproduction and heterosexuality" such that "erotic autonomy brings with it the potential of undoing the nation entirely, a possible charge of irresponsible citizenship, or no responsibility at all."[42] Female sexual autonomy, then, "signals danger to respectability—not only respectable middle-class families, but most significantly to Black middle-class womanhood." In Alexander's discussion of female erotic autonomy in the Bahamas, she notes that lesbians and prostitutes are seen as "major symbols of threat" for their "embodiment of the dangerous eroticism."[43] However, in much popular discourse, it is the dancing woman—embodying her supposed neglect of motherly duties and lack of sexual chastity, and standing in apparent contradiction to colonial middle-class mores—who symbolizes a threat to Kittitian and Nevisian citizenship.

Working within the frame of respectability and reputation, scholars of Caribbean women's issues (such as Carla Freeman and Belinda Edmondson) have broached the topic of a broadened notion of resistance and unconventional avenues toward respectability. As these scholars have noted, the outward performance of female sexual prowess works in direct contradiction to typical ideals of respectability. While globalized movement and change have long been parts of both the Caribbean economic context, the "flexibility" brought about by neoliberal economic policies has begged for research that, in Freeman's words, "shed[s] light on some of the ways in which respectability is sought, contested, and is actively re-constituted in the contemporary context."[44] In this way, Freeman sees respectability as no longer functioning solely as a form of gendered oppression and sexualized nation building. Instead—in line with ideological notions of the neoliberal agenda's emphasis on individualism—she suggests that various actors employ respectability differently as a tool. Naturally, some are in positions to utilize it to more beneficial ends than others. With this in mind, Freeman focuses on professionalism as taking the place of respectability insofar as professionalism is considered a way of circumventing the traditional respectable role of the keeper of private aspects of daily life (including staying at home with children, cooking, cleaning, and attaining patriarchal, familial association with the male head of household who financially maintains the family by working outside of the home) through the accumulation of wealth and status via traditionally male roles.[45]

In her work on middle-class or middlebrow culture on islands such as Jamaica and Trinidad, Belinda Edmondson also suggests that in these larger Caribbean nations, traditional respectability has been replaced by American-style professionalism. This professionalism is "informed by a familiarity with American manifestations of middle-class culture," such as reading romance novels and participating in beauty pageants, where the beauty pageant "covers roughly the same terrain as the romance novel—social aspiration, nationalism, and pleasure."[46] Respectability through professionalism in some Caribbean contexts refers to the power to consume American goods and affect a sense of African American middle-class femininity. In the contemporary moment, colonial respectability can be seen as the specter of ongoing anxieties about modernization, economic growth, nationalism, and cultural authenticity, which manifest in self-realized gender roles.[47] It is this self-realization that catalyzes nationalist discourse around the "cultural dance" portion of an annual beauty pageant, while individual performances of local, secular dance are the subject of discussions of fast girls and bad parenting. Next, I discuss one local site of online engagement, at SKNVibes.com, and annual ritualized public performances, queen shows, where those discussions of improper parenting commonly occur.

The Toon Center and the Rhetoric of Delinquent Women

The Toon Center is a popular aspect of SKNVibes.com, the most prominent news and entertainment website in St. Kitts–Nevis. Every day, a cartoon depiction of local cultural criticism is posted, and not surprisingly, many of the topics in the comments section—particularly immediately after carnival and Christmas—concern the behavior of women. Specifically, the cartoons often critique women's association with local music. One cartoon, "Is This What We Encourage?" (posted on January 3, 2014—the day after the end of carnival season), depicts two women dancing on a stage surrounded by conservatively dressed parents and children. One dancer is crouching and facing away from the crowd; the second is standing on her head, smiling widely with one leg in the air. Both women have been drawn with motion lines around them to suggest that their bodies are shaking (fig. 2.6). The eyes of the children are drawn as literally bulging out of their heads. "Is this what we encourage?"

The comment section was split. On the one hand, this type of dancing is inherently and explicitly sexual to the point of vulgarity and is a problem that plagues not just St. Kitts and Nevis but Afro-descendant people on a global

FIGURE 2.6. "Is This What We Encourage?" Published in "Toon Center—Is This What We Encourage?," *SKNVibes*, January 3, 2014, https://www.sknvibes.com/toons/details.cfm?Idz=98. Reproduced with permission from SKNVibes.com.

scale. One commenter suggested that allowing children to view this type of dancing is a major factor in the prevalence of pregnancy in young girls:

> I am so glad that the cartoonist did this. From watching and reading the cartoon I realize the emphasis is on the CHILDREN carried those kind of places by ADULTS to watch those kind of VULGARITY or ADULTS behavior. Now, I saw an incident on Dec. 26th, 2013 @ Party Central, where these women was wuking up on stage and the DJ called a 9 year old girl to participate in it. I started shouting out to him, "tek she outta ah it, that's not her place to be." That was very distasteful. lord forbid, in the next year or 2, she belly big, everybody wants to know what happen. If we as adults exposed children to these things, what do we EXPECT, that they act all holy, NO!! Adults, those behavior by children are not CUTE or a LAUGHING thing. STOP IT!! let them take their time to grow and enjoy childhood. I HATE it with a PASSION.

> NOTHING BUT STRIPPERS GONE WILD! NOT A LAUGHING MATTER, BUT A BIG DISGRACE TO OUR RACE!

> Its not only in Basseterre. Its wherever we gather & they are trying to pass this dry s@x off as dancing and it is NOT! It is a disgrace to see our young girls and old women too lowering themselves to this kind of behavior. Its very circus like and I don't see animals behaving this way![48]

On the other hand, as one comment demonstrates, the other side of this discussion recognizes the possibility for other interpretations of this type of dance. Without specifying exactly who the "we" represents in the historical approximation of this type of public dance, one commenter asks: "Would you prefer we waltz or do the 2-step? The problem is not in and of itself the dancing but our societal values that are warped to place sexual currency to our actions. In some cultures nudity is a way of life yet remember in some countries women would be stoned for indecency simply for showing their eyes. We exported this dance to the world and then reimported it as vulgarity."[49]

In posting local values and criticisms as "warped," the commenter suggests there was an original or unaltered set of values that would have regarded the display in the cartoon—or at least the display that occurred on December 26, 2013—as culturally relative. In contrasting this dancing, which has been referred to as "vulgar," with a codified European dance such as the waltz, and with what is an equally codified and generally non-Caribbean folk and popular dance (the two-step), the commenter subtly references a hierarchical valuation of European—or at least non-Caribbean—movement and music over that which is emanating from St. Kitts–Nevis. Of particular interest here, however, is how and why this type of discussion takes place because of, on, and in Black women's bodies.

Another cartoon furthers the critique of female bodies and their expected roles. Entitled "Parenting Standards out the Window," it depicts two relatively scantily dressed, pregnant women interacting in a nightclub setting (fig. 2.7). One woman proclaims her love for the band—presumably a wylers band—and the other agrees, commenting that she wanted to get in her last "jam" (dance session) before the arrival of her baby. In the background, another young woman stands next to a stroller. Many of the commenters agreed that this type of behavior is a widespread problem, is indicative of skewed priorities, and is proof of the questionable parenting often blamed for many of the social ills—particularly violence, theft, and teen pregnancy—that are perceived as plaguing the nation:

FIGURE 2.7. "Parenting Standards out the Window." Published in "Toon Center—Parenting Standards out the Window," *SKNVibes*, December 11, 2013, https://www.sknvibes.com/toons/details.cfm?Idz=86. Reproduced with permission from SKNVibes.com.

This picture is so true. The young people them feel like them going die if they miss a session. And when they children are born they want them to be different when they don't set an example.

Oh plz, a large number of Kittitian women have no moral code, no respect, no principles, nothing and that goes for pregnant and non pregnant.

skn woman and dey low standards all bout de place wid big belly in de dance

and when jam sweet them a worry and say mine you push me dung when they should be home . . . and if them get shub want cause big scene[50]

The idea of these women's pregnant bodies even occupying the space of the dance is indicative, as one person wrote, of a lack of morals, respect, and principles. Another commenter suggests that people who participate in jam sessions or attend dances have some degree of ambivalence toward their own participation. In noting that young citizens behave as though the dance were very important to them but wish for a different set of priorities for their own children, the commenter elucidates the ingrained notions of shame and female appropriateness that underlie many interpersonal interactions despite the nature of the actions themselves. These ingrained notions inform most of the other comments, which are representative of the informal discourse surrounding women, music, and dance in the region. Music—the sounds, the spaces, and the dances—constitutes one site of struggle over the regulation of sexuality or the performance and rehearsal of rituals of regulation.[51]

Tings Change, Part 2: Queen Shows and the Pedagogy of Desire

In the discourse surrounding women's bodies and behavior is a tension between public displays of immorality by Black women as the product of innate degeneracy and as an effect of an unwelcome foreign imposition. Women are harbingers and markers of change. Regarding the way women dance publicly in St. Kitts and Nevis, my uncle Irving noted:

> There's a saying in the Caribbean: "Where tings does start is not where it does end." It started one way, and now it's a completely different thing. It started as sensualism and turned into extreme sexualism bordering on vulgarity . . . I guess the music has a lot to do with it. Music has such power.[52]

The power of music to influence—to infect, to contaminate—is a guiding principle by which beauty pageant contestants are expected to perform. On beauty pageants in the US Virgin Islands in the 1990s, Cynthia Oliver writes:

As a training ground for upward mobility, the contest imposes restrictions to which contestants must be willing to adhere. These strictures eliminate the "rude gal," the Carnival "mas dancer," and the "dance hall queen," women whose values or talents are explicitly based on their abilities publicly to demonstrate their sexual prowess. The pageant queen is the antithesis of this woman. She is not asexual but rather is, as Williams suggests, "in control." Upper-middle-class and elite women do not perform their sexuality in public. They indicate. Their dancing in public spaces offers a measure of sensuality. Where "wukkin up" or "goin' on bad" (explicit imitations of intercourse) might be the most obvious demonstrations of what a woman's hips and legs can do sexually, the "cultured" woman "wines" swaying her hips gently in a smooth figure eight or a circle. She gestures somewhat demurely toward sexual possibility, not allowing herself to get worked up, to really sweat. She remains cool, dignified, and controlled while demonstrating an obvious knowledge and valuing of calypso and its accompanying dancing. She is not trying to say that she is not a part of local culture but instead communicates that she knows it well and still can hint at the sexually knowledgeable woman who lies underneath her veneer, unleashed only under the most personal of circumstances.[53]

This is the pedagogy of desire.

My interlocutors who participated in queen shows suggest that the performance of "not allowing"—both symbolically with their movements and more literally in song lyrics and dramatic monologues—is also a central feature of Kittitian-Nevisian pageantry and a marker of respectability. Performing respectability in the queen show—as with any regime of differentiation—often includes scathing (if humorous) critiques of the degenerate, unappealing Black woman figure as scapegoat for the nation's ailments. This is an interesting reprisal of a popular form of Neagar Business, where lower-class men discussed, made jokes about, and theatricalized circulating gossip about members of the upper and planter classes, and sometimes others of their own class who were not adhering to the social codes of the time. While lower-class women were typically present for festivities, the actors and musicians in Neagar Business troupes were almost invariably men. Within the troupe, at least one man was designated to play a woman, donning a dress or skirt and padding his body to create exaggerated breasts or a bottom as necessary for each skit.

Queen shows, as they were imported with carnival from Trinidad, were intended to function as an elevated alternative to the "lower" forms of Christmas entertainment. The first carnival queen show was held on December 31, 1957, in Basseterre's Warner Park—the same park that housed the celebrations of Princess Margaret's visit in 1955 and Queen Elizabeth's in 1966.[54] The 1957 show showcased the daughters of St. Kitts' wealthiest white and mixed-race

FIGURE 2.8. Judy Mestier (*left*), the first winner of the St. Kitts Carnival Queen title, 1957. "Carnival – New Years Day," Historic St. Kitts (National Archives, St. Kitts & Nevis), accessed March 13, 2023, https://www.historicstkitts.kn/events/carnival. Image courtesy of the National Archives, St. Kitts and Nevis.

residents, and much of the commentary describing the evening's events likened the contestants' "charm and grace" to that of Princess Margaret. The winner, Judy Mestier, was described in the *St. Kitts–Nevis Tribune* as fine as "Dresden China" with beautiful qualities like a "moonlight nocturne" (fig. 2.8).

The late 1950s also saw the peak of nationalist and pro-independence sentiments, which had grown exponentially in the preceding decade. St. Kitts' most expansive labor movement—the impetus for its first proletariat political party—had begun in earnest in the late 1930s. By the late 1940s, it was headed by Robert Llewellyn Bradshaw. The year 1951 saw what Vincent Hubbard has described as "the greatest shift of power in St. Kitts since Europeans had displaced Indians in the early 17th century"; all Leeward Island citizens received popular suffrage and "were able to vote and control their own destiny."[55] Bradshaw, who by 1952 was leader of both the Trade and Labour Union and the Workers' League, the governing political party in St. Kitts, was also a vocal supporter of the pending West Indies Federation. Ultimately, the Federated West Indies project failed, although during its short-lived tenure, Bradshaw served as minister of finance from 1958 to 1962, when the federation dissolved.

As the Black middle class grew, and Black Kittitian-born governmental representation was installed, critiques of lower-class expressive forms shifted to focus on poor Black women and girls.[56] By the 1960s, when the talent portion was added as a standard segment of pageants, performances that critiqued the behavior of outsiders—particularly lower-class, "unrespectable" Black women—became a normal feature of the queen show. Sometimes the depictions were empathetic: a grieving mother laments not having sent her sons to Sunday school because they are both imprisoned criminals, or a schoolgirl details the hardships created by mothers who allow their daughters to be sexually abused in exchange for money. But the underlying theme was that Black women who are bad mothers are a significant source of national ailments.

This performative formulation bears resemblance to Roger Abrahams's description of symbolic landscapes in St. Vincent in the 1960s: "It is only the most egregiously rude—the thief, the vexatious fellow, or the child who has no sense—who directs community contempt on himself and reflects badly on the woman who has raised him. She can control the *melée* (malicious gossip) only by making a kind of repeated public confession, called a cursing, that the boy is unmanageable even in her yard; by this the community ascribes the fault, at least in part, to *bad spirit* in the child and not to bad upbringing."[57]

We might read these queen show skits as a ritualized performance of a similar kind of motherly grievance on a contemporary public stage. Warner Park is a multifunctional space: it has been an arena for royal pomp and circumstance; it has hosted decades of cricket matches; and every year it turns into Carnival Village, the official space where events such as the Calypso King and Queen finals, the Soca Monarch and Miss Talented Teen competitions, and the National Carnival Queen Pageant take place. As is customary for this latter event, one band provides all the live music for the pageant and offers a twenty- to thirty-minute performance before the "evening wear" segment, which is typically followed by pronouncement of the winner. Green House—billed "The Number 1 Rock and Reggae Band from St. Kitts and Nevis"—provided the musical accompaniment in 2012–2013.[58] The polished band played a number of American R&B and Top 40 hits between pageant segments. The band's set list included a rendition of Psy's "Gangnam Style"—complete with carefully approximated Korean lyrics—and a fifteen-minute loop of the chorus of Rihanna's hit "Shine Bright Like a Diamond" to accompany the evening-wear parade. Green House's accompaniment added a Black, American, and upscale feel to the event. Like many of the Caribbean events broadcast on American TV (particularly BET), a foreign-looking, light-skinned, young woman from Barbados hosted the event. Her presence seemed to be an affront to many in the audience who wondered why a Bajan (Barbadian) would host *their* national queen pageant.[59] Throughout the evening, she was the butt of many of the crowd's jokes. For example, when she paused briefly after stumbling over her words, a man yelled toward the stage, "You suppose' to come from Barbados and you cyan' read?" At one point in the evening, the host playfully remarked that she heard "St. Kitts and Nevis people can wine almost as good as Bajans." She didn't use the correct nomenclature for persons from St. Kitts and Nevis, and in response, one woman in the crowd stood up and shouted, "They let you come here when you ain' even know we are Kittitians and Nevisians?" With a fake, high-pitched British affect she added, "And we don't *wine!*" Leaning back slowly into her chair, she concluded in a deep, comical Kittitian accent: "We does *wuk up!*"

Rattling the Barricades

The participatory nature of the National Carnival Queen Pageant is evidence of the fully local and folklorized nature of the event. For audience members, the queen show has an air similar to any rowdy calypso show of the season. Each time I attended a calypso show with my cousin Fiona, I was tickled by the vigor of her participation. We'd arrive early to get seats toward the front of the stage, chatting and laughing with other early arrivals, and grab concessions before the start of the show. By the middle of the first calypsonian's song, Fiona had both feet stuck between the poles of the metal fence between audience and stage, leaning the top of her body over to yell more directly and emphatically at and with the performers. I could not anticipate what she might say. Anything from "Dat ain' de right key!" for a performer singing under pitch, to more traditional exclamations, like "Kaiso!" would fly out in her distinctively husky voice. While I knew about calypso, had memorized lyrics of Lord Kitchener and Mighty Sparrow songs, and had a solid grasp of the tradition's history, I had not experienced calypso as a live participant in the intense, swirling, loud context of a carnival-time calypso tent. Fiona laughed at me in the way that big cousins do. Gripping the top of the metal fence, she chastised me playfully, shaking with each word. "You're supposed to yell back, Jess!"

The metal barricade, especially as Fiona used it as a platform for responses and critiques of the calypsos, was an anchor for her own stream of sound, interpretation, and improvisation. The song "By de Breath," by calypsonian King Konris, wittily describes how Konris is so ahead of his competitors that they are gassed and spent in an attempt to keep up with him. He sings "They breaking a sweat, hear them" as backup singers breathe heavily and rhythmi-cally.[60] Fiona, by the second chorus, was shaking her water bottle around, yelling, "Baai! Gee dem dis! Look like dey need some wata!" (Give them this! It looks like they need some water). While Fiona, then in her early forties and a respected high school teacher, would not be spotted during J'ouvert with her legs on a metal fence, something about her engagement with the barrier, her playful touch and utilization of it, reminded me of other engagements with those metal fences I had seen in the days and years before.

To Fiona, the metal barricades invited a kind of engagement with the performance on the other side. The materiality of individual barricades—portable, relatively transparent—meant that the instrument was more symbolic than anything else. It was clear that what such barricades signaled was a recurrent pretext for what they were actually used for. The metal fences are among the physical things that transform the various spaces, like Fort Thomas Hotel and Warner Park, into venues for the kinds of events that mark the recurrence of different seasons on the islands—Christmastime, carnival season, the "off-season" music festivals in the summer. The same barricades mark the winding path new arrivals are forced to traverse from the sweltering tarmac of Bradshaw International Airport to the customs kiosks.

Being perpetually marked as outsiders and anomalies, Black women are in close conceptual proximity to colonial categorical boundaries policed through discourses and performances of restraint, morality, and contagion. Pushed into those positions, Black Kittitian and Nevisian women have historically stood on, wrapped around, danced on, and shouted from the barricades, rattling the fences and making these boundaries useful by highlighting their contradictions. This enactment of oomanship is predicated on a learned "ability to read a concrete situation of power and consciously choose an ideological position that poses the most adequate opposition to [a] power configuration."[61]

Conclusion: Oomanship and the Ideal Beauty Pageant Queen

The ideal image of the beauty pageant queen is characterized by a certain level of extreme bodily control via willpower, wisdom, and training. For Tishima Browne, her body moved slowly, and seduction lay in her reservedness. To conjure the pathological Black woman, Browne threw her body around wildly and made specific reference to the speed of the music, which carried diseases of the body (chikungunya) and the mind (schizophrenia). The degenerate Black woman, in her portrayal, also affected a sense of pathological speed in her moving quickly and unselfconsciously between the carnival road to the bank lobby, where her fast walking—another form of bodily speed with social meaning—was read as a farce. If the seventeenth-century notions of creole contagion were predicated on the idea that New World inhabitants contaminated the "pure" aesthetic, social, and cultural forms of the Old World, Browne's representation of the pathologically ill Black woman gestures toward similar ideas.

Within Browne's performance, we are able to see an explicit castigation of Black women in relation to fast, regional music—laying out often unspoken yet ever-present ideas. She emphasizes that the music and the women who dance to it are ill; the pathologically fast music constitutes a unidirectional relationship wherein male musicians tell women to engage in socially deviant behavior and the women comply without question or regard—like a game of Simon Says. Browne invokes professionalism as an area where women participate in another kind of socially deviant speed, because their professionalism is fundamentally incompatible with having "your bottom in de road."[62] Browne briefly mentions the bad behavior of men, but she emphasizes that women's pathological behavior begets the wrong kind of attention (in the bank and elsewhere) and precludes participation in other respectable institutions such as marriage. In noting that some women want to be married but behave in a manner that attracts that wrong kinds of men—"rats"—Browne's monologue participates in a much larger body of social commentary that dangles aspirational and respectable social mores (like a professional job and heterosexual, monogamous marriage).

It is important to note that Browne did not write the monologue herself. Beauty pageant contestants throughout the Caribbean region are groomed and trained by an extensive team of "handlers," many of whom have participated in pageants themselves as contestants, talent producers, costume designers, or coaches. So we might better understand Browne's monologue as an amalgamation of ideas meant to do a particular kind of nostalgia work in holding up national ideologies. She took on a deep Kittitian accent and drew the crowd in through the idea of superlocal knowledge. As an ambassador of St. Kitts–Nevis, her job requires knowing local culture, and that requires demonstrating that she is aware of local values—especially with regard to Black women, who function as an almost singular barometer of the nation's moral status. Despite changes in contemporary social politics and norms— including the general acceptance of professional women (e.g., women who own homes and cars and are financially autonomous)—the moral status of the nation becomes even more bound up with the status of "respectable women," as St. Kitts and Nevis becomes more visible and accessible in the global tourism and economic scene.

Key to Browne's performance is that she was portraying a woman whose ideas of what is socially acceptable and which kinds of music promote respectable behavior were presumably formed during a much earlier time, before independence. She portrayed a body that was too frail to comfortably dance to the tempo of contemporary Caribbean music. However, if, as Browne's performance suggested, the mas dancer and the bank clerk are understood to an older generation as socially incompatible, then the silhouette of new representations of Black womanhood are steeped in familiarly paradoxical worldviews. Oomanship, then, as a subjectivity, as a form of personhood, cannot be measured by any one act or even any pattern of acts. It must be measured by the autonomous decision to perform different, seemingly antithetical ways of being, particularly with an awareness that a set of physical parameters (a Black, feminized body) precludes equal recognition. Oomanship describes a set of ideals and philosophies that articulate an optimistic sense of Black women's survival.

Browne's monologue similarly hinges on a shared understanding of wylers as containing nested deviations from expectations. Before 2015, wylers was widely considered derivative, backward, indicative of a diminished musical capacity, and a product of decolonial nationalism's failure to provide the sonic corollary of a foundational myth. Many of these critiques have been mapped on to temporal norms—locally constituted temporal thresholds or frames—that posit wylers and its adherent sonic and bodily practices as "too fast." The following chapter expands the temporal scale of this political context.

Wylers and the Tempo of Development

Chocolate's Joke

On a weekday morning in late December 2012, I sat at the newly erected outdoor bar at the deepwater harbor where large tourist ships dock in the heart of Basseterre. Because no tourist ships had arrived at Port Zante that morning, the scene was relatively quiet, despite the general buzz of Christmastime excitement around the island. One of the tables next to the bar was taken by four young men who were drinking brown mixed drinks out of small plastic cups. They playfully argued, as men do in St. Kitts, while sharing some fried chicken. They passed the bucket around the table along with a roll of paper towels that kept threatening to blow away with each passing breeze. The chalkboard sign that the day prior had advertised "Rasta Rum Punch" and "$1 Sex on The Beach Shots!" was lying flat on a stack of wood pallets tucked behind the side of the bar. The day before, the broad pavement was a busy promenade for bikini-clad, sun-reddened tourists. That day, it was virtually empty except for two women in work uniforms who sat on a bench that offered a shady spot for a midmorning meal. I quickly realized that my presence was noted when a man who appeared to be in his early twenties pushed the chicken bucket toward me.

"You want a piece?"

I declined and smiled. After a limp handshake and brief introductions, he told me to call him Chocolate.

"Let me buy you a drink," he insisted.

Awkwardly navigating the space between ethnographer and young woman alone at a bar, I asked for a soda.

Incredulously, he yelled, "You are on vacation! Take a real drink!" as the bartender gently placed the open bottle of Peardrella in front of me.

Unsure how to respond, I turned my head and thumbed the corner of my notebook. Through the flaps of the umbrellas shading the empty chairs around the bar area, I could see the ombré sea sparkling under the hot sun. I sank into the metal bar chair to toggle the day's ethnography to-do list: sit at the bar and find people to talk to, eat lunch at the snackette a hundred yards away, go to the final round of the Soca Monarch competition later that night. I wanted to protest that I was not on vacation, but what evidence did I have to the contrary?

Only a little defensively I explained I was in St. Kitts doing research on local music—"band music." One of Chocolate's friends was seated a few tables away, watching us as he chugged a Carib beer. He called out, "What she lookin' for?" Without hesitation Chocolate, smiling, thrusted his hips forward, rhythmically chanting, "she lookin' for that 'ding, dinga, ding.'" Both Chocolate and his friend laughed hysterically at the joke.

In the early years of the 2010s, it was hard not to feel impatient and a little incredulous that the music playing on the radio, blasting out of cars on the street, and rattling sound systems set up in central Basseterre was somehow also a kind of sonic elephant in the room. At the beginning of each conversation I would find myself spewing a series of adjectives to help the person I was speaking with pinpoint which "local" genre I was referring to. Most often, the words "band music," would do the trick, at which point my interlocutor would typically respond in a way that let me know that they understood what I was talking about while still declining to refer to it by any name: "Oh! Dat 'boom boom boom' in me head ting?" or "Dat jump up ting?" or "Dat shub back ting?" Wylers is not something that comes from a speaker system, riddim box, or musician, but something that lives in the listener's head. The listener's own perception, the connections and continuities the listener brings, is what makes it wylers. Said another way, so much of what people want from wylers is *energy*.

When Rankin Skeff stopped by the small crew gathered by the bar, Chocolate pointed him out to me and encouraged me to "ask *him* about music," especially because he would be performing in the Soca Monarch competition that evening. Despite being a contestant in the 2012 Power Soca finals, Skeff made it clear that "we music . . . is not soca." He added: "It doesn't have the real soca rhythm. The beat is different." After a lot of small talk, about which Caribbean island had the best KFC, and other breezy topics, I walked with Skeff toward the other side of the marina in search of more local food options.

We were standing in line at Mrs. Moore's Eat to Live snackette on the far edge of Port Zante when I asked him to explain what the difference was between the soca rhythm and "*this* one." It was unfair of me to ask him to produce the rhythm while soca classics from bands like Burning Flames and Byron Lee were playing over loudspeakers outside the shops flanking the walkway. But I was anxious to have someone pin down for me exactly what "the beat" was. "I can't do it here, but you can hear it." He explained: "It's like salt fish. Everybody in the whole Caribbean got salt fish. But here it's juicy and nice with red gravy—tomatoes or ketchup or what have you. In Trinidad or Jamaica it ain' so. It's drier."

When salted codfish is soaked and boiled, chipped into small flakes, and sautéed with herbs and aromatics like thyme and garlic, what happens next depends on who and where you might be. These probabilities represent individual and collective acts of local creativity: in Jamaica, people add ripe ackee to make the national dish; in Trinidad, scotch bonnet for saltfish buljol; in St. Lucia, they serve it over a steaming plate of boiled green banana. Home chefs in St. Kitts and Nevis let the pot simmer until a few handfuls of chopped tomatoes turn into a flavorful gravy. By the time a dark island of grease had started to form on the bottom of the brown paper bag with Skeff's saltfish and johnnycake sandwich, I understood that asking about the difference between a soca beat and the one I was seeking was as misguided as asking about the difference between ackee and tomato.

Later that evening, Skeff performed "No Rag, No Flag," an ode to the distinctiveness of Kittitian-Nevisian revelry. In the midst of honorable attempts to infuse overt and acceptable versions of national culture into these shows, Rankin Skeff's "not really soca" performance disavowed the rags that are emblematic signifiers of mainstream soca and national flags as dignified markers of local identity in favor of young people "getting on bad." His set looked sparse in comparison to the stage shows of other entrants with dozens of ensemble members, full-body paint, and pyrotechnics. The chorus of the energetic anthem stated his cause: "We don't want no rag / we don't want no flag / All we want is soca music and we gettin' on bad." Onstage, Chocolate and about eight other young men and one woman stood ragless and flagless, wukin up fast and hard.

Footage from the event pans away from the stage dancers when a man drinking from a massive plastic tumbler lifts his leg up and joins the wining woman and another waist-pelting man in a kinetic, onstage threesome.[1] It was youthful, playful, and intense. Although certainly not subtle, the performance sought to bypass a symbolic middleman (a rag, a flag, a plan) in service of representing a less translated invocation of local music. The winner of the Soca Monarch finals represents St. Kitts and Nevis at the regional competition during Trinidad's carnival, so to advance, entrants must balance international legibility and island distinctiveness.[2]

I do not know whether Skeff would have classified his song as wylers, even if what he sang was "not really soca." It did not have a high-pitched riddim or the many digitized sounds that are telltale timbres of local music. He did not have one of the crystallized Kittitian or Nevisian bands behind him whose names are synonymous with the Kittitian-Nevisian popular music scene: Small Axe, Nu Vybes, Grand Masters, Kollision, Odisi. However, all the dense and lively improvisation on the drum kit was turned up loud while the bass and keyboard kept a dark ostinato running. There did not seem to be any real stage direction, and it did not surprise me to recognize a few of the men onstage as my drinking buddies from eight hours prior. The scene, the movements, the interactions between the dancers, their obedience to the beat—all were as central to what was the performance of disregard for order, rules, and professional representation; it was the stuff of wylers, even without the name.

Chocolate's joke—that I was really searching for "dingaling," or sex, and not just music—was the stuff of wylers, too. The quick dance he did to stylize his wordplay resembled the ones of other young people to demonstrate that they were talking about wylers. What I thought was just an uncomfortable sexual reference was that, and it was also a reference to a chant he heard at a jam once. Among other things, wylers is a working set of performance practices and sonic markers—manners of aesthetic representation—through which Kittitian and Nevisian youth challenge accepted patterns of Kittitian-Nevisian sociality. Wylers, like Chocolate's joke, is what Mary Douglas called "a play on form." She explains, a joke "brings into relation disparate elements in such a way that one accepted pattern is challenged by the appearance of another which in some way was hidden in the first."[3] The overlap between his friend's question of "What she looking for?" and the lyrics of a chant provided an opportunity to voice—playfully and irreverently—the otherwise unspoken assumptions and gender dynamics swirling around our interaction.

How does characteristically youthful play on form participate in enduring debates about the relationships between music and modernity, speed, and development? This chapter centers musical speed as an essential experiential element of music in St. Kitts and Nevis. Contrary to circulating narratives, wylers musicians and producers do not consider the style a modern intervention, nor do they understand their music to be a response to contemporary social conditions. Wylers musicians assert, through their music, that postcolonial Kittitians and Nevisians are descendants of various kinds of speed that are historically and experientially rooted in the condition of being an Afro-descendant on their specific islands. Wylers musicians see themselves as protectors of an inherited essential musical sensibility. Critiques of wylers, however, have suggested that the excessive perceived tempo of the music and its reliance on percussion and rhythm lacks a musical and economic sense of direction that is not only a deviation from the expected path of musical development, but is also a product of the failures of postcolonial development as a political project.

Dagah and Development

Sometime between our meeting in the late morning and his performance at the Soca Monarch competition that night, Chocolate walked me a couple hundred yards away from the bar to meet "another music guy," Dagah.

"It's Dagah, like 'dagger' but how we say it," Dagah said, preempting any confusion. In his early twenties and dressed in baggy jeans with a crisp, fitted baseball cap, Dagah was a hip-hop artist and manager of an urban clothing store on Port Zante called iRep. A play on Apple's extremely successful product lines, the iRep store sold pricey, locally oriented St. Kitts–Nevis themed merchandise, such as T-shirts with 869, the St. Kitts area code, and jackets and bikinis that read "St. Kitts: Est. 1492." Offering additional novelty items such as high-heeled shoes, makeup, costume jewelry, false eyelashes, CDs of local music, and tickets to upcoming events, the iRep store was a youth hub.

When I told Dagah I was researching local music, he immediately began listing a diverse array of artists who influenced his own work, including Stevie Wonder and the Beatles. When I clarified that I was interested mostly in "band music," he commented that even though many "love to jump up and dance and party to it for carnival, a lot of people don't really like it. Like, the music itself is dumb." When I pushed him for an explanation of what he meant by "dumb," Dagah explained that the guys who play it "aren't really musicians, for real," they just learn how to play what they need in order to perform the band's songs. To make his point, Dagah pointed to a stack of Nu Vybes CDs, a new release of one of the popular wylers bands: "You see these? These don't sell," he suggested, because very few people outside of DJs and those who live abroad seek to own this music or to listen to it outside of the carnival season.[4] I hastily bought a CD.

Dagah encouraged me to buy tickets for Inception Fete, then in its third year—the "hottest event right now"—where he would be performing later that week. As a rapper, he was excited to be onstage at the kind of venue where hip-hop could "fit in." He lamented that he knew a much larger Kittitian and Nevisian audience would appreciate his music if they were open to the idea of a Kittitian hip-hop artist. Young people in St. Kitts more readily accept local artists who make reggae or soca than those who seek to adopt contemporary American styles such as hip-hop and R&B, although they are happy to consume American hip-hop and R&B produced outside of St. Kitts and Nevis. In hopes of creating a local "urban music" record label, Dagah was working closely with another young Kittitian artist, Dejour, sixteen years old at the time, who was pursuing his own career and performed regularly as both a background singer and as a solo artist during Dagah's shows. Dejour's voice provided the crooning R&B vocals that adorned many of the tracks on Dagah's album *The Patriot*—which was already playing in the store when Chocolate and I arrived. During my time standing at the front counter of the iRep store, Dagah mentioned several times that his and Dejour's detractors say that their performances are not "real hip-hop" and that people from St. Kitts–Nevis cannot be "legit" in their rap performances. In response, Dagah noted that he believed as a Black, native-English-speaking man, he is entitled to hip-hop and should be welcomed to participate in its culture without restriction or question. He added, "Guys like Eminem and stuff, white rappers, or French African rappers—I deserve to do hip-hop more than them. Hip-hop is more mine than theirs."[5]

The venue of Inception Fete, complete with its VIP section, professional lighting, and extremely trendy audience, was promising for Dagah. His aspirations to participate in what was understood as an American genre seemed more at home at a venue that was not torn about its allegiance to a celebration of middle-class consumption and its attendant aesthetic and material imperatives. Inception Fete's red-carpet entrance and paparazzi-style photo background were one part of what was billed as an all-inclusive event, mirroring the kinds of promises made to tourists who visit the islands. Within the hotel industry, the all-inclusive resort model was created in part to provide busy, new-aged tourists of the 1980s the ability to have multiple tourist experiences in the span of one short vacation. Similarly, events like Inception Fete (tagline: "10 Fetes in One!") promise patrons a traditional enough carnival experience, with multiple soca and dancehall acts, the provision of branded waving implements, and copious amounts of alcohol alongside the material trappings of bourgeois modernity. Then, at the end of a long night, the bands play after, as Mention says, "everyone done drunk."

When I attended the Seventh Inception Fete in 2016, it was called the Johnny Walker Black Label Inception Fete, as the company had become a "title sponsor" for two years. That year, after the red carpet, and in addition to the commemorative mug and unlimited whiskey, I had the option of receiving a free "mini mani/pedi" and an "express massage" from the standby technicians and therapists in tents directly inside the venue gates. I opted, instead, to simply pick up my complimentary goodie bag of locally handmade soaps. When I reached out to the spokesperson for the event (whoever was manning the Facebook page) asking about the origins of the event, they said that while the emphasis during carnival used to be "traditional mas and folklore, pageants and calypso shows, there were really no fringe activities like in other destinations . . . adding them to our calendar of activities . . . improved the overall Carnival product or experience."[6] These kinds of changes have been key to development as an ideology on these islands.

Inception Fete mixes parts of J'ouvert, New Year's celebrations, a concert, and a road jam into a "carnival product" through its promotion of what Percy Hintzen calls "the 'style' or 'taste' of the new post-colonial elite."[7] The addition of spa services and top shelf liquor sponsors to carnival events in the broader Caribbean is "patterned after their counterparts in Western Europe and North America."[8] However, these middle-class aspirational tastes and patterns of consumption can no longer be "understood as 'foreign', 'white' or 'colonial.' They are the 'styles' and 'tastes' of development, and modernity's prerequisites for equality."[9] Hintzen offers a succinct explanation of the relationship between modernity, coloniality, and the ubiquity of development in the English-speaking Caribbean in the immediate aftermath of independence:

> To be "modern" was to be "equal." For the community of Afro-creole nationalists, equality (with Europeans) came with the material life conditions and productive technology of Western Europe and North America. This was the promise of development. . . . The cultural, social and symbolic capital of the post-colonial elite derived from privileged access to the resources of the colonial metropole. Social capital was accumulated primarily through their European [and American] education and training. The acquisition of cultural capital derived from their socialization into the dominant European [and American] forms. The authorial power of these elites in the post-independence state created the conditions for the re-authentication of European [and American] forms now incorporated into the "style" or "taste" of the new post-colonial elite. The social construction of this dominant group as a 'nationalist' elite negated the force of challenges to their legitimacy based on claims of the perpetuation of white (colonial) supremacy.[10]

Music, still, remains a site of contestation and tension between the ubiquity and naturalization via localization of "foreign" styles through globalization and the local desire and necessity for a cohesive national identity. As it relates to Dagah as a rapper, there is a tension between the reconciliation between contemporary urban Black, masculine American style, and hip-hop culture more broadly, as a legitimate and appropriate mode of middle-class aspiration. Even in the midst of the ongoing valorization of the "North," hip-hop music in general has come to represent what Hintzen calls "the pathologies of western capitalism such as drug consumption, gang violence, environmental degradation, the cult of individualism, and the glorification of profit over welfare and social security."[11] Evading associations with these pathologies while promoting an elite version of carnival-adjacent activity, events like Inception Fete feed the on-the-ground need to demonstrate that the trappings and imperatives of development as modernity are compatible with the national and ethnic traditions of the islands—"modernity is as much mine as it is theirs."

Events and carnival experiences like Inception Fete, created by a group of party promoters, highlight how considerations about what kinds of music people *want* are as dependent on what they want to listen to as what they want to buy. Dagah's declaration that wylers CDs "don't sell" had much wider connotations about the music's literal worth and value, both materially and aesthetically. The thing that most carnivalgoers want from wylers is an experience that cannot be transferred to the kind of CD that sits on the counter at a novelty store. Despite the relatively low CD (and now digital music) sales, wylers is considered an essential music at carnival events. On the flier for Inception Fete there are categories for the various kinds of artists that are set to perform: "Soca, Dancehall, DJ's" and at the bottom it reads, "and we can't forget The Bands." Their being listed, oftentimes not even as individual bands but, instead, as an entity, aligns with the way I see wylers functioning as a space of vernacular temporality, especially in the context of relatively rapid and all-encompassing development on the islands. But where development may be understood as the imposition of development's acceleration onto local forms, wylers musicians and audiences understand a sense of speed, broadly and aesthetically defined, as endemic to the people of St. Kitts and Nevis.

Inception Fete, December 30, 2012—Basseterre

Holding a microphone close to his mouth, Gregory "Mr. Mention" Hobson, the lead singer of the Nu Vybes Band International (a.k.a. De Sugar Band), commented on the scene in front of the stage:

> When de music sweet, no barrier can stop the gyal dem from reaching. You see Suga Band? We Sweet. We have to apologize for the gyal dem behavior at the Inception. When the things dem sweet, they say dey cyanan't do without the barrier break down. Sorry officer.

Police officers in army fatigues, with pistols at their waists, stoically supported the metal barriers that maintained the five feet between the lip of the concert stage and the heaving crowd while enthusiastic dancers in the front rows used the hefty metal fence to keep their balance. When the music got particularly good—"sweet"—dancing women assumed different precarious positions as they worked their bodies, sometimes in a freestyle display of

wining, wukin up, bouncing, and jiggling, other times heeding the instructions of the chants booming out of the speakers stacked high on the stage
above: "Siddung pon it like a—Bend down. Touch de ground!"

When the song ended, the dancing stopped. Women pulled their skirts
back down, picked their pum-pum shorts out of cracks and crevices, wiped
sweat, chugged water, and laughed at the version of themselves they left in
the last sprint of music and dance. Soon, the ping-pongy chromatic descending octave and the four-on-the-floor bass drum—a pared-down version of
the previous riddim—saturated the warming early-morning air. "If you come
to Inception to party . . ." The drummer started to improvise on the snare,
and other quirky sound effects accented each rhythmic phrase. Dancers also
performed their own ramp-up, moving in measured and more restrained
ways—their feet pedaled and heads coolly bopped. "I wan' see everybody
han' inna de air right now! One, two, one, two, three! Put dem up!" That final
"up" landed on a downbeat that brought back the full band—riddim box,
keys, rhythm guitar, bass, and background vocals. Bodies once again started
to move, this time jumping up and down on every beat, waving flags, drinks,
and white glow-in-the-dark batons provided by Flow (a local cell phone company and one of the event's many sponsors). "Put dem up! Put dem up!"

Because I caught a ride with my Auntie P, who was adamant about being up for a service at the Anglican Church the next morning at eight, I was
among the less cool people who showed up to the fete before midnight. Lucky
for me, this also meant that I didn't wait very long in the line to receive my
complimentary plastic Johnny Walker mug along with the unlimited whiskey
included in the price of admission of 175 Eastern Caribbean Dollars. By the
time Nu Vybes was at the end of its set, it was shortly after six in the morning;
I had been on my feet for more than seven hours. I watched this scene from
the steep hill that leads down to the grounds of Fort Thomas Hotel.

Built in the nineteenth century on a spot fifty-six feet above sea level, Fort
Thomas was a spot from which militia men could survey the ocean for in-
coming attacks. In the late 1960s, a sixty-four-room Holiday Inn was built on
the site. After it shuttered in the 1990s, it became unofficially known as Fort
Thomas Hotel. The large open area stretched to the edge of the inlet of Lime-
kiln Bay on the southeast side of the island and was the initial location for the
St. Kitts Music Festival in 1994. After catching my third wind—and fortified
by a Styrofoam cup of fish stew—I was in a prime location for taking in the
scenery through the grayish haze of predawn. As the sun rose behind Nevis
in the distance, the small lights dotting the sister island disappeared into the
silhouette of Nevis Peak across the water. All around, the field's sparse grass

had been trampled and mixed with spilled drinks and humidity; the ground's soft mud was caked onto my feet and legs.

In the section behind the rows of women who were rattling the crowd barrier, a group of men swung their arms forcefully to the rhythm of the music in what's known as a "bull ring." Shoulders bumped chests; fists met rib cages. Those who had enough moved through the crowd to a safer space. Mere feet from a military officer in a green beret, one man hit another particularly hard, and it looked like a fight would break out. A tall man with his locs tucked into a stocking cap placed his palm firmly on the heaving chest of the offended party, tapping gently in an apparent effort to defuse the situation. He stood between the two men as the music stopped again. In the relative calm between bursts of speed and sound, the members of the bull ring dispersed to other parts of the field.

We Have Always Been Fast

I spoke to Mr. Mention, lead singer of Nu Vybes, almost ten years after my initial request to interview him, and he confirmed what was clear to me from the hill of Fort Thomas Hotel: so much of what people want from Nu Vybes as a band and wylers as a genre is *energy*:

> We come out fast—168, 165 [beats per minute] is the fastest. That's not even that much faster than other soca, it just feels faster. It *tricks* the ears. It makes it sound like it's going faster. It sounds like acceleration—the drive. That's our culture. That's what we create down here. You can't explain your creation. It's not about intention. That's just our culture. *We have always been fast.*[12]

When Mention emphasized "that's just our culture," I reflected on feeling that he had been getting impatient with me, and not without cause. I had been messaging him intermittently, with increasingly more information about how he might know or place me within his very wide network of acquaintances and connections on the island and throughout the Caribbean diaspora. Finally, I asked my cousin, the brother of an ex-partner of one of Mention's former bandmates, to reach out to him to beg him to respond to my messages. When he learned that I could see his home from Auntie P's porch, I had finally established enough proximity (and applied enough social pressure) that he agreed.

He was pleasant on the phone, and we exchanged small jokes about how good he had been at dodging me. It surprised me when he thanked me for whatever potential publicity our conversation and my writing might provide.

After so much time, so many attempts, my anxiety about having him say something direct, concise, or specific—to act as an authority on this matter—snuffed out any semblance of nuance to my questions. So, when I asked, "Is the intention of the music to be fast?" I cringed at my own forwardness and expected the forcefulness of the question to cause our conversation to end early. I was relieved when he laughed at his own frustration and sat with the question a little longer, pushing back against my reliance on a characterization of the music as "fast":

> It's fast, but it also has a lot of music in it. It's not just a fast bit. It's music. The style of the riddim that's so drivey overrides the music, so that they can't grasp the music. Because what grasps them first is what they're not accustomed to, which is the style of rhythm and the tempo. They just can't hear it. Because what is so amazing to them is the tempo. We get that from everywhere, overseas, other islands. It's a very active music. Not fast. But driving.

Anticipating my next line of questioning, he continued:

> How do you explain drive? When you're driven toward something. That's what the music is. It has a high energy. It is Pep. That's the best way to put it. *Very* high energy. When you look at Kittitians, we jam like no other. It doesn't look like it's driving them crazy? That tempo, that riddim, it works together to create energy. We don't take a break because it's all about momentum. It's a part of us.[13]

In my experience at carnival, fringe events like Inception Fete, and packed beachside bars on Frigate Bay's Strip, wylers did make people go wild. There was clearly a visceral connection, a loose contract, between the behavior of the audience and the tempo of the music. The "drive" is the product of the densely layered sound of the riddim, the rhythmic lines played from the riddim box, and the bass, which in St. Kitts–Nevis refers interchangeably to the kick, or "foot," drum or electric bass.[14] The drive, then, isn't directional; it is momentum, mobilization, in its capacity to move—emotionally, affectively, spiritually. Wylers' elicitation of feelings characterized by a sense of speed is an aestheticization of the drive toward various sensual attachments. Steve Goodman calls this "affective mobilization": "the intensity [of music] now has to match the drive of big drum, steel band, string band. All those things even before the combo band. We build our music around those things. Elements of how they played, formulate the new soca. . . . [T]hat's what we came from: steel band, big drum, even way before brass band. That's why we embrace it in the music today. Over the years, music has gotten faster [but] it's not just a fast bit. It's music . . . and you can't create something out of nothing."[15]

Matching the drive has less to do with matching the tempo, measured in beats per minute, or specific rhythmic figures. Instead, "intensity" relates to a process of capturing the "distilled essence" of the music.[16] As Mention emphasized, "The elements may change, but the drive, the groove, that's what we aim for." Wylers music is created to evoke the same kind of sense of speed and response that these carnival-time forms did throughout the island's Afro-diasporic history.

In response to the idea that the tempo of wylers is new, he said, "We have always been fast." Recognizing the perceived tempo of wylers as part of a larger genealogy of speed, Mention noted:

> Even when [music] was a lot slower than it is now, it was still always faster than the other islands. We always had, even before the drum machine, been rhythmic. Most of we brass band had elements different from the original drumming [big drum]: conga, iron, cowbell, plus all the other [electric] band instruments. We not gonna leave out anything, we just add it. That's why our [music is] more rhythmic—it just has more elements. More sounds.[17]

Mention and other wylers musicians—singers and producers, in particular—suggested that the "stacking" of sound is essential to what creates a sense of drive and acceleration that, as dance music, creates a sense of speed. As a highly technological style, riddims are created as heavily layered ostinati that feature distorted and stretched sounds on top of a full electric band setup. One producer, Leonard "Jam Crew" Lestrade noted, "We always playing with the timing." He explained how in the early 1990s, when keyboards came with preset sounds, local producers would play with the affordances of MIDI technology which allowed them to decrease the period of each repeat. Instead of using these sounds exclusively as ornamentation or isolated sound effects, they could speed up repetition, making each occurrence of a sound happened so quickly it sounds like a sustained pitch. This produces an effect that resembles the trembling sound of a steel pan. These kinds of techniques, which have become more complex as technology has made procuring sounds easier, allow musicians to create the sense of acceleration that feels "right." The deep, pulsating kick drum against the affected sounds creates additional layers of tempo—microtemporal events that, combined, create the signature feeling and sound.[18]

Anatomy of a Wylers Song

A contender from the 2014–2015 carnival season aptly illustrates these musical dimensions. "Shake Your Bumpa" by the Grand Masters Band, a perennial

FIGURE 3.1. Transcription of the chorus to Grand Masters Band's 2014 "Shake Your Bumpa."

rival of the Nu Vybes Band (fig. 3.1). This song features a riddim (the prepro-grammed backing track) with characteristic wylers instrumentation, includ-ing a synthesized metallic percussive sound and other another high-pitch, highly textured melodic lines. As unique, synthesized sounds crafted in house by the band's producer or keyboardist, the high-pitched melodic instruments in wylers are sustained through ultrafast repetition of the initial attack—like a steel pan. What sounds like a sustained pitch via repeated strikes creates a pulsating effect, similar to the bumpy sound of a pea whistle, that imbues the riddim's melody with an internal energy that is amplified. A sole male vocal-ist singing about—and to and for—women's dancing backsides is backed up by a chorus in three-part harmony on accented words. The song recording, at 162 beats per minute, is decidedly upbeat. However, the perception of the tempo is augmented by the recurrent chromatic passages that add to the feeling of building, moving, and accelerating throughout.[19] In the recording, the bass line moves between octaves frequently and at times mirrors the vocal melody. On top of the riddim, an acoustic drum set improvises freely, adding to the frenzied texture. The use of Kittitian-Nevisian creole, as demonstrated in the words "grung" (ground), "dung" (down), and "tung" (town): (Ladies on de grung when they jam dung tung / Ladies on the ground when they jam downtown), is particularly striking against the melody of the verse, a minor third below the chorus, which borrows from the 2013 hip-hop song "Holy Grail," by Jay-Z featuring Justin Timberlake.

What cannot be captured in a wylers studio recording (or transcription of recordings) is the broader context of a jam session—any live performance event (sometimes impromptu) at which many ideas for any song are tested and developed. One of the most salient features of a jam session is the ubiquity of chants performed improvisatorially and intermittently throughout. As Mr. Mention noted to me: "Chants are big part of we culture. *That* gets the people wild." Chants are hooks that are provocative, catchy, and emblematic of the here and now of the performance. Mr. Mention describes it thus: "Four bars on a riddim. A chant is a jingle. If it's an entity, and you want to keep relevant, you have to acknowledge what your audience likes. We keep our audience happy. It's *fun!*"[20]

Chants and the improvisational performances that engender them are fleeting in the sense that only the ones that garner the most reactions at the right time of the carnival season are turned into a recorded song with verses and a chorus. However, wylers enthusiasts do not easily forget their favorite chants from many years ago, and the recorded version of the song is often an inadequate marker of the most striking and addictive features of an especially beloved performance. Remember here that it was a chant from a particularly memorable jam that was the basis of Chocolate's joke at the bar. When Mr. Mention chants over a sprinting riddim, "Sugar band you too bloodclot sweet / Sweet like rice and peas" or "Too much a sweetness, too much a sweetness / Suga band ah give you diabetes," he takes the backdrop of a riddim that audiences are familiar with—because they have heard it at another jam or because it has been playing for several minutes—and injects newness and lyrical and rhythmic unpredictability while opening up new possibilities for meaning for each reveler. This setup of expectation and its playful, associative, rhyming, salacious deviation is an essential feature of Kittitian and Nevisian performativity.

Wylers is not concerned with being one specific tempo; instead, techniques of arrangement, instrumentation, curating, and performance work together to create a general sense of speed as an experience of change. Speed, here, refers to a relative disjuncture of temporalities. Phenomenologically, as direct experience, speed refers to the moment when someone recognizes motion. It is in the moment of acceleration or change of tempo or direction that speed is acknowledged. Speed, then, is a "relational ontology," meaning that it is "the ontology of the specific relation of a set of objects and actors." In St. Kitts and Nevis, there is an interchangeability between the word "speed" and "tempo," not as the description of a characteristic of all movement but as the indication of a specific "material phenomenon attested to by subjective insight."[21] Speed, understood in this way, is a bringing to consciousness of a form of change in motion. In this way, a sudden switch in key, stopping the music at the high point of the chorus to start again, chanting a rhyme that repeats a phrase from a completely different context (like an earthquake public service announcement or a commercial), brings disparate, seemingly isolated sounds and ideas into a relation of disruption without erasure, disjuncture without rejection.

Wylers is a sound of relation. Recall the 2012 song "DCH," by Small Axe Band, that I described in this book's introduction: originally a public service announcement for earthquake readiness. The Labour Party, led at the time by Dr. Denzil Douglas, had been criticized for promulgating ideas and practices reminiscent of the colonial planter class.[22] Among these colonial tendencies was the promotion and valuation of the foreign above the local. Many political developments forwarded by Douglas's government had been cited as demonstrations of Douglas's lack of commitment to St. Kitts and Nevis and his overwhelming disregard of the local community. In 2012, for example, to repay domestic banks for sizable loans taken out by the St. Kitts–Nevis government, Douglas proposed a "land-for-debt" swap program. There was a major public outcry against the program, which would settle an approximately $700 million debt for 1,200 acres of former sugarcane fields.

The common assumption had been that the land would be sold to foreign investors, without local interests in mind. A former leader of the People's Action Movement was quoted in a 2012 newspaper as saying, "The Prime Minister is jeopardizing the ability of Kittitians and Nevisians to have land to build homes, start businesses, go into farming or to will to their children and grandchildren."[23] Fears ran high that this proposed debt-restructuring effort was eerily reminiscent of the social and economic dynamics of the late nineteenth-century, post-emancipation era when the formerly enslaved were still landless and endured only minimally improved conditions despite the historical political change. Members of Douglas's cabinet (led by Dr. Timothy

Harris) submitted a motion of no confidence against Douglas's leadership on December 11, 2012. The motion was never addressed. In the wake the vote of no confidence, Douglas repeatedly urged his supporters, during his weekly radio show *Ask the PM*, to "drop, cover and hold on" to him as he weathered the political turmoil. More than just a quotation of the sound du jour, Douglas's invocation of the hyperlocal and current through wylers was intended to do important localizing and authenticating work against accusations of his increasing foreign interest.

Or, consider another instance of relation. In February 2023, the Kore Band from Nevis started a jam at the bar Jim Jim's with a riddim and chant loosely—raggedly, irreverently—on Andra Day's 2015 single "Rise Up." The original song, a stirring ballad, was conceived by songwriter Day as "a sort of prayer" on the heels of learning of a friend's cancer diagnosis. Transducing the sentimental connotation of the 2015 song with lyrics like "Siddung pon de ting and make it rise up / Shub back on de ting and make it rise up / Work up on de ting and make it rise up," the performance is scandalous and startling, potentially humorous, and ultimately catchy as highly syncopated riddim studded with high-pitched ascending accents beneath the chant.

The performance and aestheticization of this kind of speed as "we culture" may be better understood, as Raymond Williams writes of culture, as "a special kind of map" through which societal, economic, and political "changes can be explored."[24] As a map, wylers might chart a vast geography of relation where traditional sounds like the big drum and the steel pan and new technologies like drum machines are stable nodes on a grid of traditional to modern longitude or European to African or undeveloped to developed latitude. That drive, though, its insistence on a consistent movement toward, may require a different navigational tool for its apprehension.

The geographer Philip Steinberg, in theorizing an "alternative ontology of connection," turns to the modeling techniques of oceanography.[25] Eulerian fluid dynamics is predicated on objects that are fixed in the water, like a buoy. Lagrangian fluid dynamics, in contrast, traces the paths of "floaters" or particles, and "objects come into being as they move (or unfold) through space and time." "Movement," from this perspective, "is geography." From this view, a mapping of wylers as culture would recognize all the materials, the subjectivities, sounds, experiences, texts, and techniques of "mobilization and modulation" that Steve Goodman has called "virologies of the Black Atlantic" as mobile and coconstitutive of the nationalist critiques, and traditionalizing discourses that counter it.[26]

Even as wylers is distanced from traditional and local styles because of its status as "modern," but not effectively nationalist or developed, some listeners and promoters of wylers and other small-island genres seek an alternative mapping of Caribbean music that can account for its tempi and pace, perennial sites of alternate island times.

Created for postcolonial youth by postcolonial youth, wylers music aestheticizes motion, change, and evolution as emphasized and locally inherited constants—a sense of awareness and subjectivity—through the elicitation of speed.[27] Wylers musicians and producers assert that the sounds and styles associated with wylers are obvious iterations of the same geometry of sounds, movements, and patterns of performativity on which earlier manifestations of Kittitian and Nevisian music were modeled. In a UNESCO documentary about the evolution of music in St. Kitts and Nevis, Mr. Mention responded to the assertion that wylers is "modern" music: "Music is music. There's nothing new under the sun so to speak, just a different time . . . Wherever there's advancement there's a certain amount of change. This music still remains the music. I . . . see it as the same now . . . So there's a difference but not that much of a difference to speak in terms of "modern." Because what is modern? You know?"[28]

In contrast, the previous generation's failure to hear wylers within a development model has precipitated critiques that cast the music as constituting a drastic break in the trajectories of the most immediately recent era of Kittitian-Nevisian political and social life. Where the development model is predicated on tracing a recognizable continuity of content, wylers musicians hear their relationship to the past as one of form. Through the performance and curation of experiences of speed, as a more capacious, locally emphasized and meaningful form, wylers musicians and audiences constitute a sense of cohesion—historically and regionally—that offers an alternative model to the constrictive logics of development.

In the following section, I describe the point of view of my uncle, Irving "Santoy" Barrett, a Nevisian who has been a gigging musician and teaching artist for all his adult life. Born in the 1960s, Uncle Irving is a member of the "statehood era," the time of quasi independence from the late 1960s until 1983. He is an arranger and a specialist in the native Nevisian bamboo fife who is responsible for implementing "indigenous music education" for primary school students on both islands; he also toured with Ellie Matt and the G.I.'s Brass for several years as a trombonist.

Uncle Irving and the U-Turn

Uncle Irving and I were seated on the balcony of the Circus Grill, a popular destination for tourists in Basseterre hoping for a good view and local eats.

The sidewalks were lined with vendors selling a little bit of everything: bags of precut and peeled sugarcane, glow sticks, and homemade hot sauces in plastic water bottles. Uncle Irving, my father's youngest brother, had taken the lunchtime ferry over from Charlestown, Nevis, to play fife in the annual children's masquerade later that day. Given his stature as a respected educator, it is not surprising that he knew or had heard some bit of news about almost everyone we spotted from our elevated perch. A sound system loudly sent that year's wylers road march anthems throughout the busy streets. We people-watched over two Carib beers and a curry goat roti while we discussed the merits of contemporary music. When I told him that I wanted to talk about "this" music (pointing indiscriminately in the air), he launched into an explanation that spiraled and flowed into several other conversations:

> This is so much faster than my time. It's a very new music . . . When I look at it, I realize it's an approach, it's almost like a U-turn to a more African-oriented music . . . You used to have Ellie Matt and the G.I.'s Brass. They made music you had to sit down and really construct. Now with this [wylers] music you are on the same chord for eight measures? People would have dismissed that in the 1970s and 1980s as a lack of music literacy . . . not necessarily fast but *extremely* fast. I guess because I'm so steeped in the original calypso thing—I am steeped in the music of the 1970s, 1980s, and 1990s: Sparrow, Chalkdust, Sugar Aloes, Calypso Rose. There is a generation gap that is very pronounced in the music. The music that your mom and your dad would have enjoyed is different. It's different in tempo. I left in the late 1980s and came back in 2000 and realized the music went from what it was to something less sophisticated. I was shocked.[29]

Uncle Irving compared music from previous decades to wylers as objectively more sophisticated and complicated because of the deployment of standard harmonic progressions. He also commented on the lack of politically relevant lyrics and described his discomfort with overtly sexual dancing. His argument, however, was largely about progressions on two scales: at the scale of the music itself and on a larger scale of historical narrative and development over time. For Uncle Irving here, to be African in orientation is to have a musical sensibility guided primarily by rhythm and percussion and less by harmonic and melodic imperatives. His description of wylers as constituting a U-turn is based on a processual understanding of music as progressing toward an aesthetic goal in audibly discernible ways.

The argument in musicology about the teleology of Western classical music versus the more immediately experiential popular music can be traced in one of its twentieth-century iterations to Leonard Meyer's work on the relative value and greatness of goal-oriented classical music in relation to the "primitive" and monotonous sounds of 1950s rock and roll.[30] The contemporary version of this idea in St. Kitts and Nevis, however, is less rooted in a dichotomy between popular and classical. In a national and cultural context where development as progress is a prevailing frame for understanding the passage of time, wylers songs fail to develop musical ideas that constitute a viable, commodifiable, and exportable product.

A U-turn also suggests that there is a trajectory or a path according to which music is able to develop within St. Kitts and Nevis and wylers has deviated from it by going in the opposite direction. Despite the recognition of music as an endlessly creative medium, music in St. Kitts and Nevis is understood as developing along a very specific trajectory toward the destination of global popularity and entrance into the attention market as a desirable product. It is too fast precisely because of the way it moves away from markers of teleological development in music.

Uncle Irving identifies what he sees as a moralistic change, which is mirrored in musical changes that he laments as equally disappointing and shocking. This understanding of modern music and its effects on the youth is not simply due to a generation gap. There are also religious groups in St. Kitts and Nevis that decry the heathenistic nature of all of carnival—especially the music and attendant dancing. During my conversation with Uncle Irving, we were interrupted by my cousin, who stopped to say hello. Making small talk with the young man with her (whom she identified as her high school friend from before she moved to Indiana), Uncle Irving asked if he was enjoying the carnival festivities. The boy said that he does his best to steer clear of the "heathen activity" that plagues the island during the time. Uncle Irving reflexively offered him a brief but stern lesson about the history of the music and dance practices of the enslaved Africans on the two islands, who celebrated their emancipation from the bondages of slavery with similar sounds and movements. He stressed that what we call "carnival" is just a name for a much deeper, "indigenous" practice of African heritage.

The idea of carnival-like celebrations as a marker of emancipation, while not quite the case on St. Kitts, was certainly true on Nevis, where Uncle Irving was born and lived after decades in the United States. Culturama, the biggest event of the year on Nevis since 1974, was the brainchild of a group of returning Nevisians who had gone abroad for higher education. It was created as a means of resuscitating old performance genres, such as Christmas sports, and other dramatic arts. At the time, St. Kitts had already established a national carnival, which Nevisians felt was not equipped to adequately represent or include them—an imbalance of power entrenched into political activity and many social attitudes as well. Aside from providing a separate space

FIGURE 3.2. Ellie Matt and the G.I.'s Brass Band, ca. 1977. Uncle Irving Barrett, age twenty, is center, front row, touching the ground. Ellie Matt stands second from right, in glasses. Courtesy of the National Archives, St. Kitts and Nevis.

for folkloric revival, Culturama addressed growing concern about the loss of local "culture" in the face of increased migration and global influence. In 1977, *Culturama* magazine wrote: "In many Caribbean islands much of the culture is no longer enjoyed by the locals. Instead, it is geared towards entertaining the many tourists on our shores. Hence, the youths do not have a chance to look into the past and see what their great-grandparents used to enjoy, what was 'their own.' There is now a total lack of cultural awareness in our midst. We have no values, nothing to call 'our own' anymore."[31]

Karen Fog Olwig, an anthropologist whose research focused on conti-nuity and change as organizing features of culture on Nevis, remarked that in the mid-1980s, "the main principle behind [Culturama] activities is that they must portray 'traditional' Nevisian culture. . . . [Music] is supposed to be dominated by string bands and calypsos rather than brass bands and elec-tronic disco rhythms."[32] During my lunchtime chat with Uncle Irving in 2012, he confidently grouped brass bands such as Ellie Matt and the G.I.'s Brass into the conversation of tradition, indigeneity, and culture in ways that would have been unheard of thirty years prior (fig. 3.2).

Looking out across the Circus, I was surprised by the sharp sound of a whip cracking on the pavement below. A man dressed in a colorful shirt and ankle-length pants walked slowly down the street with his bull—a man dressed in a black-and-white cow outfit—trailing behind him. "They must be tired because they ain't doin' nothin'," Uncle Irving remarked. The two were stragglers from the Monkey Hill troupe, one of the bull play troupes that have been a staple of Christmastime performance and sport since the early twen-tieth century. The whip as a percussive instrument is no doubt a reminder of the enslavement that begot the traditions Uncle Irving had described to the young carnival critic.

For Uncle Irving, the bull troupes and other folkloric arts, such as the string band and the fife, were important because of their relationship to the past on the islands—a local past closer than precolonial Africa and one that constituted a sense of continuity through folklorization. Ellie Matt and the G.I.'s Brass, along with other brass bands of the 1970s and early 1980s, represented a musical "evolution" that combined rhythmic interest with "color, texture, timbre, and harmonic intelligence." Uncle Irving described the music of Ellie Matt and his band as being like "a quilt that patched together different kinds of sounds and musical ideas to make something beautiful." In contrast, wylers was "a quilt with only two colors."

Irving rationalized that the direction of contemporary musics was the result of migration, saying:

> They have more media outlets, more radio stations, more television stations—more access to the media. You have the advent of the internet so their minds should be broader than ours. But the music isn't reflecting that. It's so limited. But so many of the important musicians left after the 1980s. There was a void. Out of the void came this music.[33]

The void created by immigration, particularly in the decades leading up to independence, had become a part of life on St. Kitts and Nevis. During the first thirty years of the twentieth century, "the tempo of life on the islands had thereby become geared to the presence or absence of migrating men."[34] Little had changed by the 1980s. However, aside from the absence of this group of men, it is possible to consider that, in the mid-1980s—when, arguably, the vision of a self-determined Caribbean political reality was already foreclosed by the failure of Grenada's revolution (memorialized in a calypso by Ellie Matt)—there remained the possibility of alternative modes of self-determination on the islands, particularly within the porous parameters of small-island soca and the inevitability of its being swept up into the larger "world music" portfolio. The lack of formal education spoke, in a sense, to a kind of neglect that was creatively fertile. As Uncle Irving noted, "They did the best with what they had" to create this style of music. Uncle Irving not only thinks about the music differently; he hears it differently, too. For him, the vertical movement of harmonic interest is prioritized over other, more linear ways of hearing progress, movement, unfolding, or beauty.

When I reconnected with Dagah via WhatsApp ten years later, he was disappointed to remember that he had offered a "salty comment." Not surprisingly, in the intervening decade, he came to see his relationship to St. Kitts, the Americas, Blackness, and avenues for his own musicality differently. Being "in a different place mentally" led to a realization. "I come from a soca background but I was running away from it. . . . People wanted to see if I was still Caribbean, and it was hard to convince them."[35]

Dagah's comments about wylers are, more than a denigration of a genre, a representational move meant to mediate his proximity to the ideas associated with it or his fear of the ideas that could be associated with wylers' production and reception. Dagah's relationship to Blackness and Americanness suggests something about his own sense of belonging to an archipelago and archipelagos within the legacy of New World racial formations. Connected in a complex network of Blacknesses and associated musical styles, Dagah's authority as a musician, especially a rapper, was based on his successful navigation of his own place in the diaspora. On the topic of musical performances of share diasporic legacy, Fred Moten and Stefano Harney suggest that "flight from externally imposed regulation . . . is the ongoing performance of a shared diasporic legacy that is always articulated in close proximity to intradiasporic conflict."[36] Under the shared scaffolding of our Blackness, Dagah's insistence on a distance from wylers was matched by equal and opposite effort to convince him of my Caribbeanness. The description of the political atmosphere surrounding the emergence of wylers as a new sound in the following section puts Dagah's concerns about his own association with the style into better view.

Out of a Void: Development, Drugs, and Crime

Despite wylers' inarguable embeddedness in the sonic landscape of St. Kitts and Nevis, some critics argue that, instead of the music being a creative and obvious outgrowth of the styles before it, it represents an unpredictably and unfortunate deviation from the otherwise progressive evolution of local music. Wylers simultaneously represents sonic and temporal excess: it is "too fast" and the product of extreme lack—it came "out of a void."[37]

Specifically, wylers has been historicized as a product of the failure of development, as a political process, to improve the lives of citizens in the wake of the nation's independence in 1983. The mid-1990s was a tumultuous time of political and social upheaval for the entire federation. On St. Kitts, the atmosphere turned violent when, following the 1993 election, which produced no clear majority, the prevailing political parties—the People's Action Movement (PAM) and the Labour Party—hurled accusations of misconduct at one another. Instead of calling another vote, the subsidiary representative governing body of Nevis (Nevis Reformation Party) aligned with the PAM to push that party into power. Labour supporters "took to the streets, and St. Kitts was engulfed in a series of protest marches."[38] Church leaders and private-sector representatives facilitated dialogues between key members of the political parties. After a meeting at the Four Seasons Hotel on Nevis, it was decided that PAM would stay in power for only two years and another election would be held in 1995.

By the mid-1990s, the importation and trafficking of illicit drugs had become one of the most important issues in the islands, socially, economically, and politically. Located between South America and the continental United States, St. Kitts was a convenient point for cocaine and marijuana transshipment, which caught the attention of US officials who were monitoring the situation closely and feared that St. Kitts–Nevis would become a narco-state. In the summer of 1994, more than a ton of cocaine hidden on a beach disappeared, and shortly thereafter, Vincent Morris, son of then deputy prime minister Sidney Morris, and his fiancée were found murdered, abandoned in a torched car in a sugarcane field. In the months that followed, the superintendent detective investigating the murders, Jude Matthews, was shot seventeen times in his driveway on his way to deliver documents regarding the case to the court. Shortly after the assassination, in November 1994, two of the deputy prime minister's other sons were jailed, having been found in possession of 121 pounds of cocaine and guns. Given their familial ties to local elites, they were immediately granted bail despite the severity of the accusations. Many of those in prison grew angry at the blatant favoritism and incited a riot that severely damaged the Basseterre Prison and resulted in the escape of over 150 inmates. One man, David Lawrence, was charged with the murder of Detective Matthews. However, after three separate trials and three hung juries, Lawrence was not convicted.

At the time, St. Kitts and Nevis was still in the relative infancy of its tourism economy, and much of the publicity in foreign newspapers had shifted from touting the majestic wonders of its tranquility as a backdrop for vacation to, among other things, exposés on one man who represented what seemed like the inevitable contamination of St. Kitts and Nevis by the drugs and gang violence that had ravaged other West Indian islands and their diasporic outposts. Charles Miller, known as "Little Nut," was a Kittitian who left for Jamaica as a teenager and joined one of the deadliest Jamaican posses at the time. A known murderer and drug lord, Miller was granted immunity by the US government and put into the witness protection program, only to reemerge in his birthplace as a dangerous kingpin. Crime existed in St. Kitts and Nevis before Charles Miller, of course. Economic initiatives such as the Investment for Citizenship program, which ultimately sold St. Kitts–Nevis passports to anyone for a fee, were, especially in their early years, used by shady businessmen who sought to evade the laws of their home jurisdictions. But Little Nut did bring a particular brand of menace that was unusual for these islands. Public murders and suspicious disappearances were new to Kittitians and Nevisians. Miller's drug-money-fueled lifestyle and his untouchable persona as a dark-skinned Black man without other ties to the respectable middle-class elites was new to the local social scene, too. When he was questioned about his involvement with the murder of the superintendent detective in 1994, he said, "The problem is that I am too black, too young and too successful for the local elite." In 2000, Miller was finally extradited back to the United States, where he was imprisoned on drug charges. A newspaper reported a general sense of relief around the island: "It is as if a noose has been removed from the neck of a lot of people."[39]

Despite removing Miller—the most notorious and violent of the criminals in St. Kitts and Nevis—the islands continued to be plagued by crime, violence, and the proliferation of street gangs. In late April 2010, the newly appointed minister of national security, the Honorable Sam Condor, held a press conference calling for national collaboration on the new Zero Tolerance Policy regarding the "escalation in violent crime" in the federation.[40] Fighting crime had become a key issue for government officials, particularly around election time. Losing kids—especially young men—to "the street," gangs, or senseless violence was a source of significant fear for adults on the islands. Fingers were pointed in many directions to find a culprit for these transgressions. Some suggested that the waning role of the church in family life was the reason for crime. Others suggested that it was the continued degradation of the nuclear family and especially the high rate of single, unwed mothers who neglected to provide the appropriate upbringing for responsible and upright citizens. Others blamed the music.

Responding to an online news journal article about the press conference, a commenter, "Sad Citizen," offered suggestions for curbing the crime. First on the list was controlling the music that "stimulates" criminals: "I would like to give some tips to help start the control of crime. 1. Music. . . . . loud music until the wee hours stimulates the criminals. The Strip should be closed by 2.a.m and the music lowered at midnight. 2. Traffic. . . . . . the traffic laws should be enforced. 3. Children of 14 and sixteen should be off the street unless with a parent. Certainly not in the bars. 4. Forget politics! We are losing our country, our tourism, our lives, our children!"[41]

The musicians I spoke with all suggested that local music gained a reputation as "too fast," as "wylers," when producers began using the riddim box in the 1990s.[42] The experimental sounds being created with novel technology coincided with the escalating plague of drug trafficking and crime. The energy of wylers—particularly as it manifested in the body—was interpreted as a product of its contemporary environment.

In an interview a decade before his death in 2019, Kenrick Georges, a multi-instrumentalist who was the composer and lyricist of the official St. Kitts and Nevis national anthem, commented much to the shock of the ZIZ TV interviewer that "the government has failed miserably" at supporting the arts: "When you're independent, what you should do is pay attention to your cultural development—developing our culture and our arts. We have achieved in other kinds of development—infrastructure and things like that—but not developing culture."[43]

I came across this interview after his untimely passing, but Georges had made clear to me, in a brief interaction five years prior, that wylers, too, was the product of such massive failure. In 2014, I reached out to him to discuss ways of transcribing examples of the fife and drum tradition. After our conversation he reminded me—sternly but not uncaringly—that I was "wasting time" studying wylers because it was "idiotic at best." Instead, he suggested, young people on the island should be invested in projects like the one he was currently working on, which included orchestral arrangements of popular soca and calypso songs.[44] A respected and lauded composer, arranger, teacher and musician, Georges had already recorded several albums of this kind. The tagline of the last of these compilations from 2018 reads, "Experience a new concept; a different way to listen to music; savor the new flavor."[45]

What allows this kind of music to register as "new" while wylers is understood as a metaphorical U-turn back to the old? This is the quintessential expression of the major tension between wylers musicians (and their supporters and defenders) and their detractors. These ideas about the shape and direction of local music that are tied inextricably to local conceptions of and investments in development as a "powerful semantic constellation."[46]

While there is not a specific category of "developed" music like there is of "developed" and "underdeveloped" countries, there are at least two avenues toward musical development in St. Kitts and Nevis. The first is through valorization of and subsequent adoption as legitimization of hegemonic European (or "northern") forms of music making.[47] The second form of musical development is more obviously related to other nodes and forms of development, as it is inextricably tied to the music's ability to produce international economic capital. In the following section, I detail the incorporation of the steel pan into the mainstream of Kittitian-Nevisian musical idioms as a salient example of development via the adoption of hegemonic forms. Then I discuss the historic success of Ellie Matt and the G.I.'s Brass of the 1970s and 1980s as an example of the latter mode of musical development.

The Development of the Steel Pan

The steel pan was brought to St. Kitts from Trinidad in 1949. Admiring young-sters referred to it as the "ping-pong" owing to its tinny, resonant timbre.[48] By carnival in 1950 there were steel pan bands—mostly made up of young boys—representing each of the different neighborhoods around the island. Many of the bands were named after iconic American brands, such as the Coca Colas and the Boston Tigers. The latter was created by Valentine Morris, a prominent bandleader and superintendent of the prison system in St. Kitts and Nevis (fig. 3.3).

Despite the steel pan's immediate popularity among the islands' Black lower and middle classes, it was not until 1955 that steel pan music was ac-cepted as a legitimate form fit for consumption outside of a carnival. Much of the ambivalence toward steel pan music was due to the type of people it represented. Morris, remembering the difficulties he faced trying to find per-formance venues as a steel pan player, noted, "These so-called 'upper-class' people didn't want to have no part of it."[49] In the 1950s, paying gigs for lo-cal musicians, outside of the small tourist scene, were largely held in school-houses and sponsored by elite white or mixed-race Kittitians with political power and access to economic capital. People in that socioeconomic and racial group "wanted the orchestral music. The steel pan had young black people playing it. They didn't want that." In 1952, the Boston Tigers had re-ceived a few opportunities to play for free at these types of dances to gain

FIGURE 3.3. Valentine Morris (*left*) with friends and handmade steel pans, ca. 1950. "Three Men with Steel Pans," National Archives St. Kitts and Nevis, January 15, 2018, https://www.nationalarchives.gov .kn/883. Courtesy of the National Archives, St. Kitts and Nevis.

exposure. It was not until 1955, however, that steel pan music made some headway: the elite classes "realized that classical, semiclassical music could have been played on pans," Morris recalled. "That's how we broke through." The steel pan's ability to play what Morris called "musically complex" styles granted it a degree of legitimacy that aided in its acceptance as more than just a youthful Black pastime.

Sitting on his breezy porch, I stopped Mr. Morris in his recounting to ask what "semiclassical" music referred to. "Bach and Beethoven, Minuet in G. Not Tchaikovsky," he said, adding that "the first song to be played on the pan in St. Kitts was 'Georgie Porgie Pudding and Pie,' but they saw we could do more than that." Essentially, the steel pan became accepted as a legitimate instrument when it moved from "ping-pong" percussion to a harmonic instrument. In the 1950s, small orchestras that played waltzes and Cuban son were the main forms of musical entertainment, and by 1955, steel pan orchestras joined orchestral ensembles in providing the entertainment at local dances. In the 1960s, Valentine Morris made an important decision to, as he put it, "move on." "Most steel pan players in the 1950s were using tonic sol-fa"—or "tonic sulfur," as it is often called in St. Kitts and Nevis, a British method of teaching songs using solfège syllables and movable do, as their primary method of teaching, learning, and arranging steel pan songs. "I didn't want to stay there like that," he recalled.[50] A desire to learn how to read music led him to lessons with Edgar Challenger in the early 1960s. Challenger was a schoolteacher and prominent historian who would become one of the first elected officials to serve under the government of St. Kitts, Nevis, Anguilla. After spending years learning the trumpet under Challenger's instruction, Morris created the Val Morris Orchestra, a ten-piece ensemble that played popular dance-band music from around the region, which, because of American and European tourism, was heavily influenced by American dance-band music.

Before Captain Morris would continue with the interview, he wanted to know "exactly what" qualified me as a musician. I told him, "I am a vocalist, and I play some piano."

"Some? Can you play in any key?"

I laughed; he did not.

"You know how you can learn to play anything in any key?"

I smiled and said nothing.

"You practice."

I laughed politely as he pointed to his granddaughter inside, visible through the living room window, practicing on an upright piano.

Ellie Matt and the G.I.'s Brass

The other route to participation in national development projects, in the 1960s through 1980s, was through legitimization via access and proximity to international money. This typically took the form of mainstream US and European recognition and acceptance, which is the route Ellie Matt took and is one of the reasons Ellie Matt and the G.I.'s Brass is heralded as among the best and most influential musical acts from St. Kitts and Nevis. In the early 1960s, orchestras such as Val Morris's were the main source of live dance music on the islands. But by the middle of the decade, combos—such as Comet's Combo, founded in 1966 as the first electric combo in Nevis—came into vogue and all but replaced the older acoustic orchestral sound. Electric combos were made up primarily of bass guitar, rhythm guitar, keyboard, drum set, and a lead guitar; they covered Jamaican music styles and popular Trinidadian calypso alongside soul and R&B hits. By the 1970s, larger combos—also called brass or brass bands—which incorporated large horn and wind sections—gained in popularity. Eventually, these ensembles began including vocals into their sound, continuing to cover American Top 40 songs and putting forth a regional, calypso-influenced sound. The most famous of the combos was Ellie Matt and G.I.'s Brass ("G.I.'s" being short for "Group Impressions"), which was formed in 1969. Elston Nero, the band's leader—an instrumentalist, arranger, and a prolific calypsonian with ten Calypso King and seven road march titles under his belt—performed steadily throughout the region and in the diaspora through the 1980s, when he was the music director on the Mighty Sparrow's Japanese and European tours in 1988.

While 1957 marked the first government-organized carnival in Basseterre, St. Kitts, 1971 was the first year of "National Carnival." The implementation of National Carnival came on the heels of major political change. In 1967, St. Kitts, Nevis, and Anguilla became an associated state; after much social protest, Anguilla seceded from St. Kitts and Nevis to remain under the colonial protection of Britain. The years between 1967 and 1971 were politically turbulent and carnival celebrations were unstable: there was no carnival in 1967, and in 1970 there were two carnivals, each held by opposing political parties. In light of the resurrected and unified National Carnival of 1971, Ellie Matt was quoted as having said that it was a time for musicians like himself to focus on "our own materials, and play our own songs."[51] While his band did continue to cover other songs in addition to composing and performing original pieces, it could be said that the era heralded the international dissemination of a particular style of Kittitian-Nevisian music.

If G.I.'s Brass was representative of a distinctive Kittitian-Nevisian sound, then a salient portion of that sound was achieved through utilizing a faster tempo than was in fashion at the time in the places that were cultural referents. Take for example G.I.'s 1976 hit "Shake Your Booty," a cover of KC and the Sunshine Band's song from earlier that the same year. According to Mick Stokes, one of G.I.'s lead singers and drummers: "Shake Ya Booty was what [G.I.'s Brass] actually broke into the American market with. We added a calypso flavour and the white people loved it along with the blacks. It was number #1 on the radios for three months. The white people loved it when we visited the US and promoters fought to book us . . . We had a following."[52]

This kind of international success—including when G.I. won the Brass-O-Rama competition in Trinidad in 1973 (especially as a "small island" band)—marks Ellie Matt and his music as contributing to a larger development project. This fact is evidenced not least by the historicization of his figure in official text, but also by the plethora of awards and medals Nero amassed for his dedication to "nation building" and "cultural development" over thirty years.[53]

Sounds of Development and Its Deviations

If disparate styles such as the steel pan orchestra and the brass band sound of Ellie Matt are accepted as legitimate forms of music, then what does development sound like? Jocelyne Guilbault's discussion of zouk as a part of Antillean Creole "open specificity" in the context of world music demonstrates how recognizable rhythmic patterns and different types of instrumentation inherent to zouk are culled and hark back to various homelands throughout the Caribbean and its diaspora.[54] Zouk's popularity lies in its recognizability as a mixture of various rhythms and sounds that have a diverse set of referents. For different people in parts of the Caribbean and the rest of the Afro-diasporic world, these overlapping rhythms and referents constitute entry points for broad listenership. In the same way that, as Wayne Marshall suggests, hip-hop, R&B, and dancehall mixes from the early 2000s "primed" American audiences for the later explosion of reggaeton by familiarizing them with relevant rhythms and lyrical flows, Guilbault suggests that the "family resemblance" of the Haitian biguine rhythm and the chouval bwa of Martinique within zouk creates an engaging point of reference and site of ownership for a wide range of listeners.[55] The sheer speed of wylers, in contrast, obscures many of those points of reference. Herein lies one of the main points of convergence between national development and musical development in terms of teleological ideologies: beyond a national development project, the speed of wylers has opened the genre up to criticism that even at the song level, wylers fails to develop.

4

Archipelagic Listening from the Small Islands

June 2019, Santa Marta, Colombia—we are the only ostensibly Black people on the short flight from Bogotá to Santa Marta. As the small crowd of travelers exits the airport, a taxi driver, Juan, approaches us with a smile. After a brief exchange—some Spanish, a bit of English, a lot of arm movements—Harrison, my two children (four-year-old Zora and eleven-month-old Malcolm), my mother, and I climb into Juan's van. "Where are you from?" he asks. "¡Soy de San Kitts—San Christopher!" my mom responds in the assertive voice she reserves for meeting new people and reading the Sunday morning liturgy at church. Juan, offering an international gesture of Black solidarity, rubs the dark skin on his forearm. "Somos caribeños." We all laugh.

When I met a scholar from Cali, earlier that year, she warned me, in private, that the only other Black people I would meet in Santa Marta would likely be acting as security guards at the entrance of my hotel. "You might feel out of place." Initiating our first encounter in Santa Marta, Juan performs familiarity. Shortly into our drive, he insists we stop for beers to enliven the fifteen-minute trek from Simón Bolívar International Airport to our rental in Pozos Colorados, the capital of Magdalena and the second-oldest city in the Americas.

He hops out the van, hustles into a store on the side of the road, and within minutes he is back handing out cold beers to all the adults in the vehicle. "Águilas y champeta" Juan says before turning up the stereo. Up in the front seat, my mom responds to champeta as something that sounds sweet to her, "like calypso," she says, rocking from side to side as she sways her seated hips. "Like soca," I add, half-inquiring, half-correcting. I ask Juan, who's now singing, and he asks why I am not using an app to figure it out. Encouraging, not dismissing, he tells me to just look it up. "Champeta," he sounds out slowly. "Cham-peh-tah." After we all piled out of the van, Harrison dapped Juan up, pressing a small wad of fresh pesos into his palm, and they embraced briefly. "Somos caribeños," Harrison said, holding his hand over his heart. I was watching this interaction with interest. I am generally amused by Harrison's ability to navigate unfamiliar spaces with such confidence. He is always dapping up somebody, making a new friend, being drawn into conversation by strangers. As a result, we have been unofficially gathering data about the different kinds of daps and handshakes Black people greet one another with in various urban spaces. In St. Kitts, for masculine adults, after the initial hand gripping, it is customary to bump fists. In Philadelphia, Black men more often shake hands. In Chicago, the dap starts as a horizontal high-five and slides out smoothly until finger pads meet. For Harrison, a Black man's dap is global language with different accents, a song with many regional variations.

Later that same day, as we stroll through one of Santa Marta's small cobblestone streets, a young teenaged boy leans against the doorway of a home. He seems to be responding to a question from inside the house when he describes us, the obvious foreigners, as "pelomalos," or "bad haired." I do not sense personal distaste in his tone. He is simply stating fact within a specific cultural context of anti-Blackness: we are Black—kinky, "bad hair" Black. Growing up in the North Bronx in the 1990s, I spent most of my time around Caribbean people. I was no stranger to comments about the nappiness of my hair. In a "Caribbeanized" New York, the same hierarchies and distinctions which had been entrained in various islanded spaces within the region were poured into the urban, melting-pot ethos of the city. This distinction, one that marked me and my coarse-haired family as notably and obviously Black, was the flip side of the same shared currency that made "somos caribeños" a meaningful refrain during our short time with Juan.

Those interactions in Santa Marta stuck with me. I have continued to replay them in the years since. I repeat snippets of these minute interactions in my mind to figure out what or if they might mean. My engagement with my own memories and a few notes typed into my phone shift from passive reminiscence to something more like replay, that "careful looking" Tina M. Campt describes as a potential precursor to "listening to images." To Campt, images, especially the "historically dismissed" ones she focuses on, are not silent objects of visual perception but quiet instruments that produce knowledge; they make sound, if we listen. And listening to them "is a practice of looking beyond what we see," focusing instead on "other affective frequencies."[1] In its counterintuitive conceptual leaps, Campt's figuration of listening to images resonates with Kate Crawford's own reconceptualization of online participation as a kind of listening. She writes, "If the activities commonly described as lurking and non-participation are understood as forms of listening, they shift from being vacant and empty figurations to being active and receptive processes."[2] In both formulations, listening is an act that remaps perceptions of relation.

Something else about these interactions—the warm unity subtended by musical recognition of Black Caribbeanness (via champeta) on the one hand, the casual, mundane experiences of racist categorization on the other—feels familiar. This feeling, of meaningful connection and abject difference, a reaching and pulling toward a shared something while being set apart, constitutes my own experience of relation, across a broadly construed Caribbean, as a kind of paradox. In this chapter, I describe archipelagic listening as a tool for grasping this paradox—grasping, but also articulating, analyzing, comprehending it as a *paradox of aurality* distributed in a multidimensional field. I think of aurality here much as Jerome Camal does. Drawing on the work of Jairo Moreno and Ana María Ochoa Gautier, Camal describes aurality quite simply as "a less-than-transparent sonic field of relation."[3] Inhabiting such a field, listening to and within it, is an inherently poly-temporal experience. As Alexandra T. Vasquez argues, aurality holds together "flashes, memories, sounds" alongside traditions of creativity "at the service of instant allegory" to signify meaning and possibility at other registers.[4]

Listening in detail, then, gives us more access to multiplicity itself: multiple signs, multiple histories, multiple noises. This is especially important when listening to what Antonio Benitez-Rojo calls the "rhythmic complexity . . . that gives pan-Caribbean cultures a way of being." "This polyrhythm of planes and meters," he writes, "can be seen not just in music, dance, song, and the plastic arts, but also in the cuisine—the *ajiaco*—in architecture, in poetry, in the novel, in the theater, in bodily expression, in religious beliefs, in idiosyncrasies, that is, in all the texts that circulate high and low throughout the Caribbean region."[5] This "polyrhythm of planes and meters," this speed of "instant allegory," all these connections and disjunctures: they constitute aurality's field as a field of images, affects, memories, utterances, fabrications, movements, riddims.

It is into this field that I want to bring archipelagic listening as another tool of relation, one attuned to what is small and fast, and hence easily dismissed, unrecognized, or uncategorized—the "diminutive" register toward which so many Caribbean writers of the globalized, creolized 1990s turned. In what follows, I'll describe generative instances of archipelagic listening—my own and others'—that sound an island-to-island relationship between contemporaneous locales and subjectivities. I'll briefly return to champeta, which I did eventually "look up" as Juan suggested, as a site where soca, as Antillean music, especially from the small islands, became an emblem of an alternative and relationally modern Caribbeanness. Finally, I'll move to a description of Large Radio, an online community of historians who practiced a literal and deliberate version of archipelagic listening to rethink a Caribbean music history that could not hear them.

Champeta music can be traced back to the 1940s in Cartagena, where phonographs, or picós, were central to working-class social life.[6] These picós, provided by local entrepreneurs known as picoteros, became essential for music at communal events and dances. The migration of rural Colombians to the city brought with them cumbia and other traditional styles, merging with other Latin American genres like Cuban son. The picós of the 1950s became hot spots for this fusion of urban Afro-Cuban and Afro-Antillean beats. By the 1970s, picós had become emblematic of Cartagena's unique embrace and vernacularizing of technology through their huge sound systems, loud music, and personalized decor.[7] It was during this time that picós focused primarily on exclusive tracks (music that nobody else owned or had access to), accumulating records and sounds from other Afro-descendant music practices around the world. Congolese soukous, Jamaican reggae, South African mbaqanga and Brazilian samba, for example, provided the rhythms and timbres for the soundtrack of the popular classes of Cartagena. By the 1980s, Colombian musicians were creating their own interpretations and translations of "foreign" music, beginning with an acoustic genre called chalusonga (a fusion of "chalupa," the term for a palenque rhythm, and the "conga" drum). Much of Black coastal Colombia had long embraced West Indian, Latin American, and continental African sounds as a salient and meaningful part of their embodied and sonic vernacular; however, anti-Black sentiment was a significant impediment to mainstream national recognition of champeta as a legitimate and respectable style of music and dance.

Inclusion of champeta in the spectrum not solely of Afro-descendant musics but also, more explicitly, as horizontally related, islanded Afro-Caribbean music, geographically and sonically, modified the status of the music. The West Indian archipelago provided an intelligible structure for receiving and productively hearing champeta and, thus, for dispersing and selling it. This included the creation of Caribbean music radio shows that sought to entrain the listening of a wider Colombian audience toward hearing across a broad swath of Caribbean genres. Presenting champeta as part of an archipelago of Caribbean music also included the development of a Caribbean music festival that brought Caribbean acts together on the same stage in Cartagena. Within some strains of Latin American Black music discourse, champeta is frequently described in terms of its African origins, framing it as a contemporary example of sonic African retention.[8] Within the discourse surrounding champeta, there's a subtle implication that its association with the Caribbean—a narrative crafted intentionally by promoters and producers to present champeta as quintessentially Caribbean music — is an "invention."

This nuanced portrayal underscores the strategic cultural positioning of champeta, naturalizing its African heritage while simultaneously bracketing Caribbean identity as a modern veneer. However, what these continentalist discourses miss is the "aesthetic logic" that has undergirded its development. As the ethnomusicologist Michael Birenbaum-Quintero argues, champeta "did not arise from a stylistic corpus that happened to have been assembled from particular processes of musical distribution, exchange and practice." Meaning that champeta, as modern Black sonic practice cannot be understood solely, or even effectively, as a product of specific circumstances of musical affinity or passive consumption of circulating trends. Rather, "those practices of musical distribution, exchange and practice themselves comprise *champeta*."[9] The production and consumption of champeta music take place in a specific cultural context marked by the collection of predominantly non-Spanish-language Black music records. The loud and stylized replaying and showcasing of these records contributed to the buildup of social capital and musical familiarity, setting the stage for how champeta is created and enjoyed.

Champeta is an aestheticization of *practices* of intradiasporic exchange. Colombian audiences of the 1980s and 1990s required a similar archipelagic remapping to hear champeta beyond its associations with deviant blackness or African retention. The tracing of champeta's sonic relations toward the Caribbean Sea to especially small islands like Antigua, Montserrat, Martinique, and St. Thomas encouraged audiences "to broaden a concept of the world."[10] Through archipelagic listening—a sonic mapping of experiential and affective detail beyond the facts of history—champeta, soca, and wylers come into view as islands of sound, floated by similar aesthetic logics of horizontal interrelation.

It would be easiest to suggest that the archipelagic reframing of champeta was solely a marketing device or to write it off as exclusively a ploy for capitalist expansion. But it has had historiographical effects as well. The conventional approach to documenting music history—with its focus on grand narratives and seminal works—has consistently omitted small-island musical contributions from the historical record. Intriguingly, though, many Colombian Spanish-language historical accounts of Caribbean music recognize Montserrat, especially through the soca artist Arrow, as among the most significant progenitors of soca music. I have described champeta in such detail because as a modern Caribbean Black music, it has been engaged by scholars much more robustly. There are articles and books, at least two generations of Latin Americanist scholars, and specifically, ethnomusicologists who have written and published widely on its history and development. My intention in the rest of this chapter is to perform a move guided by the aesthetic logic of Caribbean music like champeta and wylers and informed by the archipelagic framing of champeta promoters. Given that there is very little written about music from the small Caribbean islands, it is only through listening and thinking with the archipelago, listening in detail to instances of island-to-island relation, that something like a history of small-island music, specifically through the development of soca, comes into focus.

Large Radio and Remapping Soca History

A quote on the important contribution of those considered "small island" to the larger thrust of Caribbean music characterizes a significant portion of the discourse that was happening daily in forums like Island Mix and later Large Radio in the early 2000s:

> I'm not exactly sure what ur issue is with being called small island. Yes, the islands are small but think of the influence that these small islands have had in the caribbean. If jamband did originate in these smaller islands, then the other islands owe their fast pace soca sound in part to us because we small islanders have been doing it before them. To be honest, I'm very proud to have roots in a small island. Small in size, big in impact.[11]

Caribbean internet enclaves like Island Mix and Large Radio, as the Caribbean popular culture scholar Curwen Best notes, are mediums through which "Caribbean artists have sought new relationships, alliances and strategies of . . . confronting the more traditional structures and procedures that have controlled the entertainment industry." Dissatisfied with "traditional practices and discourses," he writes, "they have turned increasingly to technological advances to go where no other Caribbean artists have gone before."[12] The traditionalism of decolonial nationalism, like in St. Kitts–Nevis, put increased emphasis on relatively sanitized versions of folklorized performances and denigrated new styles and modes of behavior as backward or products of failure. However, in the cyberspace of the new millennium, "soca culture celebrated a newly found freedom" as "those people who would censure soca culture for its vulgarity and experimentation were less likely to be surfing the Net."[13] Most germane to the current discussion, Best notes that it is the "lateral shifts and interactions" that new communication technology has facilitated and amplified that "hold out most hope of success for Caribbean artists."[14] Where "soca" has become a catchall term for a wide sonic spectrum of carnival-related, Anglicized dance music, the origins of soca (its saturation in a "going to" and "coming from" discourse), have historically written small islanders out of its story of emergence. According to people I interviewed, such as the producer Jam Crew, this has provided justification for barring small-island musicians access to industry representation, collaborations, and broader recognition as legitimate music makers.

It is necessary to first understand the different relationships big islanders and small islanders (as very imperfect and transient categories) had to soca as a salient and distributed form in the 1990s before interpreting the cultural work of websites like Large Radio. The most widely recognized history of soca regards it as a sonic outgrowth of the racial and ethnic history of Trinidad. After emancipation in the British colonies (1834–1838), laborers from Asia were imported and racialized materially as exploited inexpensive labor and conceptually, as Lisa Lowe describes, as figures that would act as a "racial barrier between [the British] and the Negroes."[15] Fast-forward 150 years and the official discourse of Trinidadian nationalism referred to a euphemistic mixture, a "callaloo nation," that privileged Afro-Creole forms like carnival and calypso, and specifically the versions of carnival and calypso before the 1980s, when the lyrical sophistication and political commentary of traditional calypso gave way to a more upbeat and dance-oriented sound. More broadly, and in everyday discourse, the idea of mixing, the use of mixing metaphors, as Aisha Khan notes, "underlay[s] the ways the past is interpreted, the present assessed, and the future imagined. Mixing is both unspoken bogey and voiced barometer of modernity and progress in a milieu where race and religion—cultural distinctions in Trinidad's stratified society and key idioms of identity construction—are two dimensions of experience most receptive (some would say vulnerable) to dilutions, impurities, and fraudulence."[16] In the early 1970s, a Trinidadian calypsonian named Lord Shorty (later known as Ras Shorty I) claimed to have combined the rhythmic patterns of Indian drumming, brought to Trinidad by indentured Indian laborers in the early twentieth century, with elements of Afro-Creole calypso to create a new genre he called "sokah," or the "soul of calypso." After the calypso mania of the previous decades waned, this new, party- and dance-oriented genre appealed to a younger demographic.

Caribbean people have exerted a great deal of effort to distinguish calypso from soca in academic texts, online chat rooms, and corner cookshops, among other venues. During the 1990s, when artists from across the Caribbean such as Arrow from Montserrat, Burning Flames from Antigua, and Square One from Barbados, had wholly adopted soca as a native category of music, numerous interviews on Trinidadian and New York City public-access television shows sought to reconfirm that Lord Shorty was indeed the sole creator of the new, widespread style of West Indian music. In the early 1980s and throughout the late 1990s, Caribbean music scholars focused their attention on soca as a product of two main factors: a desire to modernize and innovate calypso to appeal to a younger audience and Lord Shorty's own description of his musical experimentations that ultimately produced a fusion of Indian and African rhythms. Lord Shorty suggested that he used the "rhythms" of the East Indian dholak and the "rhythmic structure" of East Indian music to alter what Selwyn Ahyoung would later call the "pulse anticipation pattern" of calypso to create "sokah."[17] As Shorty explained in 1997: "Let's look at it this way. When soca was first invented there was no name. There was a vibration. . . . What I did was simply take the feeling that you got from the two rhythmic structures and put them on instruments."[18]

Largely ignoring the vibratory and sensory aspects of Lord Shorty's descriptions, soca history discourse has focused on trying to discern which parts of a typical soca rhythm or the soca "beat" are of African (and African American) origin and which are a product of East Indian cultural influence. These efforts have been mostly inconclusive. Peter Manuel and Michael Largey have offered that soca's most characteristic beat "is an up-tempo reincarnation of the 'habanera' beat, which continues to surface here and there in the Caribbean, including in the Jamaica Dem Bow riddim and its derivative, reggaeton."[19] However, recalling my conversation with Rankin Skeff in chapter 3, as "soca" proliferates as a term for an increasingly wide array of West Indian party musics, a more flexible notion of "the beat" becomes necessary. Shannon Dudley's work in this regard seeks to reconcile the feeling of soca with insistence that its definition lies in "the beat." After significant rhythmic analysis, Dudley offers that soca can be defined primarily by its "kinetic quality" and "interactive rhythmic feel."[20] This is in close alignment with Lord Shorty's original definition, as captured by the term "sokah," which was based on interconnected notions of movement, the soul as a representation of the "inner-man," and the feeling of the interactions between "African and Indian rhythmic structures." Shorty noted in a 1995 interview: "Kah is the first letter in the Sanskrit alphabet. It represents movement, and soca is the power of movement."[21]

Leading up to the new millennium, the energy behind arguments about the difference between calypso and soca had largely transferred to discussions about the legitimacy of various soca songs based on tempo. The Mighty Arrow, known for his upbeat and infectious soca formula, penned a salsa-flavored soca song called "Don't Touch My Tempo." In a plea to DJs and an upcoming generation of Caribbean musicians, Arrow sings, "Don't you touch my Tempo—no, no! /Party nice, the groove, a touch of class / Don't you push my tempo so damn fast." By the time of the song's release in 1996, performance styles emanating from the bands and sounds crisscrossing across and beyond the small islands of the eastern Caribbean had already been associated with the fast-paced, "jump-up" style of soca that was the ire of calypso-cum-soca artists of a previous generation.

The 1997 hit "Bring Down the Rhythm," by the Trinidadian soca artist Ajala, exemplifies the same intergenerational dynamic at the other end of the archipelago. Sung with striking resemblance to the vocal shade of renown calypsonian the Mighty Shadow, Ajala stages an encounter with the Shadow, who represents a generation of calypsonians who saw increased tempo as another threat to calypso's popularity. Ajala sings:

> Bring the rhythm down, down, down.
> I and the Shadow conversing
> About the speed of the rhythm
> He say: "The youths have a different direction
> They confusing the whole nation
> People started acting weird
> They want to hear my rhythm instead."

In 1994 the Bajan soca group Krosfyah, led by the singer, songwriter, producer Edwin Yearwood, released the hit "Pump Me Up," which officially heralded the "Bajan invasion" in Trinidad. A year later, the national Trinidad Soca Monarch competition was revamped as an international event, and entries from outside of Trinidad could compete. While popular calypsonians were decrying increased tempo as an incursion on a good thing, some small islanders were owning speed as the very marker of their sonic identity. This history is harder to prove, however.

In contrast to the silencing produced through Trinidadian nationalist ownership of carnival and calypso, the international embrace of soca music and its absorption at light speed into the "world music" category has given some small islanders pause. The celebratory international and cosmopolitan narratives that haphazardly deploy creolization, hybridity, and melting-pot metaphors as sufficient description of the nuances of soca—of all West Indian music—do similar work of invalidating the small islands as specific and integral participants in soca's development. Some small islanders, like the ones who created the websites Small Island Massive in 2001 and Large Radio in 2005, are dedicated to another kind of listening that is predicated on their conceptions of the Caribbean, especially the small-island Caribbean, as an interrelation of island-to-island identity.

In the early 2000s, the websites Small Island Massive and Large Radio provided a much-needed space for small-island music amid the patchy archives of recordings, forums, and chat-room logs of intra-Caribbean online discourse. Stanley "DJ Stanman" Benoit (or just "Stanny"), a graphic designer from St. Maarten who lives in Miami, and Lennox Grant, a DJ based in the Netherlands, had been dedicated to amassing, curating, and disseminating music from all islands (and islanded spaces) of the Caribbean to counteract a peculiar silence surrounding the musical output from the vast majority of the localities that make up the Caribbean. In recounting the origin of the site, he noted:

> In 2001 me and my partner from the Netherlands were in college in Miami and we thinking Miami has all these Caribbean people but we never heard any music on the radio or at parties except the standard stuff: Trinidad soca and some dancehall. We from St. Maarten are used to hearing music from everywhere: Spanish music, Haitian, stuff from Nevis, Aruba, Curaçao. the Caribbean is bouillon and pelau: mix up! Everybody "from" your island is really from some other island, your grandmother, your father, everybody moving around from island to island. That's how life is for us . . . yet they [big islanders] believe they invented everything. We like, "we have to do something!"[22]

By the mid-2000s, internet innovations and the proliferation of web forums and instantaneous peer-to-peer messaging platforms such as ICQ and MSN Messenger created a new way for small islanders to "express themselves to one another" and to extend interisland contacts and connections that had been a major part of the small-island imaginary (particularly through music listening practices).[23] Around this time, traditional radio stations in the small islands were experimenting with chat rooms, augmenting the call-in format, that allowed listeners to engage with radio hosts and DJs directly and express a host of responses, including but not limited to their like or dislike of a selection.[24] Centralizing the real-time chat room, Benoit designed a streaming radio station with an embedded chat-room script where listeners posted national flags and small animated GIFs with West Indian flare. These acts of digital representation were, according to Benoit, "addictive" for the small islanders who frequented the site—"they never got anything like that before," he added. Although it is hard to say how many people were active on the site during this time, Benoit noted that the site was "shut down every month because it needed a bigger bandwidth" to accommodate all the activity. The site included a repository of tens of thousands of songs that were uploaded and regularly updated by Benoit and Grant and streamed twenty-four hours a day. Save for technical mishaps, the streaming was interrupted only when one of the regularly programmed DJs hosted a show. The site listed a weekly schedule of DJs and the particular focus of their sets: a DJ in New York "representing" St. Kitts and the Virgin Islands, a DJ in Toronto representing Antigua. More than just a sentimental effort, the DJs on Large Radio were also soliciting new tracks, in various stages of completion, from burgeoning producers on small islands without robust local record industries. This provided an essential forum for feedback, encouragement, and imaginative connections for young musicians and gave listeners an especially broad sense of the music styles emanating from various Caribbean hubs. Jam Crew recalls:

> Live DJ's every night. People in the chat room from all over. St. Martin, Virgin Islands, who name it! In this region it was like a sanctuary. Trust me, every single night is like party atmosphere. The DJ they had on there was on point.[25]

Benoit's sentiment about the movement between islands as undercutting any real argument about origins is what inspires his extremely time-consuming dedication to the site and to amassing, knowing, and broadcasting music from every Caribbean island, especially islands that have historically been understood as silent listeners to big styles and not producers of their own unique and legitimate sounds. The website underscores the importance of this point with an official tagline reading "Small Island Massive, Taking Over To Unite Caribbean People, and to show the world what small-island people can do. The Caribbean does not only consist of Four Islands. We are here to bring the REAL island Flavour to you."[26]

"More than four" according to Benoit, is the rallying cry and central concern of the work he sets out to do. He recounted, "People always ask which islands are the four in 'More than four' and it has many meanings."[27] "More than four" is a categorical rejection of the imposing synthesis of continentality as it manifests in hubs of Caribbean-diasporic relation. Benoit lamented the limited capacity of mass commercial marketing schemas that cannot account for the complexity of the Caribbean as a region, an idea, or a practice that emanates throughout the world. The most recent logo of Large Radio that Benoit designed includes a nondistinctive flag, a font that features open circles and broken lines that signify, forming legible letters, even without contiguity, and of course, a silhouette of the Caribbean archipelago as part of the site's branding. That "more than four" has no specific island referents points to the contingency of any mapping of relation and gestures implicitly to "the multiple strategies invoked to unsettle, transform, and transfigure" limiting cartographies.[28]

Throughout the COVID-19 pandemic, Benoit moved to a video-streaming format that showcased another of his repetitive phrases: "Riddim is a must."

The riddim, the running instrumental track that is the backdrop to a jam session, a fete, a chant, or a song, is understood as an essential feature to a sense of being and belonging that is crucial to members of the Large Radio community and to others who frequent fetes, concerts, and jams around the world. This slogan points to the ubiquity of riddim as a base that can turn anything, anywhere into part of a collective archive, a vast pool of material for sonic creativity. "Riddim is a must," then, gestures toward the propensity for improvisatory refashioning, as practiced by DJs, dancers, detractors, producers, instrumentalists, and incidental overhearers who perform these roles in the context of life and performance.

Historiography of Small-Island Tempo

Before Large Radio, the origins of calypso and soca as generic monikers for other kinds of small-island styles of music, like the style of Jam Band from the US Virgin Islands, the upbeat sounds coming of Antigua, or the street style of St. Kitts and Nevis were hotly debated in the chat rooms and forums of one of the most popular trans-Caribbean internet rum shops called IslandMix.com (these debates have since migrated to more instantaneous and all-encompassing social media platforms such as Facebook, Twitter, and Instagram). A great deal of the previously scattered and unwritten counterhistory of small-island music was discussed as part of the long-standing feud between "big islands" and "small islands" of the West Indies, comically referred to as the "More Than Four Missionaries" and "Trickdadians."[29] The former refers to forum contributors who sought to spread the good word that the small islands contributed fast tempo and masterful use of the drum machine, among other essential features, to the larger Caribbean musical landscape. One poster in Toronto on a June 2005 thread, for example, described the influence that St. Thomas's music scene had on the wider Caribbean sound:

> The band jamband itself has influenced so much of the caribbean music an they dont get the credit for it. back in the day when in trinidad when people were only chipping for jouvert, jamband was already jumping and waving. jamband has always have a lot of tempo in there music. its only in the last 10 years maybe other islands outside of the eastern caribbean have pick the pace with there music bim, trini, etc. the fast tempo of music has always been a part of the eastern caribbean (v.i., st.kitts, antigua, etc.) scene from way back. the likes of ellie matt and the gi brass skb. laviscount brass anu. even the artist from these islands had fast music short shirt, star shield for example. these are the people that influenced the lead singer of jamband out of the v.i., who was actually born in antigua. grew up listening to short shirt, obstinate, swallow

and so on. so he almost had no choice but to make his music with the same pace of the music he liked. to this day they still moving along with that so-called jamband style of music and it works for them.

The idea that small-island bands like Jam Band have not received "credit" for their influence is partly because unlike the "beat" of calypso or soca, tempo, especially fast tempo, is even harder to describe, define, and defend. If Trinidad's version of decolonial nationalism posited calypso (and later soca) as national property, it did so on the premise of calypso's largely text-based form. Soca, as understood as a product of African and Indian mixture, too, bears resemblance to Trinidad's national mythology. The fast tempo of small-island music, however, has mostly been described by its aberrance in relation the more serious and legitimate "big island" styles. However, small islanders have taken to a kind of historiographical work of remapping history, drawing on alternative archives and their possibilities.

In a 2003 Virgin Islands public-access interview, Nick "Daddy" Friday, the lead singer, songwriter, and bandleader of the St. Thomian band Jam Band, an offshoot of the brass band Eddie and the Movements, described the reception of his music in the late 1980s: "When we first started out playing, the style of calypso music that was liked or loved around here was the slow tempo calypso and everyone would say, 'you're playing too fast. You're playing too fast. You got to play slow like the Trinidadians. . . .' [Then] the people actually followed our music because we changed the whole trend. Everyone realized now that people were going for the faster style music. So Trinidad music changed completely over the years. From nice slow tempo to the up-tempo [of] what you're hearing [now] until they've gone *too fast*."[30] It is true that, for example, a contestant in the 2005 international Soca Monarch competition in Trinidad entered a song that had been written and performed by Friday and the Jam Band for the 1997 St. Thomas road march. Within the forums, this kind of influence, recognized by small-island musicians and devoted lay historians as central to the small-island contribution to a regional sound, was actively combated by a set of big-island defenders referred to as Trickdadians.

Trickdadians, the totalizing force against whom the More Than Four missionaries fight, were forum members who had a tendency to offer Trinidadianized versions of music history, giddily offering "proper citations" of scholarly articles and books that corroborated single-nation origin stories of regional sounds. One such Trinidadian online historian known as "SocaPhD" participated heavily in the feuds on the site in the early 2000s and agitated nationalist tensions by signing each of his forum comments with a signature that read "Hailing from Trinidad & Tobago and very proud of it!! Land of

Calypso, Steelband, Limbo, Parang, Rapso, Chutney-Soca, Soca, Jamoo, Pan-jazz and the Biggest, Best & Most Influential Caribbean Carnival in the World with no apology!"[31]

Given that the small-island Caribbean has not enjoyed a fraction of the archival and ethnographic attention that Trinidad has in official discourses and registers, much of what the "missionaries" offered in rebuttal to the grand claims and even published "facts" wielded mightily by the pro-Trinidadians was based on firsthand experience and personal musical collections. At a time when I found it impossible to contact the right people to access the audiovisual archives of ZIZ, the state-owned St. Kitts–Nevis media station, I could reliably find uploads of obscure recordings in the Island Mix forums. The following relatively minor example demonstrates the potential historiographical outcomes of the accessibility inherent to those forums.

The Tale of Two Sundar Popo

The 1971 carnival was crucial in changing carnival dynamics, which had been less of a unified event and more a series of seasonal programs and celebrations marked by the recurrence of certain kinds of performance, including calypso competitions, string band serenades, and various mumming traditions. In 1970, for example, rival political factions held two opposing carnivals, and there were duplicates of many of the characteristic events. In response, the Labour Party outlawed any carnival function not approved by the National Carnival Committee. The first, post-1970 official National Calypso King, Levi Weekes (or King Entertainer), competed with politically minded calypsos about land cultivation and the state of the nation polity. One newspaper article describing the evening and commending Entertainer for elevating the event noted, "Before [King Entertainer] entered the scene it was habitual for the vast majority of calypsonians to compose smutty tunes." Entertainer's entries, however, marked a change to more politically centered or civic-minded calypsos winning the title moving forward. Similarly, the road march competition of the same year featured a performance by a young man named Irvin Barnes, who, according to the calypsonian Ellie Matt, performed a song set to the melody of a Dominican folk tune. Instead of coming up with a new sobriquet, Barnes performed under the moniker "Sundar Popo."

By 1971, the name Sundar Popo (the stage name of Sundarlal Popo Bahora, from Trinidad) was already synonymous with a new style of Indo-Caribbean music called chutney. Named after the Indian condiment of mango, chilies, and other spices, chutney music as performed by Popo combined Creole English, Bhojpuri Hindi, and locally inflected Creole Hindi lyrics about broad topics, similar to those found in traditional Indian folksongs: love, family life, gods, and eroticism. Using sonically distinctive Indian instruments, such as harmonium, dhantal, and dholak, with the danceable syncopation of Afro-Creole West Indian music, chutney gained international popularity in the 1970s. Among the first forms of popular Indo-Caribbean music, the large populations of ethnic East Indians in the circum-Caribbean in nations like Guyana and Suriname celebrated chutney as something of their own along-side Indo-Trinidadians.

For Irvin Barnes of St. Johnston Village, St. Kitts, the name Sundar Popo resonated with him as he was drawn to the idea of Trinidadian Popo's style of chutney "wrapped in a calypso shell."[32] Kittitian Sundar Popo (Barnes), in his ostensibly well-received performance of the song "Play You Mas," experimented with contrast on various levels. When a clip of his competition performance was posted to the Island Mix forums, the poster, an especially active member under the alias "JamCrew869," mentioned that the only information he had about the recording was the squeals and laughter in the background, which according to his parents, marked when Popo was "rolling on the ground." I was intrigued by the assumed importance of such a recording, being the first national road march winner. Having little else to go on, I asked my parents if they knew anything about it and replicated Jam Crew's extra-archival process of asking his mom and dad to listen and respond to the fuzzy recording.

The 1971 carnival season was their last "at home" before immigrating to the United States. A twenty-year-old without job prospects because she was accused of supporting "The Opposition," Mom was frazzled and frightened by the smallness of St. Kitts and Nevis and the way proximity amplified political pressure. The 1971 consolidation of cultural performance through the nationalization of carnival was just one way that the state enacted everyday power over citizens. Aaron Kamugisha describes of Caribbean politics: "The small size of the populations and the ease of isolating or co-opting induvial radicals mean that power can be sure of itself with allying with practices that might damage its international human rights record. In small societies, compulsory unemployment within the entire country can be often engineered for radicals by the ruling elites, rumors engendered, and personal lives destroyed, leaving many with the choice that the Trinidad installation artist Chris Cozier once referred to as 'Migrate or Medal/Meddle.'"[33]

When I asked my parents about this moment in history, my mom, fifty years later, found it too painful to recount any specific run-ins with politics. The spectacle of Popo's performance, however, especially in the midst of political turbulence, was a bright spot in her memory. My father, a bassist and a "band man" at the time, recalled how the song's popularity after the performance meant that he had an unusual amount of gigs covering the tune at events around the islands. The tune, promoted by the chaos of this performance, had a ripple effect for musicians on the islands. As Ellie Matt writes in his autobiography, "'Come Play You Mas' was very popular hit with the people and it helped to promote my band. We eventually started to get more jobs once people realized that we were attracting a large following. During carnival we got contracts to play twice per day, sometimes three times."[34]

My mother mentioned that some who knew Barnes when he was younger saw him as an "introverted and socially awkward guy." The very image of him on the stage as a calypsonian—a persona associated with being "a rummer or a womanizer"—was an obvious contrast. The second juxtaposition was audible in his performance of the song. Pressed for more detail, they both laughed and shook their heads before launching into an impromptu show: Dad narrated, and Mom acted:

> Popo was there standing stiff and marking the beat with his arms like a British choirmaster [*Mom marches around with outstretched arms and legs à la Tchaikovsky's* Nutcracker.]
> It was like an anthem during the verses. But then, during the chorus, he would start shaking his hips wild, and jumping up and down. [*Mom crouches down and sticks her hand into her armpits, jutting her elbows out and shimmying her body with gusto.*]
> Not really dancing, you know. Just acting insane. Then, as the song went on, he was forgetting the lyrics and missing the entrances because he was rolling on the floor.[35]

Road march tunes are colloquially regarded as the anthem of that year's carnival. For the first National Carnival, the lyrics of the song were especially topical:

> I want everyone to bounce in peace and unity
> So we must forget the past and live in harmony
> For the progress of the island three
> St. Kitts, Nevis, and Anguilla in the heart of the Caribbean Sea
> Let's go![36]

The most salient feature of the recording is indeed the sound of the audience laughing and vocalizing along with the backing band during what would have been the chorus, had Popo (Barnes) remembered to sing it. Another perplexing, though generally accepted "fact" was that it had been the famous Trinidadian Popo (Bahora) who had won the first national road march competition in St. Kitts–Nevis.[37] It was not until 2014, when a Kittitian-Nevisian

News outlet published a "where are they now?" series including a post and a very brief interview with Irvin Barnes that the official record was corrected about the identity of the Kittitian Sundar Popo (Barnes). Interestingly, Irvin Barnes was not invested—or even interested at all—in the fact that he was improperly recognized.[38]

In a space where it was accepted that one might take seriously recollections, speculations, and feelings for the sake of piecing back together what is already understood to be inherently interrelated—archipelagically—isolated ideas, sounds, and objects become points of connection that may grow and morph into something that has broader implications, as was the case with the Sundar Popo mix-up. However, correcting official ledgers is not a central goal for Stanny Benoit or others who participated in these forums. It is the practice of archipelagic listening as an extension of what many of these small islanders know to be true about archipelagic inhabitance: how they understand island-to-island relation as an analogical reality at various scales. Through the triangulation of YouTube uploads, speculative inquiry, and ongoing discussion, these forums, and later the Large Radio platform, became a space for practicing and historicizing island-to-island interrelation via archipelagic listening.

When I reached out to Jam Crew in late 2014, he was among the first people to respond eagerly to my attempts to initiate conversation. When I told him about my project, my interest in the history of wylers, trying to understand why some folks suggest St. Kitts–Nevis does not have any music, he agreed that "it's like we doing the same thing." The truth was that Jam Crew had been doing it much longer, and in a broad variety of ways. Born in 1983, the year of titular independence for the Federation of St. Kitts and Nevis, Jam Crew referred to himself as an "independence baby." More than just a coincidence of his birth year, he also works tirelessly in the realm of the national to promote and share "modern" local culture. Not only was Jam Crew prominent on the online forums and chat rooms in the early 2000s, he also hosted his own online talk show, *The Little Talk Corner*, on which he interviewed people in the music industry, especially those working from the small islands. Within his wide-ranging interviews, Jam Crew, a certified producer and recording engineer, pays particular attention to explaining what certain jobs entail, such as manager or soundboard engineer, and how the music industry works (especially with regard to publishing rights and compensation) and can work even for small islanders.

Jam Crew has produced riddims and songs for artists around the region, and he was among the primary people responsible for bringing the Soca Monarch competition to St. Kitts in 2010. Crew is generally emphatic about the microhistory of wylers and its technological innovations in the constellation of small-island sounds. His generational investment in St. Kitts–Nevis plays out aesthetically in his own consistent sonic practice of re-creating riddims he deems important to the larger sweep of musical development, and it plays out politically in his advocacy of the Labour Party. When he speaks, Jam Crew dips in and out of multiple accents, songs, and sonic registers. He describes songs by first mimicking the timbre of the highest-pitched sounds of the riddim, then he adds the percussion, all with striking verisimilitude. He speaks of "old school" riddims with an awe and seriousness that stands out starkly against the backdrop of "too fast" discourse. He believes artists and other creatives in St. Kitts and Nevis "just don't know their worth." This was part of the impetus behind his dedication to discussing, archiving, producing and disseminating small-island music via the available online channels in the early 2000s. It is through his own investment in archipelagic listening, through streaming radio, interviews, extensive travel to other carnivals, but also through his own practice of making riddims and sourcing sounds from everywhere, that Jam Crew helped me to amass the partial history of small-island soca that appears in the following section. Particularly, this archipelagic listening in detail is attuned to tracing speed and experiences of sonic shock that have characterized a small-island sound.

Small-Island Soca Revolution

In small-island music circles, the Burning Flames band is regarded as a paragon. In the spring of 2021, I interviewed the members of 17 Plus, a St. Thomian band that saw local and some international success when their single, "Mary Jane" was featured in the Denzel Washington movie, "The Mighty Quinn" in 1989. Happy to speak with me about what seemed like a fleeting time in their lives, the members, especially the lead singer John Engerman, were adamant about everything their band did: having a small group of only five members, using multiple drum machines, emphasizing their individual sartorial choices within the group, was because "Burning Flames did it first."[39] The Flames, a band from St. John, Antigua, made up of three brothers and their nephew, began as family members having fun busking in the late 1970s. In the early 1980s they were a punk rock band playing covers primarily for the entertainment of mostly white tourists. The singer and keyboardist Oungku recalled: "We used to play a lot of hard rock and smash the equipment, old stuff. Then we put it back together again." Digging deep into the alternative, punk aesthetics of 1980s rock bands, they donned outlandish and sometimes comical outfits while playing covers of contemporary punk, rock, and pop songs. According to forum lore, the band stopped playing rock covers and began playing "calypso" when Antiguan audiences goaded them by saying that *couldn't* play local music. While recordings bear little resemblance to the live "jam sessions" Burning Flames are known for, the jumpy soca song "No More Rock and Roll" on the 1988 album *Light Years Ahead* is an ode to the significant transition: "You say you don't want no rock and roll / Well this is the music to rock your soul."[40]

The band emerged on the world scene through their top-selling 1989 hit song, "Worky Worky." Instantly gratifying, the track begins with three descending synth chords that dip into the harmonized refrain of the song, "Worky!" Four measures of this tugs the listener down into the lightsome, spacious riddim where the intimate playfulness between the steady bass (guitar) and the angular (snare) drum bounces along at an easy pace. Onyan's high tenor voice sweetly croons: "I know how you like romancing on the floor / Well this is the song you've been waiting for." It is a song for everyone. Wallflowers and the too-cool-to-sweat easily sway on the 1 and 3 or march in place at the top of each beat. The barely audible staccato of the electric guitar takes center stage toward the end of the song when the group's voices chant "give she work to do" in double time. Making songs for the masses was already the band's specialty, especially after Oungku spent time playing and working closely with world-famous Montserratian soca star Arrow. Before his passing in 2010, Arrow was known as an important figure in promoting small-island musicianship by recruiting musicians from around the Leeward Islands to write music, tour, and record with him. More on Arrow later.

By the late 1980s, Burning Flames were known regionally as a high-energy band that was changing the mold for young small-island bands. Bands from various islands in the Leewards regularly played at one another's carnival celebrations or hosted jam sessions in outdoor locations to show off their new style (fig. 4.1). Road march competitions, too, were an annual event for showing off new musical ideas, new clothes, and newly acquired amplification gear. In an interview after a 1988 jam session in Antigua an interviewer asked the band what makes them different from other bands. Oungku remarked:

> Talking like an Antiguan now, they say "band man." Band man, on the whole, you see them in their little vest cut and their vest cut match the trousers and the little pretty [i.e., colorful patterned] shirt underneath. And Burning Flames comes on the scene and Burning Flames change all that. Burning Flames put up their hair and put on high heel shoes, pretty, pretty trousers and a piece of cloth tied around their waist and so. People start to realize that right now you're not only hearing a band, they want to see something, too.
>
> And when Burning Flames put on all them pretty clothes and tight trousers and funny looking shoes and so, they just come to see that, and the Flames

FIGURE 4.1. "Burning Flames Jam Pond 1988," posted by the Antigua Carnival Festivals Commission on YouTube, https://www.youtube.com/watch?v=5jl4aL7NKTo.

don't stand still like other band men. We get a lot of publicity from the way we move and obviously the way we groove, with ease.[41]

In that quote, contrasting a popular model of band branding that emphasized professionalism through visual uniformity and signaled Caribbeanness through bright colors and floral patterns, Burning Flames describe themselves via language that emphasizes attention-grabbing unity in diversity. Watching footage of this 1988 interview, it is especially satisfying that while vocalist Onyan is describing the band's philosophy of style, Krokuss, the bassist, keeps waving open the lapel of his blazer to reveal a Jack Tar Village, Royal St. Kitts Hotel and Casino T-shirt, one of the first large hotels on St. Kitts and a significant venue for live musicians in the region. This kind of proof of familiarity with the archipelago, or at least an archipelago, is meaningful precisely because of its insignificance and regularity within the region. Approximately fifty miles southeast of St. Kitts and Nevis, on a clear day, Antigua's western shores come into view from various points on the surrounding islands: St. Kitts, Nevis, Montserrat, and Guadeloupe. This familiarity is embedded in the geography and metageography of the region, which recognizes a repetition and suffusion of styles, words—modes of relation—suffusing objects, subjects, and discourses across the Caribbean.

The contrast between the everydayness of the band's live shows "at home" in the Leeward Islands as compared to their recorded albums is another salient part of their centrality to regional music. In the early 1990s, rock critics were trying to figure out how to categorize them. As one newspaper put it in

1992: "The Flames are like a garage band gone eccentric. The closest North American equivalents would be Fishbone or Red Hot Chili Peppers—they've got some of the same mix of high speed, funk bottom, punk attitude, wild style, and humor. The Flames also exhibit an in-your-face irreverence and a stubborn refusal to fit easily into any one musical category."[42] The members, too, struggled to find a fitting name for their style that would differentiate the distinctly small-island, fast-tempo soca from the more sedate Trinidadian style. They experimented with "speed soca" and "C-Funk," and one review article referred to it as "P-calypso (P for punk)"; however, "the prestige markets of Jamaica and Trinidad, with their strong local music scenes, weren't paying attention. The Flames' music was too frenetic for ears accustomed to the slower rhythms of reggae and classic calypso."[43] While these kinds of representational negotiations were happening on the international scene, Burning Flames regularly participated in the musical ecosystem of the region, with their songs gaining regional traction in neighboring islands. Some Island Mix forum members reminisced about the time Burning Flames was on the road for J'ouvert in St. Kitts in 1992 and the speakers were so powerful they busted the windows out of an appliance store.

In the previous era—the pretty-shirt-band-man 1970s—dancing audiences favored brass combo bands, large ensembles that often featured upward of a dozen instrumentalists and singers. These bands and their leaders sought to create a unified energetic sound with an emphasis on sharpness and unity, as represented by James Brown. This big sound became emblematic of small-island bands, not only for the band's volume and power but also for its ability to play arrangements with many overlapping harmonic and rhythmic lines, eliciting a more energetic feel and amplified by the already comparatively accelerated tempo. The Earth Tones Brass's bracingly fast and bouncy 1973 song "Tempo" names exactly this combination of riddim (rhythm) and tempo as core features of infectious dance music: "Talking about hot and fiery / this is what you need / this kind of riddim and tempo /going to give you good speed / with a Guinness, Skull, or Carib tramping in the dance / and the music penetrating? Man you bound to prance."[44]

The new era of soca, what Kevin Burke has called "post-soca," owed most of its riddim and tempo to drum machines.[45] It was during Clarence "Oungku" Edwards's stint as Arrow's musical director (while the other members played in Arrow's band) that he recalled first utilizing a drum machine:

I got it in New York, Sam Ash to be exact, and the initial use was to work on productions for Arrow as it was only me with my bass trying to create unique bass lines and grooves (which we can now say I obviously did) and I needed something to keep a beat and timing other than a metronome. I brought it into Burning Flames a few years later. I was using it to do my work in Montserrat at least three to four years before bringing it into Burning Flames.[46]

Creative use of drum machine sounds allowed producers—a role called "riddim master" by the end of the 1990s—to incorporate heritage sounds into their new compositions. I call them "heritage sounds" because they were already part of the local sonic landscape but dispersed across various musical practices. As Oungku has suggested, "the congas, timbales, tambourine, shaker, kick, snare, toms, cymbals, even the triangle were all used in calypso and other Caribbean rhythms long before we were born but only entered the Caribbean thru electronics in the 80's."[47] More than just replacing human instrumentalists, drum machines provided an array of percussive and vocal sounds that could be layered densely in a way that was reminiscent of indigenous musical styles.

The band 17 Plus, which was formed in 1985, is credited as having been among the first bands in the Leewards to use more than one drum machine at a time in addition to an acoustic drum kit. By 1987, 17 Plus was regularly using two particular types of drum machines that had preprogrammed synthesized percussion sounds. The Roland TR-707 Rhythm Composer was a basic drum kit with distinctive kick drum, snare, and hi-hat sounds. The Roland TR-727 Rhythm Composer augmented the 707's offerings with Latin instruments such as congas, bongos, and maracas. By 1988, the Alesis HR-16 was another drum machine that offered an even larger range of drum kit sounds that included Latin—or in this case, Caribbean—percussion instruments, such as tambourine, triangle, cowbell, and agogo (a high-pitched cowbell instrument). During a live performance, the keyboardist typically operated the drum machines. Despite the harsh critiques from older generations of musicians, who suggested overreliance on drum machines made for lesser musicianship, the machines required a significant amount of attention in order to access the appropriate sound patches at any given time.[48]

The Yamaha RX-5 and Yamaha RX-7 offered sounds that remain staple auditory markers of distinctive small-island soca. These riddim boxes offered a muted, metallic steel pan sound; a synthesized Brazilian cuica drum, which, in its higher register, resembles the timbre of a fife; and several whistle sounds. Additionally, they included a host of vocal sounds, such as "hey," "wow," "woop," and "ugh," which was described to me as resembling the sound of "a man getting punched in the stomach."[49] In 1991, the genre became more solidified with the emergence of a Kittitian band called 14 Minus (a playful antidote to St. Thomas's 17 Plus), with keyboardist Ras Valley controlling the

FIGURE 4.2. Ras Valley of 14 Minus with Keyboard and Riddim Box at SKN Carnival 1993–1994. Screenshot from DaddyPlay SKN, "14 MINUS 'Live' 1993–1994, by DaddyPlay," YouTube video, August 28, 2013, https://www.youtube.com/watch?v=SUMglHP7RPE.

riddim boxes. Valley was known specifically for masterfully operating seven or more drum machines simultaneously over the course of a performance, which could range from open-air jam sessions on a basketball court to the tarp-covered bed of a tractor on J'ouvert morning.

In St. Kitts and Nevis, the small-island sound was rhythmically dense and highly syncopated, both instrumentally and with the addition of light, sexy, playful, and always-catchy lyrics. In addition to the regular verse, chorus, and bridge sections of the song, particularly popular songs included a "chant" section recited over the instrumentals that included any number of programmed riddims, live acoustic drum kit, rhythm guitar, keyboards, and electric bass (fig. 4.2).[50] Chants were, and continue to be, an especially popular way to excite a crowd during carnival. During carnival of 1993–1994, for example, 14 Minus popularized a chant to a ping-pongy, iron-heavy riddim with subterranean bass at a breathless 166 beats per minute: "Rougher than dem? Push them! Rougher than dem? Jam them! Wine your waist!"[51]

The riddim box was catalytic in the proliferation of distinct yet closely related small-island styles. Regarding Burning Flames' influence on regional music, the lead singer of Dominica's premier bouyon band, WCK, said in an interview: "I took a part of it, because it's a part of me and I mixed it with whatever else we had and it became bouyon."[52] The name "bouyon" was a late 1990s invention, but the sentiments and burgeoning signature style of the modern Dominican genre had coalesced around 1990 with WCK's "Culture Shock." The same could be said for Grenadian jab jab music, which we hear in its first drum machine iteration with signature conch shell in M.O.S.S. International's 1991 "Jambalesse Rule."[53]

In the small islands, the years between the late 1980s and the early 1990s saw a host of new small-island bands that had been energized by the commercial success of Mighty Arrow, whose 1982 single "Hot Hot Hot" was a worldwide success.[54] It became the theme of the World Cup Soccer tournament in 1983, then was covered by Buster Poindexter in 1987 and rereleased in 1994, when it charted even higher on UK dance charts than the first time. It has been featured in Miller Light Beer and Tropicana commercials and played on soap operas and in film scores. It remains soca's highest-selling record ever. Older producers referred to Arrow as the model of small-island success because he was well known for having amassed wealth from royalties and for deftly navigating copyright law. Compare this, for example, to the recording and selling experience of the first Kittitian band to record an LP, the Silver Rhythm Combo, in 1965. In an interview with the St. Kitts–Nevis National Archives about fifty years later, one of the band members recalled:

> We played a song by the name "La La Means I Love You," a song that the Jackson Five did. And we used four guys, four people to play that song . . . And when we finish playing the song, the engineer said, "Byron no' going to like this you know! Byron use a whole army to play this song and all you use four people. Byron no' goin like it." Because Byron Lee was in Canada at the time And I'll never forget, took us over a year to get our record and it was selling in Jamaica with no name on it, no label on it. Selling in Jamaica! Kittitians who was going to University in Jamaica recognized it, because they knew the songs that we played, and they told us. So we had to take the masters from Byron Lee and give them to another studio to master and press and everything. But by the time we got the record it was too late. You know what I mean, there was some diehards who wanted to have a copy but it did not sell as much as it should have.[55]

Arrow's financial success became a beacon for small-island artists who were used to being dismissed and outright cheated in some cases. He believed heartily in the inevitable ubiquity of soca as "like pop. Not just an 'ethnic' thing."[56] In a 1990 interview, he emphasized: "Music is an international language. People don't have to understand what you're saying. They respond to the melody, they respond to the beat, and if it's compatible with them, they're gone with it . . . people can relate to a phrase."[57]

Arrow understood soca as a resource for West Indian musicians to exchange on the global market their catchy chants, body-rocking riddims, and appetite for sweet melodies. These soca subgenres were honed and developed in the context of competition and one-upping other island and regional bands. Where road march competitions are literally a contest of which bands can garner the most attention, Arrow understood small-island soca to be especially compatible with the world market. However, detractors (many of the personalities from chapter 3) were bemoaning the death of the lyricism and political commentary of calypso at the hand of soca. Arrow believed this was an outdated view rooted in colonial politics:

> People tend to put the burden on the soca singer to be the mouthpiece of the people. They feel that calypso is a sacred thing, it's a cultural thing, and because we as an artist have poetic license [we have] to be the voice of the opposition. Fine. This might have been the case twenty years ago . . . the calypsonian could go and criticize the government because we lived in small communities where we were afraid to say something about the prime minister because you might lose your job or you might be victimized. I feel that is no longer . . . it's time that we have to commercialize the music. Soca music is the ultimate dance music. It has been kept down by small-minded producers who feel like they have a birthright to control soca. . . . "Hot, Hot, Hot" is a bridge for people to cross.[58]

Arrow saw music festivals as an especially powerful way to reach new audiences. In addition to the New Orleans Jazz Festival and Jamaica's Reggae Sunsplash, he performed numerous times at the Caribbean Music Festival in Cartagena de Indias, Colombia, between the festival's inception in 1982 and its final run in 1996. The emergence and international proliferation of soca in the 1980s, specifically the small-island, up-tempo, explicitly dance-oriented version of soca with sparse but highly contagious lyrics, as presented by the likes of the Mighty Arrow, was interpreted and adopted around the Spanish-speaking Caribbean. Take, for example, the merenguero Wilfredo Vargas's 1988 recording of "El sambunango teleño," where he chants over an ultrapeppy Afro-Antillean-fortified merengue, "bailemos todos el ritmo soca!"[59] In Colombia, the worldwide exuberance over the drum-machine-led, electronic-heavy soca as popularized by small-island acts had a major impact on local reception and commercial success of champeta as a horizontal contemporary to new Afro-Caribbean genres, of which soca was an especially compatible and useful example.

From St. Kitts and Nevis: Listening to the Archipelago

Archipelagic listening is a tool for the invention of a horizontal model for Black, modern, sonic interrelation. Where identity is always crafted, intentional, processual, and temporally contingent, archipelagic listening—via educational radio programs, communal listening forums, or imaginative metageographies—deploys the archipelago as a model of a hierarchical relation between discrete sound units in relation across scales of experience and time. Recourse to the island, the sea, and the archipelago can slip into an ecologically romantic determinism that gives way to ahistorical, decontextualized notions of global harmony or the return to a primordial, precapitalist tranquility. However, the archipelagic listening demonstrated in the small-island Caribbean online denizens is deployed in service of making the music and its musicking practices intelligible even in the absence of stable archive, full stories, or legitimacies. Archipelagic listening is a tool of mutual intelligibility between and among discrete, irreducible islands of sound.

Archipelagic listening resists enduring misconceptions of small islands and their interconnected inhabitances as locales where big sounds are received and localized but not as places of origin and exchange within the larger scope of the circum-Caribbean. As this book listens from St. Kitts and Nevis, it becomes clear that "island time" is a localized imbrication of a significant theme in the work of Édouard Glissant. While a previous section of this chapter clarified the relationships between islandness and other conceptions of Blackness, Glissant also suggests that there are two subjectivities that spring from differing orientations to space and time as manifested in geography and history. The first, "Root-identity," characterizing the logic of coloniality, is an authority based on origins and "filiation." "Relation-identity," in contrast, "produced in the chaotic network of Relation," is linked "to the conscious and contradictory experience of contacts among cultures," an experience he repeatedly describes as a "shock."[60] As Michael Wiedorn explains, "rather than plunging vertically along a temporal axis into the past, [Relation-identity] would reach out horizontally on a spatial axis to other, contemporary cultures in the present."[61]

These, too, are the relational routes of archipelagic listening.

If "the reality of archipelagos of the Caribbean and the Pacific provides a natural illustration of the thought of Relation," then archipelagic listening, as a listening to and in Relation, and its shocks carries similar island-to-island resonances.[62] In his treatise on sound and listening, *The Order of Sounds: A Sonorous Archipelago*, the composer and music theorist François Bonnet posits what he calls the "sonorous archipelago" as a metaphor for a vast and infinite scope of "setup[s] for the apprehension of sound." Through theoretical mapping, he makes a few important points that guide my understanding of listening here. First, he suggests that we might think of all sound as ubiquitous, particularly because absolute silence is impossible and ears do not close. In this formulation, sound, which comes into experience through listening, can be understood as an "autonomous entity fashioned by a listening," which cuts into a "sonorous flux."[63] Presenting listening as a distributed act (processual and instantaneous), Bonnet argues that the audibility of sound is made possible through preexisting mental forms, forms that are revealed through repeated encounters.[64] Listening, the process through which the sonorous becomes audible, is a process of attachment between the sensible, its articulating language, and its defining discourse.[65] This is the same relationship, though at a different scale, that Robert Walser describes when he argues that the "conventional notions of aesthetic difference" (as an articulating language) and the assumed universality of "technical perfection" (as a defining discourse) within musicological and historical analysis render the "semiotic successes" of Miles Davis, his masterful deployment of the syntax of Black music functionally "inaudible."[66] If, as Ana María Ochoa Gautier suggests, "scant" archives may still raise useful questions about the "topography of sounds in colonial situations," archipelagic listening may tell us something about how sounds are imagined in relation, particularly as it strains against other "ideological filter[s]" such as continental thinking and its related listening practices.[67]

As a theory of listening's mediation, Bonnet stretches toward an archipelagic model of listening by understanding the audible, following Deleuze and Guattari, as a territory or a territory-sound: "Above all, to define the audible as territory-sound is not to set up an abstraction, or to transmute sound into an idea of sound. On the contrary, it is to affirm and to assume that listening is a device for integration into a milieu and for the definition of plots within this milieu."[68] Where objects—not so much as things but as autonomously recognized units: a sound, a riddim, a song, a chant—"presuppose form," Bonnet reminds that in cartography, territories are joined to one another via the presupposed model and its structures. This kind of model "enchains and articulates territorial units, audible sounds, according to its own reason, according to the discourses that modulate it, and according to the worldview that governs it."[69]

Listening to make connections to develop a kind of competence, the archipelagic listening of my interlocutors, the practices of sonic enchainment, semiotic articulation, and the geography of thought that regulate them, attunes to multiple sonic and discursive horizons of relation and their possibilities.

The repetition inherent to archipelagic listening does not necessarily serve to congeal. Instead, this repetition, like that of what Antonio Benitez-Rojo identifies as the repeating meta-archipelago that is the Caribbean, "is a practice that necessarily entails a difference."[70] These horizons—like those visible from the shores and mountainous highpoints of the Caribbean islands—are constituted by trajectories modified by race, islandness, smallness, and the swelling and shifting constellation of individual and collective desires, themselves islands of other expansive archipelagos.

Conclusion: Connecting the Dots

June 8, 2023—Christiansted, St. Croix

In a large bar and live music venue on Company Street in Christiansted, St. Croix, my friend Ryan Jobson nudged my shoulder playfully as he pointed into the air. "That's you, right?" A slick Afrobeat- and dancehall-flavored tune, the 2023 hit "Talibans" by Kittitian dancehall newcomer Byron Messia, was playing over the loud sound system. Hearing a Kittitian artist outside of St. Kitts or Nevis, and no less, having Ryan, a Jamaican, put me on to a new small-island artist, were both new and puzzling experiences. I immediately googled Byron Messia and was spoiled by the glut of interviews and professional videos online. Most prevalent in my search results were conversations and responses to the idea that Byron Messia's music is not "real" dancehall. The discourse took on a familiar shape: accusations of cultural appropriation precipitated qualifying responses about the ubiquity of music and the need for regional solidarity throughout the region. Messia's own biography provided the most compelling and least refutable response. In a BBC Radio 1Xtra interview with DJ Seani B, Messia responded to questions about his authenticity as a dancehall artist. Replying to a series of pointed questions about the number of times he had been in Jamaica, Messia responded: "I've been to Jamaica three times. Once when I was born, and twice when I visited."

"So you a yaahd man, then?" asked Seani B. Messia replied that he was born in Kingston and adopted at two months old by a Kittitian woman who raised him in St. Kitts. Seani B, deploying the familiar logic of natal origin, was quick to claim and insist on Messia's Jamaican heritage and, accordingly, his legitimacy, allowing Messia to sidestep crucial initial inquiries about his entitlement to the dancehall arena. But Messia was resistant to accept such a simple notion of belonging: "'Memba, you no ketch a sense of consciousness until you're five years old. So basically, you know, the mind is a Kittitian mind, but the body is a Jamaican-born. I'm a Ja-Kittitian."

St. Kitts Music Festival, June 22, 2023—Basseterre, St. Kitts

I was back in Basseterre to attend the St. Kitts Music Festival. When I wrote about the St. Kitts Music Festival in 2012, the marketing had shifted from an international festival to one appealing largely to a US-facing Black American audience, in the image of the Essence festival in New Orleans or the jazz festivals littered around the region.[1] In 2023, the vast majority of acts were from the Caribbean as opposed to continental North America. Most surprising was that on the reggae and dancehall night, historically the most popular of the three-day festival, Byron Messia was by far the most anticipated act. The crowd seemed to tolerate the internationally known reggae performers like Koffee and Chronixx in order to get to the reason they were all there. The crowd's reaction to Messia was like nothing I had ever experienced. Thousands of people sang his songs word for word and bounced and grooved with laser-beam attention to his performance. The dozens of local professionals whose expertise was required to make such a large event run well had flocked to the stage wings to participate in the moment and cheer on their hometown talent.

My brother was at the performance, too, and said over and over again, "I can't believe I'm here for this." The statement was loaded. In the previous two years, Mother, our last living grandparent, had become an ancestor, and we both felt a bit more of the weight of holding down our cultural roots on our backs. To be "here" in St. Kitts, witnessing the first big performance of an already internationally known performing artist, was novel. That the particular artist was a dancehall artist and not soca was also unexpected, but perhaps not to the "country" youth who came out in numbers to support Messia. That late-June weekend also marked the decriminalization of marijuana in St. Kitts–Nevis—part of a larger wave of decriminalization reform across the region. Were my uncle Michael still alive, these kinds of changes would not have been marked in the topography of the land on one of his round-the-island drives, but they felt no less ground shifting and glaringly obvious.

While Messia's rise to global circulation and a widely international audience was something different for St. Kitts and Nevis, Messia's aversion to ready-made market terms and genres follows the pattern of the repeating islands of the Caribbean. Reminiscent of a 1970s Lord Shorty or the Burning Flames in the early 1990s, Messia preempted affirmations of his music as squarely dancehall. "I'm trying to run with a new wave—a new sound, and

I'm trying to label it as 'Dance-Soul,' so it's a mixture of that Soul feeling and Dancehall."[2] I am drawn to the fact that Messia wanted to mix the *feeling* (and not the sound) of soul music with dancehall. While discussions of these kinds of moves are generally put in terms of widening audiences, cosmopolitan aesthetics, or the homogenizing thrust of music's globalization, attention to the archipelago and recognition of self-conscious moments of Caribbean musical change reveal a different orientation to the creolizing force. When Lord Shorty and Byron Messia have talked about the soul feeling, it has not been an attempt to zoom out, a search for the least common denominator of musicality. Instead, the sounds of modern Caribbeanity, informed very much by the social and historical context of the Caribbean, have been forays into sounds that are more specific to some version of a rooted and routed self. For whatever is hazy about the specific rhythms, timbres, or mechanics that identify a soul feeling, the reception of soca and Messia's new form during the St. Kitts Music Festival points to attempts to sonically discern more about the corrugation of the island's periphery than to fabricate a contiguous mass of hybridized sound.

Times have changed. The forums of IslandMix.com and the locally produced documentaries and short articles that sought to refute the one-island origins of soca oftentimes used insider knowledge of trips Lord Shorty took to other Caribbean islands to infer more regional and less staunchly national listening practices. At the time of this publication, "links" between artists from different parts of the region are highly publicized events, streamed lived, recorded, and reposted ad infinitum in specialized clips on TikTok and other social media platforms. The ubiquity of all listening is a given, and still, discourse about musical interchange that focuses on the singular origins of things and people—*where did it come from*—dominates public forums. When Messia heralds something new for Kittitian artists, he does so through forms of creativity and play that display his "Kittitian mind." The lyrics are explicitly violent (not about real events, Messia says, more of a metaphorical "warning") and recognizably Kittitian in their organization, with line after line of metaphor, double entendre, and joking. According to Messia, "Talibans," a song that would catapult him onto London billboards and Times Square marquees, "wasn't even something serious. I never wrote down the lyrics for 'Talibans,'" he said. "It's based on pure inside jokes."[3]

All around us at the St. Kitts Music Festival, twenty thousand people bounced together: singing, and moving, and belonging to it all. The energy between the crowd, Messia, and the sound was electric when he finally performed "Talibans" at the end of the set. The ground yielded to the downward thrust of our gathered motion. I had changed, too. The exhilaration and deep sense of belonging that drew me to large crowds, loud music, and collective dancing in the 2010s had morphed into something that felt much more like trepidation and worry. My feet were tired. The energy of the collective body could not sustain me; it could barely reach me. Feeling like one of the only people in the space who did not know the lyrics was disorientating. After Messia's set, when the congealed mass of audience dispersed for refreshments, I looked over to my cousin Darnel and asked, "Are we old now?" Expressionless, his signature style, he nodded: "Yeah."

Old Now

During one of my conversations with Uncle Irving in 2012, he looked at me seriously and asked, "You ever hear the old saying: 'Where tings start is not wey deh end?'" I thought he was kidding and responded with a too-long chuckle. In the recording, I can hear the sharp inhale marking the exact moment when I realized I was laughing alone. The maxim seemed too obvious to be useful and not true enough to be widely applicable. More than a decade later, the saying has gathered weight. To be awake at three in the morning, to feel my way through a jam session, to be on top of new trends, to listen to music intentionally and repetitively enough to learn lyrics, to be visible as a peer in the joking and experimentation—these things made certain connections, a particular kind of experience of the music, accessible and desirable. What I felt comfortable understanding as a perennial relationship to the islands of St. Kitts and Nevis, and the essential features of local music there, has taken on a different shape in the temporal containers of my thirties. My interlocutors too, have refigured their relationships to wylers, to speed, and the various island times they occupy.

In the summer of 2023, Jam Crew, took on a role as the chair of the streets activities, including significant events like J'ouvert, the road march, and the various parades, for the St. Kitts–Nevis Carnival Committee. His passion for wylers and island culture, which started with banging out wylers rhythms on school desks and raucous road jams so loud they blew the glass out of local shops, looks much different these days. He described his more distant interest in newer wylers: "The young boys dem . . . they using too many samples now . . . And they gone *too fast*."[4] He described an exemplary scene, in a wide-ranging, multimodal diatribe, much like Tishima Browne's monologue:

> Kollision Band was playing 190 [beats per minute] this past Christmas. That? That'll kill somebody heart: send your heart out your mouth. I said, 'well look

at that kinda speed there!' That was *fast*. The drummer was live, keeping that kind of speed. He's in his early twenties though. You can't do that at forty. Try that in your forties and they'll have to have the hearse outside de jam. Dem kinda speed? I'm not jumping up to that. I'll die. But you see, when they pump it up to dem speeds there, they're just experimenting with us. They want to see, "How they going to act?"[5]

Connecting the Dots

Toward the end of his set at the June 2023 St. Kitts Music Festival, Byron Messia stood at the edge of the stage and spoke directly to the crowd, addressing the fact that as a hometown hero, he no longer resided in St. Kitts: "This place is home. When you see me out there in other places, wherever, know that I'm just out there trying to connect the dots." I was struck by this statement because it reminded me of my own work at various scales of distance and analysis. In this book, I have tried to draw together a relatively wide set of historical parameters to say something about a place I have understood as "home," although I have never permanently lived there, although my human connections to the land and culture are passing on, and even though I have heard and felt strains of home, especially through music, in many places in the Americas.

More than two decades into the twenty-first century, still, each beat in wylers represents a threat to tell the truth about contemporary relationships between local sounds and local behavior. The tempo of a woman's body—whether in 1955 or 2015—marks one form of barrier between perceived failures of past generations and the hopeful promises of future political sovereignty. In St. Kitts and Nevis, these representations of women, the rituals of womanhood they share intergenerationally, and the discourse surrounding Black girls' and women's bodies are as integral to the imagined community of the nation and the imagined moral health of Kittitian and Nevisian citizenship as the big drum is.

Following the tension between public displays of immorality by Black women as the product of innate degeneracy and the effect of an unwelcome foreign imposition, women are harbingers and markers of change. Interpolating these political parameters to respectable womanhood, the threat of musicality, and the awareness that women are responsible for holding, and sometimes adjusting, such boundaries is a guiding principle against which beauty pageant contestants are expected to perform. Living between seemingly incompatible or incongruous cultural and social structures is an integral feature of St. Kitts and Nevis. Black women experience the nation at its categorical limits. Their particular worldview, captured by the notion of oomanship, is one that promotes or necessitates rattling the barriers as a form of survival.

The creativity on display in barrier rattling is the basis of what Gregory Hobson described as "we culture." It, like a groove, is when survival becomes something other than itself. These creative acts (like wukin up or performativly *not* wukin) highlight how easily appropriated metal barricades are: taken as symbols of or totems against dangerous kinds of temporality like repetition and contagion; deployed as tools for sounding the depth, or measuring the capacity of the racialized and gendered parameters of postcolonial small-island belonging, Black Kittitian and Nevisian women highlight the metachronographic nature of national and regional discourse.

Between the addition of new experimental sounds created by the riddim box and the escalation of drug trafficking and crime, the contemporary fragile political and social environment of the mid-1990s in St. Kitts–Nevis cast a shadow on the energy carried by wylers, particularly as it manifested on the body. Wylers was no faster than the calypsos of two generations prior, but it was perceived to be temporally and sonically excessive, and not just "too fast," but also morally degraded as the product of developmental failure. Wylers' perceived speed is part of a larger genealogy of speed in St. Kitts–Nevis music.

Archipelagic listening makes the small island knowable, decipherable, and thus able to carve out its own creative space for new genres, using the tools of the riddim box, synths, MIDIs, and the fusions of jam band music, wylers, and other small-island musics. Further, archipelagic listening accounts for modes of contemporary Caribbeanness that exponentially refract the archipelagic relations that exist in St. Kitts–Nevis, taking seriously recollections, speculation, and feelings to piece back together what is already understood there to be inherently interrelated—archipelagic In the online digital forums of Large Radio, IslandMix, and their ilk, we come to understand the generational antecedents to the Kittitian and Nevisian youth who deployed speed as a way of not just observing but rattling, teasing, and improvising on the limits of islandness and limiting geometries of temporality as foundational fictions of colonial history.

Acknowledgments

I extend my deepest gratitude to those who have played pivotal roles in bringing this book to life. Many of those influential figures have departed this earthly plane, yet their impact remains immeasurable. A heartfelt thank you to my ancestors Simeon Swanston, Emily Beard, Julia Leader, and Cyril Leader. May your legacies live on.

Research for this book began when I was a graduate student in ethnomusicology, and special acknowledgment is due to Deborah Thomas, Guthrie Ramsey, and Timothy Rommen. Thank you, Tim, for intentionally making space for me. You have provided a model of mentorship that I am proud to emulate. I am also indebted to my graduate school professors Jairo Moreno, Carol Muller, and John Jackson, who provided intellectually rich spaces in which the embers of this work first took form. I extend an especially heartfelt thanks to Professor Annie Randall of Bucknell University, who first introduced me to ethnomusicology through the work of Kyra Gaunt, whose affirmation of Black girlhood changed my life.

I have shared pieces of this work with many different audiences. I am enormously appreciative to colleagues and mentors during my time at Rutgers, including Yolanda María Martínez-San Miguel, Michelle Stephens, Yarimar Bonilla, and all the participants of the Center for Cultural Analysis's Archipelagoes seminar. Thank you for generosity. To my colleagues at the Franke Institute for Humanities at the University of Chicago, thank you for your critical engagement with my work. I have found the Society for Ethnomusicology and the Caribbean Studies Association to be rich and supportive venues for making sense of my wildly divergent ideas. Thank you to everyone who maintains a sense of caring curiosity in these spaces.

I extend my appreciation to thought partners at the University of Chicago, including colleagues in the department of music: Philip Bohlman, Anna Shultz, Travis Jackson, Martha Feldman, Seth Brodsky, Jennifer Iverson, Paula Harper, Robert Kendrick, Steven Rings, Thomas Christiansen, and Lawrence Zbikowski. Thank you to my brilliant friends in Caribbean studies: Danielle Roper, Kaneesha Parsard, Ryan Jobson, Adom Getachew, Ruthie Meadows, and my extended UChicago community, Eve Ewing, Yanilda Gonzales, Adrienne Brown, Nadia Chana, and Lindsay Wright. To my writing comrades, especially Braxton Shelley, whose ability to make sense of fragments and reassure me of their relevance is unmatched, *thank you.*

As a teacher at the University of Chicago I have had the privilege of learning from and thinking with thoughtful and engaged graduate students. I am especially grateful to the members of the first iteration of the Sounding the Archipelago seminar: Jon Bullock, Anjelica Fabro, Eric Kirkes, Erol Koymen, Ailsa Lipscombe, Joseph Maurer, Will Myers, Eva Pensis, Hannah Rogers, and Andrew White, and students of my Aesthetics of Speed seminar: Catrin Dowd, Jonah Francese (to whom special thanks goes for his help with image permissions), Anna Gatdula, Caleb Herrmann, Hannah Kim, Adam Phillips, Andrei Pohorelsky, and Jacob Secor.

I owe my sanity to my team of friends and neighbors who have celebrated wins and reminded me regularly that life, love, and work are a unity. Thank you to Susie Fogle, Lauren Franzen, Solonge Herbert, the ladies of Woodlawn Double Dutch. I am so grateful for the support of Brittany and Nathan Biggs: thank you for being our Midwest family. To my girls, Rudo Mawema Gray, Nayo Matthews, and Zakiah Baker, thank you for talking me through the tough spots. A special thank you to my grad school soul mate, Evelyn Owens Malone, whose support and camaraderie sustained me throughout the book's creation (and re-creation and re-re-creation).

In St. Kitts and Nevis, I extend a sincere thank you to Valentine Morris, David Freeman, Leonard Lestrade, Irving Barrett, Creighton Pencheon, Irvinsia Warner, "Zack" Nisbett, Gregory "Mention" Hobson, and the late Victoria O'Flaherty of the St. Kitts–Nevis Archives. A thousand thank-yous to my aunt Paulette Leader for her unwavering support and for acting as hostess, chauffeur, chef, and field assistant during my trips to St. Kitts–Nevis. Special thanks to my cousin Darnel Leader for his lifelong dedication to cousin tomfoolery and ridiculousness. To all my aunties, uncles, first, second, and third cousins, and official and unofficial godparents, I thank you for sending pictures, old books, sharing thoughts, anecdotes, advice, and, above all, your love. I have been buoyed again and again by your affirmation.

This work was made possible by funding from the University of Pennsylvania Fontaine Society and the School of Arts and Sciences Dissertation Research Grants. Additional support came from the Mellon Foundation, the Rutgers Department of Latin American and Caribbean Studies, the University of Chicago Franke Center for the Humanities, and the Center for the Study of Race, Politics, and Culture. Thank you to the three anonymous reviewers for their insights, suggestions, and critical wisdom, and to the Chicago Studies in Ethnomusicology series. A heartfelt thank you to my editor, Mollie McFee, whose guidance and encouragement were a lifeline.

This book is dedicated to my family—the Swanstons, the Leaders, and the Bakers. Thank you to my parents, Yvette and Lincoln Swanston, for their encouragement, and to my brother, Andre, for setting the bar high and helping me over. Harrison Baker, thank you for making this endeavor possible and for sharing your deep appreciation for the power of Black life and Black love. Zora and Malcolm, you keep me poised toward a brighter future. Thank you for choosing me.

To everyone who has touched my life, sparked ideas, or shared kind words—thank you. Your influence is woven into the fabric of this work.

Notes

Preface

1. Abrahams, liner notes to *Nevis & St. Kitts: Tea Meetings, Christmas Sports, & the Moonlight Night*.

2. Association for Cultural Equity, "'Our Mission.'"

3. Sands and Lyons, "A Working Model for Developing and Sustaining Collaborative Relationships," 26–39.

4. Averill, review of *Caribbean Voyage*.

5. Abrahams, *Nevis & St. Kitts*, liner notes.

6. Hall, *Five of the Leewards*, 169.

7. See Hubbard, *History of St. Kitts*; Archibald, *The Legacy of Dr. Simeon Daniel*.

8. Olwig, *Caribbean Journeys*; Curtis, *Pleasures and Perils*.

Introduction

1. J'ouvert is a contraction of the French "jour ouvert," or "day open." For more on J'ouvert and carnival in Trinidad, see Cozart Riggio, *Carnival*. Carnival as a practice in the Caribbean has been described by many scholars as a site of resistance because of its roots in two particular traditions of dissent: Canboulay and masquerade. Many scholars have focused on the carnivalesque, a term coined by Mikhail Bakhtin, who wrote of the ways that European carnivals were typically times of turning the normal social order on its head. Scholars of Caribbean carnival, especially in Trinidad and Tobago, where carnival is a national symbol, have argued that a Bakhtinian carnivalesque can describe carnival in the Caribbean. For Milla Cozart Riggio and others, the wildness of carnival is central to its history as a pre-Lenten festival in medieval Europe. Since its inception, carnival "has always licensed the crossing of many kinds of boundaries—between classes or estates, genders, races, ethnicities, carefully guarded geographical territories or neighborhoods" (13).

2. Sugar Mas is the common name for St. Kitts–Nevis National Carnival. The "Sugar" refers to St. Kitts' long history as a sugar producer. "Mas" is a shortened version of "masquerade," a generalized term that refers to music, dance, and costume or masking practices that characterize festival events like modern carnival and date to creolized forms that emerged in the context of the plantation.

3. Road march entries receive points on the basis of the number of times each song is played at various allocated judging stations along the carnival parade route, and winners are announced

at the end of season, after New Year's Day. Since 2014 there has been a change in the judging of road march entries. To combat the "monotony" that resulted from DJs "trying to make sure their favorite tune was playing when the troupe passed the judging stations, they have lessened the number of judge points to two and the two stations are now further apart. This way, there can be a greater variety of songs played on the parade route without interfering with the road march competition." St. Kitts Nevis Carnival, "Judging Criteria for Road March."

4. Corporate sponsorship has become an essential feature of carnival, in St. Kitts–Nevis and elsewhere. The J'ouvert package I purchased had been sponsored by the now-defunct LIME Corporation, a British telecommunications company that serviced St. Kitts–Nevis from 2008 to 2015. In 2015 LIME's parent company merged and the LIME name was retired. Haas, "Time to 'LIME' at Cable & Wireless."

5. "Chook" or "jook" (both rhyme with "look") in the Anglophone Caribbean refers to the act of puncturing or injecting. Chooking as dance broadly refers to thrusting penetrative pelvic movements. The relationship between pelvic movement and injection is also found in the vacunao of the guaguancó dance style of Cuban rumba. See Daniel, *Rumba*. "Shubbing back" means "shoving back" or pushing one's backside out. "Wuk" is a locally accented way of pronouncing "work."

6. Bernabé et al., *Éloge de la créolité*.

7. Abrahams, "Questions of Criolian Contagion," 77.

8. Hall, "Cultural Identity and Diaspora," 395.

9. Goveia, *Slave Society*, 121.

10. Nero, *Under de Breadfruit Tree*.

11. Doggett, *Electric Shock*.

12. Kamugisha, *Beyond Coloniality*, 174.

13. Whittaker, "Climate Change Adaptation," 22.

14. Crichlow and Northover, *Globalization and the Post-Creole Imagination*, 112.

15. Small, *Musicking*.

16. Creighton Pencheon, interview by Jessica Baker, July 14, 2010, Basseterre.

17. Pencheon, "The Bull Play of St. Kitts."

18. In their essay collection on the Lesser Antilles, Robert L. Paquette and Stanley L. Engerman explain the grouping of the Leewards and Windwards as follows: "References to various subgroups of islands in the Lesser Antilles can also be confusing because of the conflicting naming practices of the Europeans. Today's generally accepted definition of the Windward and Leeward Islands originated with the British presence in the Caribbean. The Windwards start with Dominica in the north and end with the Grenadines in the south. The Leewards comprise those islands between Dominica and the Virgin Islands. They were named for having a supposedly more sheltered position from the trade winds, which prevail from the northeast, despite the islands' location to the north, not to the west, of the Windwards. The Spanish, during their conquest and settlement of the Americas, called all those islands along the northern coast of South America, away from the trade winds, the Islas de Sotavento or Leeward Islands. They called every island from Trinidad north to the Virgin Islands the Islas de Barlovento or Windward Islands. Dutch expansion in the Caribbean in the seventeenth century left its imprint on two widely removed groups of islands. Saba, St. Eustatius, and the southern part of St. Martin (St. Maarten) form one part of the Netherlands Antilles. Although the Dutch called these islands the Bovenwindse or Windwards, they lie within the northern range of the British Leewards. Aruba, Bonaire, and Curacao, the so-called ABC islands along the northwestern coast of Venezuela, form the second part of the Netherlands Antilles. The Dutch followed Spanish reasoning by

naming them the Benedenwindse or Leewards." Paquette and Engerman, *Lesser Antilles in the Age of European Expansion*, 12–13.

19. Brathwaite, "World Order Models, 57.

20. Stephens and Martínez-San Miguel, eds., *Contemporary Archipelagic Thinking*, 3.

21. Dator, "Frank Travels," 339.

22. McGregory, *One Grand Noise*, 94.

23. Hofman et al., "Island Rhythms."

24. Hofman et al.

25. Goveia, *Slave Society*, 171.

26. Dator, "Frank Travels," 1.

27. For more on Caribbeanization, see Sutton and Chaney, *Caribbean Life in New York City*.

28. Manuel, Bilby, and Largey, *Caribbean Currents*.

29. Dudley, "Judging 'by the Beat.'"

30. Weintraub, *Dangdut Stories*, 15.

31. Crichlow and Northover, *Globalization and the Post-Creole Imagination*, 18.

32. Crichlow and Northover, 70.

33. In the 1960s, when the British Virgin Islands were undergoing rapid development into competitive tourist sites, wealthy business owners advocated for importing low-wage labor. The most obvious source of workers was the neglected colonial outposts of the British Caribbean. As noncitizen, seasonal workers in the Virgin Islands, eastern Caribbean islanders like Kittitians and Nevisians were often pejoratively referred to as "down islanders," a navigational term, or "aliens." I learned of these navigational markers when in Miami in 2013 a man from St. Martin told me he used to "cruise all around them 'down islands' until they started to have too much crime."

34. Rohlehr, *Scuffling of Islands*, 11.

35. Puri, *Caribbean Postcolonial*.

36. Guilbault, "Politics of Labelling Popular Musics in English Caribbean."

37. Jones, "Practicing Jametteness," 107.

38. Gilroy, *There Ain't No Black in the Union Jack*, 273.

39. Gilroy, *Black Atlantic*, 38.

40. Glezos, *Politics of Speed*, 24.

41. James Phipps, interview by Jessica Baker, July 15, 2010, Gingerland, St. Kitts.

42. Iyer, "Improvisation, Temporality, and Embodied Experience," 161.

43. Kornbluh, "Order of Forms," 15.

44. Curtis, *Pleasures and Perils*, 20.

45. Crooks et al., "Growing Up Too 'Fast.'"

46. Valentine Morris, interview by Jessica Baker, December 31, 2012, Basseterre.

47. Helen Gilbert defines "fass" as "interfering, meddlesome, quick to intrude in others' business." See Gilbert, *Postcolonial Plays*, 177.

48. Glezos, *Politics of Speed*, 65. Where speed as velocity is a measurement of change over time, speed is not something that can be attributed to an object (an object cannot have speed). Speed as velocity, then, is a measurement of relationship between two objects.

49. Glezos, 67.

50. Glezos, 21.

51. Sterne, *Audible Past*, 6.

52. Britton, "Globalization and Political Action," 1.

53. Britton, 1.

54. Glissant, *Faulkner, Mississippi* (1996; repr., Paris: Farrar Straus & Giroux, 1999): 117, qtd. in Wiedorn, *Think Like an Archipelago*, 39.

55. Britton, "Globalization and Political Action," 14.

56. Wiedorn, *Think Like an Archipelago*, 7.

57. Aliocha Wald Lasowski, "La philosophie d'Édouard Glissant," *Critique* 750, no. 11 (2009): 971–80, at 977, qtd. in Wiedorn, *Think Like an Archipelago*, 114.

58. Glezos, "Ticking Bomb: Speed, Liberalism and Ressentiment against the Future," 163.

59. Benítez-Rojo, *Repeating Island*, 79–80.

60. Brathwaite tells a story about watching an old woman sweep the shoreline daily. He wonders, "Why's she labouring in this way?" He realizes eventually that "her feet, which all along I thought were walking on the sand[,] were really walking on the water and she was travelling across the middle passage, constantly coming from where she had come from." Brathwaite and Mackey, *ConVERSations with Nathaniel Mackey*, 33.

61. Sethares, *Rhythm and Transforms*, 75.

62. Levine, *Forms*, 3.

63. Walcott, "Isla Incognita," 52.

64. Roberts and Stephens, introduction to *Archipelagic American Studies*, 20.

65. Roberts and Stephens, 25–26.

66. Mandelbrot, *Fractal Geometry*, 1.

67. Roberts and Stephens, *Archipelagic American Studies*, 21–23. Mandelbrot's innovative mathematics identify the infinite lengthening of geographic measurements—specifically the circumference of islands—when accounting for increasingly smaller units of measurement. Roberts and Stephens emphasize the usefulness of Mandelbrot's fractal infinitude of the island not as competitive to the explorer's larger continent, which the explorer believes is knowable, and whose knowability the explorer projects onto the island, but instead Mandelbrot's fractals "attest" to the final unknowability of the world's smallest geographies.

68. Mandelbrot, *Fractal Geometry of Nature*, 75.

69. Mandelbrot, 26.

70. Acevedo-Yates, *Forecast Form*.

71. Murray-Román, "Rereading the Diminutive."

72. Gilroy, *Black Atlantic*, 102.

73. Gilroy, 110.

74. Kun, *Audiotopia*.

75. Mandelbrot, *Fractal Geometry*, 75.

76. Brathwaite, "World Order Models."

77. Brathwaite, "Caribbean Man in Space and Time," 90.

78. O'Flaherty, "Kittitians and Their Archives," 231.

79. Glissant, *Traité du tout-monde*.

80. I draw "islanded temporalities" from McCusker and Soares, *Islanded Identities*.

Chapter One

1. Samuel "Irving" Barret, personal communication with author, August 5, 2010, Charlestown.

2. Samuel "Irving" Barret, personal communication with author, August 5, 2010, Charlestown, Nevis.

3. Jones-Hendrickson and Caribbean Studies Association, "Bradshawian Synthesis."

4. In 1871, after decades of colonial administrative reconstruction, the institution of the Federal Colony of the Leeward Islands united the separate colonial presidencies of Antigua, Dominica, Nevis, St. Kitts, Anguilla, and the British Virgin Islands. In an 1882 act of further consolidation, St. Kitts, Nevis, and Anguilla were united under a single administrative seat in Basseterre, St. Kitts. In 1951, when British colonies won universal suffrage, tensions mounted surrounding the lack of equal political representation for Nevis and Anguilla. The consolidation and dissolution of the Federation of the West Indies further entrenched Anguilla's administrative dependence on St. Kitts. In 1958, a petition signed by 3,546 Anguillans in favor of succession received no response from Kittitian officials. In February 1967, when St. Kitts, Nevis, and Anguilla became an associated state, agitated Anguillans staged a series of protests and violent disruptions that later escalated to a military event including a brief British invasion. For a more robust description, see Webster, *Scrap Book of Anguilla's Revolution.*

5. Browne, *From Commoner to King*, 91.

6. Browne, 91.

7. While most accounts of Bradshaw's aesthetic choices emphasize its Britishness, it is worth noting that Marcus Garvey was known for dressing in the regalia of high-ranking British military officials, and the spectacle of his personhood and various public appearances was a significant part of his "brand" as an important orator and thinker. The Dominican dictator Raphael Trujillo's similar sartorial choices and spectacular presence (like Garvey, often replete with live musicians preceding his appearances) signal a particularly Caribbean brand of ostentatious political figure that cannot adequately be summarized in terms of British imitation.

8. The full text of Garvey's speech was reprinted the following day, on November 3, 1937, in the daily St. Kitts *Union Messenger*, in the article "Marcus Garvey Visited St. Kitts." The paper's editor J. Matthew Sebastian was president of the African Legion's Universal Benevolent Association, which published the daily paper, and is widely considered the founding father of the Labour Movement of St. Kitts–Nevis. Interestingly, Garvey had written to Sebastian on June 10, 1937, five months ahead of the visit, asking him to make arrangements for a speaking venue with ticket sales to help defray the costs of Garvey's visit, but Sebastian and the *Messenger* administrator decided not to promote it ahead of time to avoid anticipated unrest. Historic St. Kitts (National Archives, St. Kitts and Nevis), "Our People." For more on how Sebastian laid much groundwork for Bradshaw, see Marthol, *Meet My Father*, 18–21.

9. "Bukra" is an Afro-Caribbean colloquialism for a white person, particularly one in power. Mills, Jones-Hendrickson, and Eugene, *Christmas Sports in St. Kitts–Nevis*, 18.

10. Beckles, "'Riotous and Unruly Lot,'" 511.

11. Ligon, *True and Exact History*, 45.

12. *Laws of Nevis*, 131–32. Interestingly, while public recreational drumming was banned in Nevis, the very act of emplacing such laws included their being "published in Charlestown by beat of drum" (210).

13. It should be noted that while the more rhythmically active drum of a big drum ensemble is typically referred to as a "kettle" drum, in actuality, a snare drum is often used. It is unclear whether there was a switch in instrumentation over the course of history or whether this is another example of the colorful development of Kittitian-Nevisian colloquialisms. Reference is made to this difference in terminology in Cramer-Armony and Robinson, "St. Kitts and Nevis," 414. These types of big drum ensembles and the masquerading they accompany are prevalent on many other islands of the eastern Caribbean. See Nicholls and Nunley, *Jumbies' Playing Ground*. Additionally, in Montserrat, the big drum ensemble includes "a fife, a kettle drum played with

two sticks to give an infectious syncopating rhythm, a boom drum, a boom pipe which emits a 'boom' sound and a shak-shak or maracas." See Fergus, *Montserrat*, 242. There is little extant literature that discusses the music of Christmas carnival celebrations; however, literature and ethnography suggest that Kittitian-Nevisian big drum ensembles do not utilize the boom pipe (baha), shakers (shak-shak), or maracas. These instruments are, though, typically played in local string bands or scratch bands. I also witnessed big drum and masquerade troupes use an empty glass bottle as the melodic instrument in lieu of a fife.

14. Once exclusively a male sport, some of the masquerade troupes throughout the 1990s and early 2000s feature a historically significant proportion of girls and young women.

15. Mills, Jones-Hendrickson, and Eugene, *Christmas Sports in St. Kitts–Nevis*, 51.

16. Mills, Jones-Hendrickson, and Eugene, 51–52.

17. Nicholls and Nunley, *Jumbies' Playing Ground*, 131.

18. Miller, *Carriacou String Band Serenade*, 124–25. Karen Fog Olwig has suggested, following the bachelor's thesis of Joyah Sutton, that the string band ensemble has Latin American roots and may have found its way back to St. Kitts and Nevis via return migration of men who worked in Panama and Cuba at the beginning of the twentieth century. Olwig, *Global Culture, Island Identity*, 189.

19. The term "bajo" (bajo or baja) comes from the Spanish word for "low." It has been suggested that the instrument is named after the flauta baja or low flute of South America.

20. Mills, Jones-Hendrickson, and Eugene, *Christmas Sports in St. Kitts–Nevis*, 9.

21. Mills, Jones-Hendrickson, and Eugene, 9–10.

22. Mills, Jones-Hendrickson, and Eugene, 18.

23. I saw this in a snippet of the Union Messenger from December 12, 1956, shown to me by the national archivist. The *Union Messenger* was first put out by the Universal Benevolent Association as a monthly magazine beginning in 1921, then an eight-page weekly in 1922 before its final iteration as a daily in December 1930. J. M. Sebastian was the paper's editor until his death in 1944, when former assistant editor Joseph N. France took over. The Universal Benevolent Association had been absorbed by the St. Kitts–Nevis Trades and Labour Union in 1940, but the *Messenger* kept publishing until 1961. Meanwhile, the union began its own paper in 1957, *Labour Spokesman*, also edited by Joseph N. France. The *Labour Spokesman* is often described as having evolved from the *Union Messenger*, but it is worth clarifying their mutual existence and affiliation in the period 1957–1961. See Garvey, *Marcus Garvey and Universal Negro Improvement Association Papers*; Marthol, *Meet My Father*, 18–21.

24. Carlton, "Relaxed Pace of St. Kitts Is Beginning to Pick Up," A37, A52.

25. Nandy, *Tao of Cricket*, 5.

26. James, *Beyond a Boundary*, 165.

27. Treaster, "What's New under the Sun."

28. DeLoughrey, "Island Ecologies and Caribbean Literatures," 301 (original emphasis).

29. Roberts, *Borderwaters*, 162.

30. Gillis, *Islands of the Mind*, 63.

31. Mintz, *Sweetness and Power*.

32. Maldonado-Torres, "Thinking through the Decolonial Turn," 3.

33. Lewis and Wigen, *Myth of Continents*, ix.

34. Thomas, "Time and the Otherwise," 181.

35. Thomas, 181.

36. Sharma, *In the Meantime*, 7–9.

37. Kubik, "Phenomenon of Inherent Rhythms," 33.

38. Kubik, 40.

39. McElroy, "Managing Sustainable Tourism in the Small Island Caribbean," 3.

40. These three islands were the first destinations to have a "small stream of wealthy visitors." McElroy, 3.

41. Moore and Byron, *Interviews with Lee L. Moore*, 88.

42. Moore's strategy played not only to wealthy tourists but also to those tourists who were interested in affecting an air of wealth and exclusivity. A 1983 *New York Times* article directs tourists to more isolated islands for a more impressive vacation: "It seems just yesterday that a long weekend in St. Thomas or a week's stay in Jamaica gave one a certain sunny status during the winter months. But today, with direct flights from so many United States cities to the Caribbean, the dedicated practitioner of one-upmanship must drop the name of some hideaway and proceed to tell how difficult it is to get there from here. Just how difficult? A less than straightforward journey is what you must expect if you want to pass up the nonstop-flight havens like Barbados or Trinidad for the tranquillity of such islands as Dominica, St. Vincent, Little Cayman and Mustique, where big jets can't land. There's no problem if you are steering your own plane or yacht. But other travelers have to fly in a small aircraft holding 10 or so passengers to complete the journey, or wait for the ferryboat that is the only transportation to some smaller islands." Carr, "Practical Traveler."

43. See Garvey's "1937 Speech in St. Kitts," in Garvey, *Marcus Garvey and Universal Negro Improvement Association Papers*.

44. Robert Kelly, personal interview by Jessica Swanston Baker, December 20, 2012.

45. The all-inclusive tourist hotel model is a prime example of what the tourism scholar Auliana Poon famously coined as the "new tourism" of the 1980s and 1990s. In addition to the all-inclusive's "islanding" of tourists via physical separation, the model also emerged in response to other market factors. Specifically, as Poon notes, throughout the 1980s, demographic shifts occurred in the North American market, including "the rise of double-income-no-kids-yet (dinkies) households and upwardly-mobile professionals (yuppies). These groups are different from the homogenous mass of sun-lust tourists of the previous two decades. They have different time constraints, different income scenarios and tend to be more activity-orientated. The all-inclusive vacation concept, with its freedom, flexibility, and activity-orientation aptly fitted their vacation bill." Poon, "Innovation and the Future of Caribbean Tourism."

46. Kelly interview.

47. Kelly interview.

48. Timothy Taylor's tripartite schema of authenticity is useful here. Island insularity as a stand-in for timelessness creates what Taylor calls "authenticity of primality." Taylor, *Global Pop*, 26.

49. Rommen, "It Sounds Better in the Bahamas," 442–44.

50. Susan Harewood and Mimi Sheller have demonstrated how the "all-inclusive" model as deployed in Jamaica and, later, in the Bahamas created "spatial/temporal enclaves that carved out tourist performances and territories largely cut off from the surrounding locality, and from local inhabitants." Harewood, "Listening for Noise"; Sheller, qtd. in Guilbault and Rommen, "Introduction," 19. In particular, they consider the political and social realities of postcolonial discontent in places like Jamaica, and the infrastructural roadblocks in countries like the Dominican Republic, that the all-inclusive model circumnavigates by providing all the amenities for a tourist (restaurants, entertainment, and activities) in one enclosed space.

51. Victoria O'Flaherty, personal interview by Jessica Swanston Baker, July 1, 2019. See also Mills, Jones-Hendrickson, and Eugene, *Christmas Sports in St. Kitts–Nevis*.

52. In line with these durational changes, Millington and James have suggested that the change from a wooden kettle drum to a metal one (which is significantly louder) has changed the role of the fife from a melodic one to largely ornamental one. Millington and James, "Mummies and Masquerades." Rhythmically, this gave the fife a percussive sound that peeps through the short breaks in the rolling rhythm of the kettle drum to be effectively heard, instead of floating on top of the drum in the way that can be heard in Alan Lomax's recording from Nevis in 1962. See Lomax, "Masquerade Walking Piece."

53. Winston "Zack" "Doctor of Culture" Nisbett, personal interview by Jessica Swanston Baker, July 2, 2010.

54. Mills, "Zack, Doctor of Culture."

55. Baker, "Sugar, Sound, Speed."

Chapter Two

1. Wilson, *Crab Antics*, 233.

2. Yvette Swanston, personal communication with Jessica Swanston Baker, September 16, 2023.

3. Yvette Swanston to Jessica Swanston Baker, July 4, 2011.

4. Roger Abrahams has discussed the importance of gossip to the social economy in small eastern Caribbean Islands. See, e.g., Abrahams, "Performance-Centred Approach to Gossip."

5. Kempadoo, *Sexing the Caribbean*, xi.

6. King, *Island Bodies*.

7. Richardson, "Doin' Me."

8. Abrahams, "Questions of Criolian Contagion," 81.

9. Dayan, *Haiti, History, and the Gods*, 222.

10. Anthony, "Decolonizing Narratives," 173.

11. Anthony, 174.

12. Edmondson, "Public Spectacles," 2.

13. Edmonson, 2.

14. British Parliament abolished slavery by an act that became law August 1, 1834, even though a four-year period of forced enslavement followed in the Caribbean. Across the English-speaking Caribbean, Emancipation Day is a public holiday generally celebrated on or around August 1. In St. Kitts and Nevis, it is the first Monday and Tuesday of August, also known as Culturama in Nevis.

15. Olwig, "Cultural Complexity," 116.

16. Olwig, 106.

17. Curtis, *Pleasures and Perils*, 54.

18. Curtis, 54.

19. Pinto, "Why Must All Girls Want to Be Flag Women?," 146.

20. Anthony, "Decolonizing Narratives," 252.

21. Hull, "Pung Melee."

22. Anthony, "Decolonizing Narratives," 253.

23. Tishima Browne, dramatic monologue, talent portion of 2014–2015 National Carnival Queen Pageant, St. Kitts–Nevis, my transcription.

24. Browne, dramatic monologue.

25. George, "Let Me See Yuh Hand."

26. Best, *Culture @ the Cutting Edge*, 143.

27. Manuel and Marshall, "Riddim Method.

28. It is worth noting that some part of the rhetoric surrounding this piece (called "The Celebrated Chop Waltz") is due to racist, anti-Asian stereotypes used to sell copies of its first print in 1877.

29. Browne, dramatic monologue.

30. Small Axe Band International's winning rendition of "Bottom in de Road" may be heard on various YouTube videos, including Rees Price, "Small Axe Band Bottom in de Road," YouTube video, June 4, 2015, https://www.youtube.com/watch?v=Lons94mskIE.

31. Browne, dramatic monologue.

32. See Abrahams and Bauman, "Sense and Nonsense in St. Vincent."

33. Abrahams and Bauman, 762.

34. Abrahams and Bauman, 764.

35. Abrahams, *Man-of-Words in the West Indies*, 81.

36. Browne, dramatic monologue.

37. The tempo of the original recording (and the average tempo of most recorded live performances) of "Shang Shang" (1976) hovers around 150 beats per minute, and George's "Let Me See Yuh Hand" (2001) clocks in at 160. The feel of each song is not wildly different, but "Let Me See Yuh Hand" was written as a critique of what Curwen Best has called "soca purists," who, in a protracted effort to save lyrical calypso as a Trinidadian art from obscurity, railed against the high-energy, "hardcore" soca of the late 1990s that was understood as a product of cultural impositions from elsewhere (like Jamaica and the small islands). George Sings, "My people complaining / Stop the jump and waving / Stop the hand from raisin' " / But that is we ting / Before Puff Daddy who is one of the biggest producers in America take this han' in the air ting and make a big tune / and sell it and make millions in America / and leave me hungry in Trinidad / One more jump and wave before they take it and go." George, "Let Me See Yuh Hand," track 15.

38. See Freeman, "Designing Women."

39. Freeman, *High Tech and High Heels in the Global Economy*, 214.

40. Edmondson, *Caribbean Middlebrow*, 18.

41. Recalling the earlier part of Browne's monologue describing the audacity of some Black women to show their "marked up" bottoms, critiques about the Black woman's hyperpigmentation— appearance of dark marks and scars on highly melanated skin—demonstrate the nested performances of anti-blackness and misogyny that are embedded into modern performances of regional folk heritage.

42. Alexander, *Pedagogies of Crossing*, 23.

43. Alexander, 23.

44. Freeman, "Neo-Liberalism, Respectability, and the Romance of Flexibility in Barbados," 13.

45. There is also an international aspect of professionalism by which Caribbean women affect a particular type of African American female aesthetic in their embrace of traditionally male (reputational) roles. This is a point Edmondson makes with regard to a long history of African American influence on Caribbean middle-class tastes starting at least in the early nineteenth century. Her argument runs counter to suggestions that in islands under British colonial rule, Britain stood as the only outside cultural influence. Edmondson, *Caribbean Middlebrow*.

46. Edmondson, "Making the Case for Middlebrow Culture," 13.

47. Patil, *Negotiating Decolonization in the United Nations*, 2.

48. *SKNVibes*, "Toon Center—Is This What We Encourage?" Comments left in their original form.

49. *SKNVibes*.

50. *SKNVibes*, "Toon Center—Parenting Standards out the Window." Comments left in their original form.

51. This is the case across the Caribbean but particularly in Afro-Caribbean societies. See Cooper, *Noises in the Blood*; Shaw, "Other Side of the Looking Glass"; Puri, *Caribbean Postcolonial* and "Race, Rape, and Representation"; Edmondson, "Public Spectacles."

52. Irving Barrett, personal interview by Jessica Swanston Baker, December 2012.

53. Oliver, *Queen of the Virgins*, 115–16.

54. In an essay published in honor of the fiftieth anniversary of Trinidad and Tobago's independence, Hollis Liverpool, aka Mighty Chalkdust, writes of women in soca performance and soca competitions: "Where before few women participated in the art form, there were so many females in the 1970s that a Calypso Queen contest started and the Calypso King contest had to be renamed the Calypso Monarch in 1977." Liverpool, "Calypso," 90–95, 92.

55. Mandisa and Warner, *History of St. Kitts & Nevis Carnival*; Hubbard, *History of St. Kitts*, 139–40. The labor union in St. Kitts began in 1939, when the formation of unions became legal in the Leeward Islands. Initially, Edgar Challenger headed the St. Kitts Trades and Labour Union, which grew out of the Caribbean-wide labor strikes of 1896 and 1935.

56. The mid-twentieth century also saw the most significant period of migration, especially of men who once participated in the Christmastime traditions, which were undergoing a transformation from maligned practices of an unevolved lower class to a revered vestige of local folklore. In "More Ole Time Christmas," a chapter in Mandisa and Warner's *History of St. Kitts & Nevis Carnival*, Washington Archibald writes: "The waves of emigration in the 1950s had a double effect on the culture of St. Kitts. More immediately, they drastically reduced the number of regular Christmas performers, musicians and makers of masks and whips from around the countryside and Basseterre. As these Kittitians turned their backs on St. Kitts, they left a void, which the younger generation was not willing to fill." It was on this vector of progress and change, and in response to the void in the lower classes that it created, that the first official Kittitian carnival—with carnival queen competition—was staged in Basseterre in 1957.

57. Abrahams, *Man-of-Words in the West Indies*, 151.

58. Green House Band, "Green House," Facebook, 2013, https://www.facebook.com/pages/Green-House/135109073170179.

59. In 2011, Ms. Jamaica Universe, Yendi Phillips, hosted the carnival queen competition and she did not engender as much widespread distaste. She was noticeably darker skinned.

60. A video recording of the King Konris's performance I attended is available at Sugar Mas, SKN Carnival, "Sugar Mas 41—King Konris 'Finish de Song' (LIME Senior Calypso Monarch Finals)," YouTube video, December 29, 2012, https://www.youtube.com/watch?v=z9ChT2mbXjU.

61. Tlostanova, "Transcultural Tricksters beyond Times and Spaces."

62. Browne's mention of "your bottom in de road" is also a reference to a wylers song from the same year that won the 2014–2015 road march competition, called "Bottoms in de Road," by the Small Axe Band International. It in turn borrowed the catchphrase from Iwer George's song of the same name from 1997. Small Axe Band International's winning 2014 rendition of "Bottom in de Road" may be heard on various YouTube videos, including Rees Price, "Small

Axe Band Bottom in de Road," YouTube video, June 4, 2015, https://www.youtube.com/watch ?v=Lons94mskIE.

Chapter Three

1. The portion I describe as a member of the live audience occurs at the 4:21–4:40 mark of the following video: Ryddim Magazine, "Power Segment of 2012 Soca Monarch Finals (Part 1)," YouTube video, December 23, 2012, https://www.youtube.com/watch?v=5HyH165eob0.

2. The Soca Monarch competition has been a feature of annual carnival celebrations since its introduction in Trinidad in 1993, at which point soca had already solidified as a genre separate from calypso. The Kittitian producer and music technician Leonard "Jam Crew" Lestrade brought it to St. Kitts in the early 2000s. Since the road march competition had been commandeered by bands (a change from the individual calypsonians who competed for road march through the 1970s and 1980s), the Soca Monarch competition offered a showcase and potential prize money—the 2013 price was EC$10,000—to individual soca artists.

3. Douglas, *Implicit Meanings*, 108.

4. Dagah, conversation with the author, December 19, 2012, Basseterre.

5. Dagah, conversation with the author, December 19, 2012, Basseterre.

6. Facebook correspondence between "Inception Fete" page and the author, April 12, 2019.

7. Hintzen, "Reproducing Domination," 70.

8. Hintzen, 70.

9. Hintzen, 70.

10. Hintzen, 70.

11. Hintzen, 70.

12. Gregory "Mention" Hobson, interview by Jessica Baker, November 13, 2019.

13. Hobson interview.

14. These two, riddim and bass, might be considered as forming the "acoustic image," of which "drive" is an essential feature. Where someone like Kodwo Eshun might say that the essential "rhythm and bass" of black music refers to drums and bass guitar, the words used in St. Kitts–Nevis are the same, but the configuration of meanings shifts slightly.

15. Goodman, *Sonic Warfare*, xix–xx.

16. Keil and Feld, *Music Grooves*, 109.

17. Hobson interview.

18. Leonard "Jam Crew" Lestrade to Jessica Swanston Baker, personal communication, February 20, 2020.

19. On the note of the perceived experience of speed versus actual measurable tempo or speed, wylers is a genre that is perceived as fast not only for its increased tempo but also for its other compositional techniques: within cognitive studies, researchers have found that ornamentation in melodies—the presence of "passing tones, upper and lower neighboring tones, and arpeggiated figures in addition to a basic melodic line were perceived as faster than melody lines without such ornamentation . . . and melodies played in a higher octave or brighter timbre [are] perceived to unfold more quickly than those played in a lower octave or duller timbre." Kuhn, "Effect of Tempo, Meter, and Melodic Complexity," 168. See also Geringer et al., "Effect of Articulation Style on Perception of Modulated Tempo."

20. Hobson interview.

21. Glezos, *Politics of Speed*, 20.

22. Douglas has faced harsh criticism especially since members of his cabinet (led by Dr. Timothy Harris) submitted a motion of no confidence in Douglas's leadership on December 11, 2012. The motion was never addressed.

23. Hewlett, "Government Swaps Land for Local Bank Debts."

24. Williams, *Keywords*, 16.

25. Steinberg, *Social Construction of the Ocean*, 160.

26. Goodman, *Sonic Warfare*, 162.

27. *SKNVibes*, " "De Sugar Band Lashes Out against Violence Stigma."

28. The National Commission for UNESCO released the documentary on St. Kitts and Nevis music in 2014. The official website says it "tells the story of the development of music from an economic and social perspective in the Federation." See St. Kitts and Nevis Nat Com for UNESCO, "Video Documentary on History of SKN Music." The documentary is available at SKN UNESCOnatcom, "Introduction of Modern Music," YouTube video, September 26, 2014, https://www.youtube.com/watch?v=FJrGPBwCLRA.

29. Irving Barrett, interview by Jessica Swanston Baker, December 2012.

30. Fink, "Goal-Directed Soul?"

31. Culturama Magazine, 1977, in my family's archive.

32. Olwig, *Global Culture, Island Identity*, 162.

33. Barrett interview.

34. Richardson, *Caribbean Migrants*, 130.

35. Dagah to Jessica Swanston Baker, WhatsApp, February 5, 2020.

36. Moten, *Black and Blur*, 115.

37. Barrett interview.

38. Jones-Hendrickson and Caribbean Studies Association, "Economic and Political Governance," 2.

39. Associated Press, "Crime, Corruption, Drugs."

40. McCall, "Condor Calls for Collaboration in Fighting Crime."

41. The Sad Citizen comment is referenced in McCall.

42. Gregory "Mention" Hobson, interview by Jessica Swanston Baker, December 17, 2019.

43. Cherryl Ward of ZIZ TV interviewed Kenrick Georges in 2005. When Georges died in 2019, the interview made the news rounds. See "AN INTERVIEW WITH THE LATE KENRICK GEORGES!! An Interview Featuring the Late Kenrick Anderson Georges, the Author and Music Composer of St. Kitts and Nevis' National Anthem 'O Land of Beauty,' " *St. Kitts–Nevis Times*, August 29, 2019, https://www.facebook.com/watch/?v=2325941857461256. The video originally aired on ZIZ sometime in 2008.

44. Kenrick Georges to Jessica Swanston Baker, personal correspondence, 2014.

45. Georges posted excerpts from his albums to his YouTube channel. The album art and an excerpt of this last orchestral cover of Mighty Sparrow's "The Statue" is found at Kenrick Georges, "The Statue—1st Movement by Kenrick Georges," YouTube video, October 13, 2018, https://www.youtube.com/watch?v=tZbF1sU1FJk.

46. Esteva, "Development."

47. "Hegemonic" here refers to its acceptance rather than the social status of its creators (i.e., Black music is hegemonic despite white supremacy's insistence on the genocide of Black people).

48. Valentine Morris, interview by Jessica Swanston Baker, December 31, 2012.

49. Morris interview.

50. Morris interview.

51. Ellie Matt, "Exclusive Interview by Lloyd Lazar."

52. Mandisa and Warner, "Profile of Mick Stokes."

53. In 2008, for instance, Nero was honored at the Friends of Labour–Toronto 7th Gala Awards for contributions to diasporic culture and nation building, and in 2009 he was honored in absentia "for rich contributions to musical and cultural development in the Federation." See "Friends of Labour—Toronto"; Bryant, "Nine Locals Honoured."

54. Guilbault et al., *Zouk*.

55. See Rivera, Marshall, and Pacini, *Reggaetón*.

Chapter Four

1. Campt, *Listening to Images*, 9.

2. Crawford, "Listening as Participation."

3. Camal, *Creolized Aurality*, 8.

4. Vasquez, *Listening in Detail*, 3.

5. Benítez-Rojo, *Repeating Island*, 80.

6. Picós are a network of sound system operators, DJs, record collectors, consumers and producers that promote and exchange champeta (and other afro-descendant musics) in Colombia. For more on picós, see Birenbaum-Quintero, "Exchange, Materiality, and Aesthetics"; Pacini Hernández, "The Picó Phenomenon."

7. Birenbaum-Quintero, "Exchange, Materiality, and Aesthetics."

8. See Aniyar, "La fiesta de 'La champeta.'"

9. Birenbaum-Quintero, "Exchange, Materiality, and Aesthetics," 4–5.

10. "Entrevista realizada a Enrique Muñoz, Cartagena, 15 de marzo de 2012," *Pilando Historia de UdeC Radio*, in Morales Espinosa, "Música y fiesta," 77.

11. IslandMix.com, "Jamband Style Music."

12. Best, *Politics of Caribbean Cyberculture*, 130.

13. Best, 103.

14. Best, 103.

15. Lowe, *Intimacies of Four Continents*, 24.

16. Khan, *Callaloo Nation*, 13.

17. Ahyoung, "Soca Fever," 99.

18. This excerpted passage can be found at 2:40 in Gentle Benjamin and G.B.T.V. CultureShare Archives, "G.B.T.V. CultureShare ARCHIVES 1997: RAS SHORTY I & AVION BLACKMAN," YouTube video, April 29, 2012, https://www.youtube.com/watch?v=gpLUUlX39ZE.

19. Manuel, Largey, and Bilby, *Caribbean Currents*, 287.

20. Dudley, "Judging 'by the Beat.'"

21. See full interview at Gentle Benjamin and G.B.T.V. CultureShare Archives, "G.B.T.V. CultureShare ARCHIVES 1995: RAS SHORTY I 'Interview' Seg#10f 2," YouTube video, October 2, 2010, https://www.youtube.com/watch?v=xoYM97IqrNk&t=7s.

22. Stanley Benoit, phone interview by Jessica Swanston Baker, April 8, 2017. "Bouillon" and "pilau" refer to two prevalent one-pot dishes with many variations around the Caribbean. For example, bouillon (or bouyon) in Haiti is a meat and vegetable soup; in St. Lucia, it is typically made with red beans and salted pig tails (a common combination in other island cuisines). Pilau (or pelau) (etymologically related to Persian "polow" and the Anglicized term "pilaf") is a rice

dish that includes peas or beans and an assortment of proteins. In Trinidad it is typically made with chicken or beef; in Guyana and St. Kitts it may have pig tails or tripe and is more commonly called "cook-up."

23. Benoit interview.

24. According to Benoit, Anguilla's KoolFm is notable in this regard in being one of the first convergences of new media within the Leeward Islands.

25. Leonard "Jam Crew" Lestrade, Skype interview by Jessica Swanston Baker, December 5, 2014.

26. LargeRadio, "About Us," Small Island Massive, 2014, www.smallislandmassive.com.

27. Benoit interview.

28. Crichlow and Northover, *Globalization and the Post-Creole Imagination*, 184.

29. The especially ephemeral nature of the internet as a nonarchive means that the thousands of pages of archived forum discussions between the "More Than Four Missionaries" and "Trickdadians" factions, hosted at IslandMix.com, are mostly lost.

30. "Nick 'Daddy' Friday: The Life of a Legend," PBS, https://www.pbs.org/video/showtime -trevor-nick-daddy-friday-the-life-of-a-legend-pfjbhl/.

31. He changed his handle to "SocaPro" but is still a vehement defender of Trinidadian cultural property from his home in the United Kingdom. In October 2020, he posted a long Twitter thread in response to floating "misinformation" that suggested that Lord Shorty might have been influenced by his visit to Dominica in 1975. While a Twitter thread may seem trivial, there are so few resources on small-island music that much of the work on these genres utilizes minor texts as sources.

32. *SKNVibes*, "Where Are They Now?"

33. Kamugisha, *Beyond Coloniality*, 55.

34. Nero, *Under de Breadfruit Tree*, 76.

35. Lincoln Swanston and Yvette Swanston, personal interview by Jessica Swanston Baker, June 2021.

36. Lyrics from author's recollection and from video now removed from YouTube, formerly accessible at " 'Play You Mas,' " https://www.youtube.com/watch?v=EYsz5idtZts.

37. The mistaken belief that it was the famous Trinidadian Sundar Popo (Bahora) who won the 1971 road march competition is cited, for example, in Thompson, *Reggae & Caribbean Music*, 218.

38. *SKNVibes*, "Where Are They Now?"

39. John Engerman, Zoom interview with the author, March 3, 2021.

40. Burning Flames, "No Rock and Roll," *Light Years Ahead*, produced at Sammy Fields PMR Studio, Demarest, New Jersey, 1989.

41. Antigua's Carnival Festivals Commission, "Burning Flames Jam Pond 1988," YouTube video, July 18, 2018, https://www.youtube.com/watch?v=5j14aL7NKTo&feature=youtu.be.

42. Jordan Levin, "Flames and Fortune," *Miami New Times*, January 15, 1992, https://www .miaminewtimes.com/music/flames-and-fortune-6365002.

43. Levin, "Flames and Fortune."

44. Guinness, Skull, and Carib are types of beer. The Earth Tones Brass, *Tempo*, YouTube video, https://www.youtube.com/watch?v=Ieu2YLuLMe4.

45. Burke, " 'Where Calypso Gone?' "

46. Clarence "Oungku" Edwards, phone interview by Jessica Swanston Baker, May 8, 2021.

47. Edwards interview.

48. While usually operated by keyboardists, for 17 Plus it was the drummer who operated the riddim box.

49. Leonard "Jam Crew" Lestrade, Skype interview by Jessica Swanston Baker, December 5, 2014.

50. In some cases, bands released the catchy chant portion of the song to the public via the radio or in live performances before the entirety of the song was written.

51. This chant, sung by 14 Minus and the crowd, may be heard in the clip excerpt that starts at 1:50 in this abridged video of 14 Minus playing at J'ouvert during carnival in 1993–1994: DaddyPlay SKN, "14 Minus Jouvert Clip 1993," YouTube video, June 15, 2020, https://www.you tube.com/watch?v=BcM9KcXgVfo. The full eighty-minute version shows the same scene starting at 1:00:44: DaddyPlay SKN, "14 MINUS 'Live' 1993–1994, by DaddyPlay," YouTube video, August 28, 2013, https://www.youtube.com/watch?v=SUMglHP7RPE.

52. An Antiguan communications professional interviewed the WCK singer at a reunion performance of the original "fantastic four" Burning Flames (Onyan, Oungku, Krokus, and Fox), on July 17, 2015, in St. John's, Antigua. The reunion included tribute performances from eleven other bands, some local, some celebrity, including WCK from Dominica, billed as "pioneers of Bouyon Music." Cris Warner, "Burning Flames Reunion-WCK Interview," YouTube video, July 22, 2015, https://www.youtube.com/watch?v=sNOGxXAX5NM. See also Bandsmen United, "Event: The Incredible Fantastic Burning Flames Reunion," Facebook, July 17, 2015, https://fb .me/e/5aJEBKENR.

53. WCK, "Culture Shock"; M.O.S.S. International, *Jambalesse Rule*.

54. Arrow, *Hot Hot Hot*.

55. Interview with Tamboura Kitwana, of the Silver Rhythm Combo, by St. Kitts–Nevis National Archives, *St. Kitts–Nevis National Archives*, https://www.nationalarchives.gov.kn/670.

56. Banyan Archive, "Warré Playing."

57. Interviewer Ken Corsbie asked Arrow about his career, soca, dance lyrics, and the future of soca. See Banyan Archive.

58. Banyan Archive.

59. This song was originally recorded by Los Gatos Bravos, a punta band from Honduras, in 1987. Vargas, "El sambunango teleño."

60. Glissant, *Poetics of Relation*, 144.

61. Wiedorn, *Think Like an Archipelago*, 11.

62. Wiedorn, 34.

63. Bonnet, *Order of Sounds*, 71, 105.

64. This understanding of listening is echoed in Jennifer Lynn Stoever's notion of the listening ear, which she describes as "a historical aggregate of normative American listening practices" that " gives a name to listening's epistemological function as a modality of racial discernment" Stoever, *Sonic Color Line*, 3.

65. Bonnet, *Order of Sounds*, 255.

66. Walser, "Out of Notes," 359.

67. Ochoa Gautier, *Aurality*, 34; Stoever, *Sonic Color Line*, 13.

68. Bonnet, *Order of Sounds*, 249.

69. Bonnet, 252.

70. Benítez-Rojo, *Repeating Island*, 3.

Conclusion

1. Baker, "Black Like Me."
2. Nattoo, "Byron Messia on 'Talibans.'"
3. Nattoo.
4. Jam Crew phone interview, July 10, 2023.
5. Jam Crew interview.

Bibliography

Abrahams, Roger D. "A Performance-Centred Approach to Gossip." *Man* 5, no. 2 (June 1970): 290–301. https://doi.org/10.2307/2799654.

———. "Joking: The Training of the Man-of-Words in 'Talking Broad.'" In *Perspectives on the Caribbean: A Reader in Culture, History, and Representation*, edited by Philip W. Scher, 115–28. Chichester, UK: John Wiley & Sons, 2010.

———. *The Man-of-Words in the West Indies: Performance and the Emergence of Creole Culture.* Baltimore: Johns Hopkins University Press, 1983.

———. *Nevis & St. Kitts: Tea Meetings, Christmas Sports, & the Moonlight Night.* Liner notes to Rounder Records 2002 CD. https://www.culturalequity.org/sites/default/files/2018-08/Nevis%20notes.pdf.

———. "Public Drama and Common Values on Two Caribbean Islands." In *Anthropological Realities: Readings in the Science of Culture*, edited by Jeanne Guillemin, 71–97. New Brunswick, NJ: Transaction Publishers, 1981.

———. "Questions of Criolian Contagion." *Journal of American Folklore* 116, no. 459 (2003): 73–87. https://doi.org/10.2307/4137943.

Abrahams, Roger D., and Richard Bauman. "Sense and Nonsense in St. Vincent: Speech Behavior and Decorum in a Caribbean Community." *American Anthropologist* 73, no. 3 (June 1971): 762–72. https://doi.org/10.1525/aa.1971.73.3.02a00160.

Acevedo-Yates, Carla. *Forecast Form: Art in the Caribbean Diaspora, 1990s–Today.* Chicago: Museum of Contemporary Art Chicago, 2022.

Ahyoung, Selwyn Ellore. "Soca Fever: Change in the Calypso Music Tradition of Trinidad and Tobago, 1970–1980." Master's thesis, Indiana University, 1981.

Alexander, M. Jacqui. *Pedagogies of Crossing: Meditations on Feminism, Sexual Politics, Memory, and the Sacred.* Durham, NC: Duke University Press, 2005.

Aniyar, Daniel Castro, "La fiesta de 'La champeta.'" https://www.heterogenesis.com/Heterogenesis-2/Textos/hcas/H29/Castro.html.

Anthony, Hermia Eddris Morton. "Decolonizing Narratives: Kittitian Women, Knowledge Production and Protest." PhD diss., University of Toronto, 2018. https://tspace.library.utoronto.ca/bitstream/1807/82940/1/Morton_Hermia_E_201803_PhD_thesis.pdf.

Archibald, Washington. *The Legacy of Dr. Simeon Daniel*. Basseterre, St. Kitts: St. Kitts Business College, 2010.

———. "More Ole Time Christmas." In *The History of St. Kitts and Nevis*, edited by Mosi Mandisa and Simba Warner. Bloomington, IN: Xlibris, 2010. Kindle.

Arrow. *Hot Hot Hot*. Barbados: RH Productions B 877-A, 1982. Vinyl seven-inch. https://www.discogs.com/release/7499677-Arrow-Hot-Hot-Hot.

Associated Press. "Crime, Corruption, Drugs: St. Kitts Ends Lively Election Campaign." March 5, 2000. https://www.latinamericanstudies.org/caribbean/campaign.htm.

Association for Cultural Equity. "'Our Mission': About the Association for Cultural Equity." http://www.culturalequity.org/ace/ce_ace_index.php.

Averill, Gage. Review of *The 1962 Field Recordings, 1997–2002*, by Alan Lomax. *Ethnomusicology* 47, no. 2 (2003): 272–78.

Baker, Jessica Swanston. "Black Like Me: Caribbean Tourism and the St. Kitts Music Festival." *Ethnomusicology* 60, no. 2 (2016): 263–78. https://doi.org/10.5406/ethnomusicology.60.2.0263.

———. "Small Islands, Large Radio." In *Contemporary Archipelagic Thinking: Towards New Comparative Methodologies and Disciplinary Formations*, edited by Yolanda Martínez-San Miguel and Michelle Stephens, 383–402. Lanham, MD: Rowman & Littlefield, 2020.

———. "Sugar, Sound, Speed: 'Area Code 869' and Sonic Fiction." *Representations* 154, no. 1 (2021): 23–34. https://doi.org/10.1525/rep.2021.154.3.23.

Banyan Archive. "Warré Playing and Interview with Arrow." Alexander Street, 1990. https://video.alexanderstreet.com/watch/warre-playing-and-interview-with-arrow-1.

Beckles, Hilary McD. "A 'Riotous and Unruly Lot': Irish Indentured Servants and Freemen in the English West Indies, 1644–1713." *William and Mary Quarterly* 47, no. 4 (1990): 503–22. https://doi.org/10.2307/2937974.

Benitez-Rojo, Antonio. *The Repeating Island: The Caribbean and the Postmodern Perspective*. Durham, NC: Duke University Press, 1996.

Bernabé, Jean, Patrick Chamoiseau, Raphaël Confiant, and Mohamed Bouya Taleb-Khyar. *Éloge de la créolité*. Paris: Gallimard, 1993.

Best, Curwen. *Culture @ the Cutting Edge: Tracking Caribbean Popular Music*. Kingston, Jamaica: University of West Indies Press, 2004.

———. *The Politics of Caribbean Cyberculture*. New York: Springer, 2008.

Birenbaum Quintero, Michael. "Exchange, Materiality and Aesthetics in Colombian Champeta." *Ethnomusicology Forum* 27, no. 1 (2018): 3–24. https://doi.org/10.1080/17411912.2018.1454842.

Bonnet, Francois J. *The Order of Sounds: A Sonorous Archipelago*. Cambridge, MA: MIT Press, 2016.

Brathwaite, Edward Kamau. "Caribbean Man in Space and Time." *Small Axe: A Caribbean Journal of Criticism* 25, no. 3 (2021): 90–104.

———. "World Order Models—A Caribbean Perspective." *Caribbean Quarterly* 31, no. 1 (1985): 53–63. https://doi.org/10.1080/00086495.1985.11672063.

Brathwaite, E. Kamau, and Nathaniel Mackey. *ConVERSations with Nathaniel Mackey*. New York: We Press, 1999.

Britton, Celia M. "Globalization and Political Action in the Work of Edouard Glissant." *Small Axe: A Caribbean Journal of Criticism* 13, no. 3 (2009): 1–11. https://doi.org/10.1215/07990537-2009-022.

Browne, Whitman T. *From Commoner to King: Robert L. Bradshaw, Crusader for Dignity and Justice in the Caribbean*. Lanham, MD: University Press of America, 1992.

Bryant, Melissa. "Nine Locals Honoured for Service at Investiture Ceremony." *SKNVibes*, July 28, 2009. https://www.sknvibes.com/news/newsdetails.cfm/10641.

Burke, Kevin. "'Where Calypso Gone?' Independence, Globalisation, and the Troubled State of Trinidad's National Music." *Caribbean Quarterly* 66, no. 1 (2020): 29–49. https://doi.org/10.1080/00086495.2020.1722372.

Burning Flames. "Workey Workey." *Me Na Freard*. Antigua and Barbuda: Burning Flames Music LP BF 0006, 1989. LP.

———. "Workey Workey." *Workey Workey*. Colombia: Codiscos LP 2D5 21411, 1990. LP.

———. "Workey Workey (Remix)." *Workey Workey*. Colombia: Codiscos LP 2D5 21411, 1990. LP.

Camal, Jérôme. *Creolized Aurality: Guadeloupean Gwoka and Postcolonial Politics*. University of Chicago Press, 2019.

Campt, Tina. *Listening to Images*. Durham, NC: Duke University Press Books, 2017.

Carlton, Michael. "The Relaxed Pace of St. Kitts Is Beginning to Pick Up." *Boston Globe*, November 14, 1982.

Carr, Stanley. "Practical Traveler: Getting to Those Out-of-the-Way Islands." *New York Times*, October 16, 1983. https://www.nytimes.com/1983/10/16/travel/practical-traveler-getting-to-those-out-of-the-way-islands.html.

Cooper, Carolyn. *Noises in the Blood: Orality, Gender, and the "Vulgar" Body of Jamaican Popular Culture*. Durham, NC: Duke University Press, 1995.

Cozart Riggio, Milla. *Carnival: Culture in Action—The Trinidad Experience*. London: Routledge, 2004.

Cramer-Armony, Jacqueline. "St. Kitts Mass and the Spirit of Christmas." St. Kitts Heritage. https://www.stkittsheritage.com. Accessed April 8, 2015.

Cramer-Armony, Jacqueline, and Joan Robinson. "St. Kitts and Nevis." In *Music in Latin America and the Caribbean: An Encyclopedic History*. Vol. 2, *Performing the Caribbean Experience*, edited by Malena Kuss, 414. Austin: University of Texas Press, 2007.

Crawford, Kate. "Listening as Participation: Social Media and Metaphors of Hearing Online." In *The Good, the Bad and the Challenging: The User and the Future of Information and Communication Technologies, COST 298 Conference*. Copenhagen: COST, 2009.

Crichlow, Michaeline A., and Patricia Northover. *Globalization and the Post-Creole Imagination: Notes on Fleeing the Plantation*. Durham, NC: Duke University Press, 2009.

Crooks, Natasha, Barbara King, Geri Donenberg, and Jessica McDermott Sales. "Growing Up Too 'Fast': Black Girls' Sexual Development. *Sex Roles* 89 (2023): 135–54.

Cunin, Elisabeth. "De Kinshasa a Cartagena, pasando por París: Itinerarios de una 'música negra,' la champeta." *Revista Aguaita*, nos. 15–16 (2007): 176–92. https://core.ac.uk/download/pdf/47107176.pdf.

Curtis, Debra. *Pleasures and Perils: Girls' Sexuality in a Caribbean Consumer Culture*. New Brunswick, NJ: Rutgers University Press, 2009.

Cyrus, Alston "Beckett." "Coming High." Arranged by Frankie McIntosh. *Disco Calypso*. Casablanca LP NBLP 7059-V, 1977. LP.

Daniel, Yvonne. *Rumba: Dance and Social Change in Contemporary Cuba*. Indianapolis: Indiana University Press, 1995.

Dator, James. "Frank Travels: Space, Power and Slave Mobility in the British Leeward Islands, c. 1700–1730." *Slavery & Abolition* 36, no. 2 (2014): 335–59. https://doi.org/10.1080/0144039x.2014.937640.

Dayan, Joan. *Haiti, History, and the Gods*. Berkeley: University of California Press, 1998.

DeLoughrey, Elizabeth. "Island Ecologies and Caribbean Literatures." *Tijdschrift Voor Econo-mische en Sociale Geografie* 95, no. 3 (2004): 298–310. https://doi.org/10.1111/j.1467-9663 .2004.00309.x.

Devonish, Hubert. "'Wine', Women and Song: The More Things Change . . ." *Sexuality & Culture* 15 (2011): 332–44.

Doggett, Peter. *Electric Shock: From the Gramophone to the iPhone—125 Years of Pop Music*. New York: Random House, 2015.

Douglas, Mary. *Implicit Meanings: Selected Essays in Anthropology*. 2nd ed. London: Routledge, 1999.

Duclos, Vincent, Tomás Sánchez Criado, and Vinh-Kim Nguyen. "Speed: An Introduction." *Cultural Anthropology* 32, no. 1 (2017): 1–11. https://doi.org/10.14506/ca32.1.01.

Dudley, Shannon. "Judging 'by the Beat': Calypso versus Soca." *Ethnomusicology* 40, no. 2 (1996): 269–98. https://doi.org/10.2307/852062.

Edmondson, Belinda. *Caribbean Middlebrow: Leisure Culture and the Middle Class*. Ithaca, NY: Cornell University Press, 2009.

———. "Making the Case for Middlebrow Culture." *Journal of Transnational American Studies* 2, no. 1 (2010): 1–23. https://doi.org/10.5070/t821006984.

———. "Public Spectacles: Caribbean Women and the Politics of Public Performance." *Small Axe: A Caribbean Journal of Criticism* 7, no. 1 (2003): 1–16. https://doi.org/10.1215/-7-1-1.

Eshun, Kodwo. "Swarm 3: Abducted by Audio." *Abstract Culture* (1998): http://www.ccru.net /swarm3/3_abducted.htm.

Esteva, Gustavo. "Development." In *The Development Dictionary: A Guide to Knowledge as Power*, edited by Wolfgang Sachs, 6–25. New York: Zed Books, 2010.

Fabian, Johannes. *Time and the Other: How Anthropology Makes Its Object*. New York: Colum-bia University Press, 2014. https://www.hf.uio.no/ikos/english/research/news-and-events /events/phd/2020/fabian-time-and-the-other-%282014%29-extract.pdf.

Fergus, Howard A. *Montserrat: History of a Caribbean Colony*. London: Macmillan Caribbean, 1994.

Ferrándiz, Francisco. "Open Veins: Spirits of Violence and Grief in Venezuela." *Ethnography* 10, no. 1 (2009): 39–61. https://doi.org/10.1177/1466138108094977.

Fink, Robert. "Goal-Directed Soul? Analyzing Rhythmic Teleology in African American Popu-lar Music." *Journal of the American Musicological Society* 64, no. 1 (2011): 179–238. https://doi .org/10.1525/jams.2011.64.1.179.

France, Joseph N. Editorial. *Union Messenger*. December 12, 1956.

Freeman, Carla. "Designing Women: Corporate Discipline and Barbados's Off-Shore Pink Collar Sector." *Cultural Anthropology* 8, no. 2 (1993): 169–86. https://doi.org/10.1525/can.1993.8.2 .02a00030.

———. *High Tech and High Heels in the Global Economy: Women, Work, and Pink-Collar Identi-ties in the Caribbean*. Durham, NC: Duke University Press Books, 2000.

———. "Neo-Liberalism, Respectability, and the Romance of Flexibility in Barbados." Working Paper No. 40, Center for Myth and Ritual in American Life (MARIAL), Emory University, Atlanta, April 2005.

Garvey, Marcus. *The Marcus Garvey and Universal Negro Improvement Association Papers*. Vol. 13, *The Caribbean Diaspora, 1921–1922*. Edited by Robert A. Hill, John Dixon, Mariela Haro Rodriguez, and Anthony Yuen. Durham, NC: Duke University Press, 2016.

Gautier, Ana María Ochoa. *Aurality: Listening and Knowledge in Nineteenth-Century Colombia*. Durham, NC: Duke University Press, 2015.

Geertz, Clifford. *The Interpretation of Cultures*. New York: Basic Books, 1973.

George, Iwer. "Let Me See Yuh Hand." *Soca Compilations 2*. United Kingdom: JW Productions, 2001. CD.

Geringer, John M., Clifford K. Madsen, Rebecca B. MacLeod, and Kevin Droe. "The Effect of Articulation Style on Perception of Modulated Tempo." *Journal of Research in Music Education* 54, no. 4 (2006): 324–36. https://doi.org/10.2307/4139754.

Gilbert, Helen, ed. *Postcolonial Plays: An Anthology*. New York: Routledge, 2013.

Gillis, John. *Islands of the Mind: How the Human Imagination Created the Atlantic World*. New York: Palgrave Macmillan, 2004.

Gilroy, Paul. *The Black Atlantic: Modernity and Double Consciousness*. Cambridge, MA: Harvard University Press, 1993.

———. *There Ain't No Black in the Union Jack*. New York: Routledge, 2013.

Glezos, Simon. *The Politics of Speed: Capitalism, the State and War in an Accelerating World*. New York: Routledge, 2013.

———. *Speed and Micropolitics: Bodies, Minds, and Perceptions in an Accelerating World*. New York: Routledge, 2020.

———. "The Ticking Bomb: Speed, Democracy and the Politics of the Future." In *The Politics of Speed: Capitalism, the State and War in an Accelerating World*, 10–42. New York: Routledge, 2013.

———. "The Ticking Bomb: Speed, Liberalism and Ressentiment against the Future." *Contemporary Political Theory* 10, no. 2 (2011): 147–65. https://doi.org/10.1057/cpt.2010.6.

Glissant, Édouard. *Poetics of Relation*. Ann Arbor: University of Michigan Press, 1997.

———. *Traité du tout-monde*. Paris: Gallimard, 1997.

Goldie, Matthew Boyd. "Island Theory—The Antipodes." In *Islanded Identities: Constructions of Postcolonial Cultural Insularity*, edited by Maeve McCusker and Anthony Soares, 1–40. Amsterdam: Rodopi, 2011.

Goodman, Steve. *Sonic Warfare: Sound, Affect, and the Ecology of Fear*. Cambridge, MA: MIT Press, 2012.

Goveia, Elsa V. *Slave Society in the British Leeward Islands at the End of the Eighteenth Century*. New Haven, CT: Yale University Press, 1965.

Guilbault, Jocelyne. "Interpreting World Music: A Challenge in Theory and Practice." *Popular Music* 16, no. 1 (1997): 31–44. https://doi.org/10.1017/S0261143000000684.

———. "The Politics of Labelling Popular Musics in English Caribbean." *TRANS Revista Transcultural de Música—Transcultural Music Review*, no. 3 (1997). https://doi.org/https://www.sibe trans.com/trans/article/265/the-politics-of-labelling-popular-musics-in-english-caribbean.

Guilbault, Jocelyne, Gage Averill, Édouard Benoit, and Gregory Rabess. *Zouk: World Music in the West Indies*. Chicago: University of Chicago Press, 1993.

Guilbault, Jocelyne, and Timothy Rommen. "Introduction: The Political Economy of Music and Sound." In *Sounds of Vacation: Political Economies of Caribbean Tourism*, edited by Jocelyne Guilbault and Timothy Rommen, 9–40. Durham, NC: Duke University Press, 2019.

Haas, Ryan. "Time to 'LIME' at Cable & Wireless." *SKNVibes*, November 3, 2008. https://www .sknvibes.com/news/newsdetails.cfm/7178.

Hall, Douglas. *Five of the Leewards, 1834–1870: The Major Problems of the Post-Emancipation Period in Antigua, Barbuda, Montserrat, Nevis, and St. Kitts*. St. Lawrence, Barbados: Caribbean Universities Press, 1971.

Hall, Stuart. "Cultural Identity and Diaspora." In *Colonial Discourse and Post-Colonial Theory*, edited by Patrick Williams and Laura Chrisman, 404–15. London: Routledge, 2015. http:// dx.doi.org/10.4324/9781315656496-39.

Harewood, Susan. "Listening for Noise: Seeking Disturbing Sounds in Tourist Spaces." In *Sounds of Vacation: Political Economies of Caribbean Tourism*, edited by Jocelyne Guilbault and Timothy Rommen, 107–33. Durham, NC: Duke University Press, 2019.

Hewlett, L. K. "Government Swaps Land for Local Bank Debts." *St. Kitts Nevis Times*, April 27, 2012.

Hintzen, Percy C. "Reproducing Domination Identity and Legitimacy Constructs in the West Indies." *Social Identities* 3, no. 1 (1997): 47–76. https://doi.org/10.1080/13504639752168.

Historic St. Kitts (National Archives, St. Kitts & Nevis). "Our People: Joseph Matthew Sebastian." https://www.historicstkitts.kn/people/joseph-matthew-sebastian.

Hofman, Corinne L., Alistair J. Bright, Arie Boomert, and Sebastiaan Knippenberg. "Island Rhythms: The Web of Social Relationships and Interaction Networks in the Lesser Antillean Archipelago between 400 BC and AD 1492." *Latin American Antiquity* 18, no. 3 (2007): 243–68.

Hubbard, Vincent K. *A History of St. Kitts: The Sweet Trade*. Northampton, MA: Interlink Publishing Group and Macmillan Caribbean, 2002.

Hull, Kareem-Nelson. "Pung Melee." In *The Virgin Islands Dictionary: A Collection of Words and Phrases So You Could Say It Like We*. Bloomington, IN: AuthorHouse, 2018.

IslandMix.com. "Jamband Style Music." June 10, 2005. http://www.islandmix.com/backchat/f16/thought-soca-jamband-style-music-89526/index3.html.

Iyer, Vijay. "Improvisation, Temporality and Embodied Experience." *Journal of Consciousness Studies* 11, nos. 3–4 (2004): 159–73.

James, C. L. R. *Beyond a Boundary*. 1963. Durham, NC: Duke University Press, 2013.

Jones, Adanna Kai. "Practicing Jametteness: The Transmission of 'Bad Behavior' as a Strategy of Survival." In *Carnival Is Woman: Feminism and Performance in Caribbean Mas*, edited by Dwaine Plaza and Frances Henry. Jackson: University Press of Mississippi, 2020.

Jones-Hendrickson, Simon B., and Caribbean Studies Association. "Economic and Political Governance: A New View from St. Kitts and Nevis." Paper prepared for the Twenty-Third Annual Caribbean Studies Association Conference, May 26–30, 1998, St. John's, Antigua: Caribbean Studies Association, 1998.

———. "Strategies for Progress in the Post-Independence Caribbean: A Bradshawian Synthesis." Presidential address at Ninth Annual Caribbean Studies Association Conference, St. Kitts, May 30–June 2, 1984.

Kamugisha, Aaron. *Beyond Coloniality: Citizenship and Freedom in the Caribbean Intellectual Tradition*. Bloomington: Indiana University Press, 2019.

Kassabian, Anahid. "Would You Like Some World Music with Your Latte? Starbucks, Putumayo, and Distributed Tourism." *Twentieth-Century Music* 1, no. 2 (2004): 209–23. https://doi.org/10.1017/s1478572205000125.

Keil, Charles, and Steven Feld. *Music Grooves: Essays and Dialogues*. Tucson, AZ: Fenestra Books, 2005.

Kempadoo, Kamala. *Sexing the Caribbean: Gender, Race and Sexual Labor*. London: Routledge, 2004.

Khan, Aisha. *Callaloo Nation: Metaphors of Race and Religious Identity among South Asians in Trinidad*. Durham, NC: Duke University Press, 2004.

Kincaid, Jamaica. *A Small Place*. New York: Farrar, Straus & Giroux, 2000.

King, Francine. "Marcus Garvey's Views on Fascism as They Relate to the Black Struggle for Equal Rights: An Analysis of Commentaries from the Black Man, 1935–1939." *Proceedings and Papers of the Georgia Association of Historians* 10 (1989): 26–36.

King, Rosamond S. *Island Bodies: Transgressive Sexualities in the Caribbean Imagination*. Gainesville: University Press of Florida, 2014.

Kornbluh, Anna. *The Order of Forms: Realism, Formalism, and Social Space*. Chicago: University of Chicago Press, 2019.

Kubik, Gerhard. "The Phenomenon of Inherent Rhythms in East and Central African Instrumental Music." *African Music: Journal of the International Library of African Music* 3, no. 1 (1962): 33–42.

Kuhn, T. L. "The Effect of Tempo, Meter, and Melodic Complexity on the Perception of Tempo." In *Applications of Research in Music Behavior*, edited by Clifford K. Madsen and Carol A. Prickett, 165–74. Tuscaloosa: University of Alabama Press, 1987.

Kun, Josh. *Audiotopia: Music, Race, and America*. Berkeley: University of California Press, 2005.

Landau, Carolyn, and Janet Topp Fargion. "We're All Archivists Now: Towards a More Equitable Ethnomusicology." *Ethnomusicology Forum* 21, no. 2 (2012): 125–40. https://doi.org/10.1080/17411912.2012.690188.

LargeRadio. "About Us." Small Island Massive, 2014. https://www.largeradio.com.

The Laws of Nevis: From 1681 to 1861. London: n.p., 1862.

Levin, Jordan. "Flames and Fortune." *Miami New Times*, January 15, 1992. https://www.miaminewtimes.com/music/flames-and-fortune-6365002.

Levine, Caroline. *Forms: Whole, Rhythm, Hierarchy, Network*. Princeton, NJ: Princeton University Press, 2015.

Lewis, Martin W., and Kären Wigen. *The Myth of Continents: A Critique of Metageography*. Berkeley: University of California Press, 1997.

Ligon, Richard *A True and Exact History of the Island of Barbados. History of the Island of Barbados*. London: Printed for Humphrey Moseley, 1657.

"LIME/Flow Merger Complete." *Jamaica Observer*, March 31, 2015. https://www.jamaicaobserver.com/news/cwc-flow-merger-complete.

Liverpool, Hollis "Mighty Chalkdust". "Calypso: Speaking Truth to Power, 1962–2012: Understanding a Society in Transition." In *Trinidad & Tobago: 50 Years of Independence*, 90–95. London: First Publications, 2021. https://firstforum.org/wp-content/uploads/2021/05/Publication_00657.pdf.

Lomax, Alan, ed. "Masquerade Walking Piece." Performed by Daniel Hobson, fife; David Freeman, second fife; Ernest Archibald, kettle drum; and Alfredo Morton, bass drum. Field recording by Alan Lomax in collaboration with Roger Abrahams, assisted by Antoinette Marchand. Recorded in Gingerland, Nevis, July 11, 1962. *Nevis & St. Kitts: Tea Meetings, Christmas Sports, & the Moonlight Night*. Alan Lomax Collection: The 1962 Recordings, Rounder Records, 2002. CD. Available at https://music.apple.com/gh/album/masquerade-walking-piece/1466258971?i=1466260056.

Lorde, Audre. "Of Generators and Survival—Hugo Letter." *Callaloo* 14, no. 1 (1991): 72–82. https://doi.org/10.2307/2931437.

Lowe, Lisa. *The Intimacies of Four Continents*. Durham, NC: Duke University Press, 2015.

Lucas, Elwin "Daddy Bougna". *Crowd Checking!* album cover. Small Axe Band. Old Road, St. Kitts: Tydal Wave Recording Studio, 2000. CD.

Maldonado-Torres, Nelson. "Post-Continental Philosophy: Its Definition, Contours, and Fundamental Sources." *Worlds and Knowledges Otherwise* 1, no. 3 (2006): 1–27. https://globalstudies.trinity.duke.edu/sites/globalstudies.trinity.duke.edu/files/file-attachments/v1d3_NMaldonado-Torres.pdf.

———. "Thinking through the Decolonial Turn: Post-Continental Interventions in Theory, Philosophy, and Critique—An Introduction." *Transmodernity: Journal of Peripheral Cultural Production of the Luso-Hispanic World* 1, no. 2 (2011): 1–15. https://doi.org/10.5070/t412011805.

Mandelbrot, Benoit B. *The fractal geometry of nature*. Vol. 1. New York: WH freeman, 1982.

Mandisa, Mosi, and Simba Warner, eds. *The History of St. Kitts & Nevis Carnival*. Bloomington, IN: Xlibris, 2010. Kindle.

Mandisa, Mosi, and Simba Warner. "Profile of Mick Stokes." In *The History of St. Kitts and Nevis Carnival*, edited by Mosi Mandisa and Simba Warner. Bloomington, IN: Xlibris, 2010. Kindle.

Manuel, Peter, Kenneth Bilby, and Michael Largey. *Caribbean Currents: Caribbean Music from Rumba to Reggae*. Philadelphia: Temple University Press, 2006.

Manuel, Peter, and Wayne Marshall. "The Riddim Method: Aesthetics, Practice, and Ownership in Jamaican Dancehall." *Popular Music* 25, no. 3 (2006): 447–70. https://doi.org/10.1017/s0261143006000997.

Marron, D. "Éléments pour une approche de l'archipel lyrique contemporain." Talk delivered at Literature and Music study day, École normale supérieur, Paris, March 31, 2009.

Marthol, Elise Sebastian. *Meet My Father: A Short Walk through the Life of Joseph Matthew Sebastian*. Basseterre, St. Kitts: self-published, 1993.

Martínez Miranda, Luis Gerardo. "La champeta: Una forma de resistencia palenquera a las dinámicas de exclusión de las élites 'blancas' de Cartagena y Barranquilla entre 1960 y 2000." *Boletín de Antropología* 25, no. 42 (2012): 150–74. https://doi.org/10.17533/udea.boan.11229.

Matt, Ellie. "Exclusive Interview by Lloyd Lazar with King Ellie Matt." SKNVibes. https://www.sknvibes.com/islandfacts/sitepage.cfm?p=167.

McCall, Terres. "Condor Calls for Collaboration in Fighting Crime." *SKNVibes*, May 3, 2010. https://www.sknvibes.com/news/newsdetails.cfm/14021.

McCusker, Maeve, and Anthony Soares, eds. *Islanded Identities: Constructions of Postcolonial Cultural Insularity*. Amsterdam: Rodopi, 2011.

McElroy, Jerome L. "Managing Sustainable Tourism in the Small Island Caribbean." Department of Business and Economics, St. Mary's College, Notre Dame, IN, September 2000. https://www.yumpu.com/en/document/read/46576440/managing-sustainable-tourism-in-the-small-island-caribbean.

McGregory, Jerrilyn. *One Grand Noise: Boxing Day in the Anglicized Caribbean World*. Jackson: University Press of Mississippi, 2021.

McKittrick, Katherine. *Dear Science and Other Stories*. Durham, NC: Duke University Press, 2020.

Meeks, Brian. "The Political Moment in Jamaica: The Dimensions of Hegemonic Dissolution." In *Radical Caribbean: From Black Power to Abu Bakr*, 124–43. Mona, Jamaica: University of the West Indies Press, 1996.

Miller, Rebecca S. *Carriacou String Band Serenade: Performing Identity in the Eastern Caribbean*. Middletown, CT: Wesleyan University Press, 2007.

Millington, Peter, and Caspar James. "Mummies and Masquerades: English and Caribbean Connections." Paper presented to accompany videos of mummies and related Christmas sports of St. Kitts and Nevis, at Bath International Mummers' Unconvention Symposium, Bath, United Kingdom, November 18, 2011. http://www.mastermummers.org/unconvention2011/Mummies%20and%20Masquerades%202012-05-06.pdf.

Mills, Frank L., Simon B. Jones-Hendrickson, and Bertram Eugene. *Christmas Sports in St. Kitts–Nevis: Our Neglected Cultural Tradition*. US Virgin Islands: Self-published, 1984.

Mills, Precious. "Zack, Doctor of Culture, Ready to Make His Comeback." *Labour Spokes-man*, September 7, 2018. http://thelabourspokesman.com/zack-the-doctor-of-cultureready-to-make-his-comeback/.

Mintz, Sidney W. *Sweetness and Power: The Place of Sugar in Modern History*. New York: Penguin Books, 1986.

Moore, Lee Llewellyn, and Dawud Byron. *Interviews with Lee L. Moore: Interviews, February 28–June 20, 1987, Basseterre, St. Kitts*. Frederiksted, Virgin Islands: Eastern Caribbean Institute, 1988.

Morales Espinosa, Reiner. "Música y fiesta: Un análisis histórico del festival de música del Caribe: Cartagena 1982–1996." Graduate thesis, Universidad de Cartagena, 2015. https://repositorio.unicartagena.edu.co/handle/11227/1695.

M.O.S.S. International. *Jambalesse Rule*. Barbados, 1991. LP.

Moten, Fred. *Black and Blur*. Durham, NC: Duke University Press, 2017.

Murray-Román, Jeannine. "Rereading the Diminutive: Caribbean Chaos Theory in Antonio Benítez-Rojo, Edouard Glissant, and Wilson Harris." *Small Axe* 19 (2015): 20–36. https://doi.org/10.1215/07990537-2873323

Nandy, Ashis. *The Tao of Cricket: On Games of Destiny and the Destiny of Games*. New York: Oxford University Press, 2000.

Nattoo, Michael. "Byron Messia on 'Talibans' and His Meteoric Rise in Music." *Clash*, May 22, 2023. https://www.clashmusic.com/features/building-a-new-genre-byron-messia-interviewed/.

Nero, Elston St. Clair (Ellie Matt). *Under de Breadfruit Tree: An Autobiography*. Self-published, 2021.

Nicholls, Robert Wyndham, and John Nunley. *The Jumbies' Playing Ground: Old World Influences on Afro-Creole Masquerades in the Eastern Caribbean*. Jackson: University Press of Mississippi, 2012.

Nu Vybes Band. "Tempo (Of My Life)." *Higher Ground*. Sandy Point, St. Kitts: 1998–1999. CD.

"Nu-Vybes Band Launches First Music Video." *D'Soca Corner Archives* (blog), July 4, 2006. https://www.trinijunglejuice.com/socacorner06.html#nuvybes_musicvideo.

O'Flaherty, V. B. "Overcoming Anonymity: Kittitians and Their Archives." In *Community Archives: The Shaping of Memory*, edited by J. A. Bastian and B. Alexander, 221–34. New York: Routledge, 2009.

Oliver, M. Cynthia. *Queen of the Virgins: Queen Shows, the Popular Women's Theatre of the US Virgin Islands*. Jackson: University Press of Mississippi, 2003.

Olwig, Karen Fog. *Caribbean Journeys*. Durham, NC: Duke University Press, 2007.

———. "Cultural Complexity after Freedom: Nevis and Beyond." In *Small Islands, Large Questions: Society, Culture and Resistance in the Post-Emancipation Caribbean*, edited by Karen Fog Olwig, 100–122. New York: Routledge, 2014.

———. *Global Culture, Island Identity: Continuity and Change in the Afro-Caribbean Community of Nevis*. New York: Routledge, 2005.

Pacini Hernández, Deborah. 1993. "The Picó Phenomenon in Cartagena, Colombia." *América Negra* 6 (1993): 69–115.

Paquette, Robert L., and Stanley L. Engerman. *The Lesser Antilles in the Age of European Expansion*. Gainesville: University Press of Florida, 1996.

Patil, Vrushali. *Negotiating Decolonization in the United Nations: Politics of Space, Identity, and International Community*. New York: Routledge, 2007.

Pencheon, Creighton A. "The Bull Play of St. Kitts: Origin of the 'Cowhead' Figure in Kittitian Folklore." PhD diss., Jamaica School of Art, 1986.

Pinto, Samantha. "'Why Must All Girls Want to Be Flag Women?'" *Meridians* 10, no. 1 (2010): 137–63. https://doi.org/10.2979/mer.2009.10.1.137.

Poon, Auliana. "Innovation and the Future of Caribbean Tourism." *Tourism Management* 5, no. 3 (September 1988): 213–20. https://doi.org/10.1177/004728758902700397.

Puri, Shalini. *The Caribbean Postcolonial: Social Equality, Post/Nationalism, and Cultural Hybridity.* New York: Palgrave Macmillan, 2004.

———. "Race, Rape, and Representation: Indo-Caribbean Women and Cultural Nationalism." *Cultural Critique*, no. 36 (1997): 119–63. https://doi.org/10.2307/1354502.

Regis, Necee. "Taking It Slow and Simple on the Caribbean Island of Nevis." *Washington Post*, October 17, 2013. https://www.washingtonpost.com/lifestyle/travel/taking-it-slow-and-simple-on-the-caribbean-island-of-nevis/2013/10/17/ca6132e8-3201-11e3-9c68-1cf643210300_story.html.

Richardson, Bonham C. *Caribbean Migrants: Environment and Human Survival on St. Kitts and Nevis.* Nashville: University of Tennessee Press, 1983.

Richardson, Xavienne-Roma. "Doin' Me: Millennial Women's Expression of Sexual Agency in St. Kitts." *Journal of Black Sexuality and Relationships* 9, nos. 3–4 (2023): 45–78.

Rivera, Raquel Z., Wayne Marshall, and Deborah Pacini Hernandez. *Reggaeton.* Durham, NC: Duke University Press, 2010.

Roberts, Brian Russell. *Borderwaters: Amid the Archipelagic States of America.* Durham, NC: Duke University Press, 2021.

Roberts, Brian Russell, and Michelle Ann Stephens. Introduction to *Archipelagic American Studies*, edited by Brian Russell Roberts and Michelle Ann Stephens, 1–56. Durham, NC: Duke University Press, 2017.

Robinson, Tracy. "A Loving Freedom: A Caribbean Feminist Ethic." *Small Axe: A Caribbean Journal of Criticism* 11, no. 3 (2007): 118–29. https://doi.org/10.1215/-11-3-118.

Rohlehr, Gordon. *A Scuffling of Islands: Essays on Calypso.* San Juan, Trinidad: Lexicon Trinidad, 2004.

Rommen, Timothy. "It Sounds Better in the Bahamas: Musicians, Management, and Markets in Nassau's All-Inclusive Hotels." In *Sounds of Vacation: Political Economies of Caribbean Tourism*, edited by Jocelyne Guilbault and Timothy Rommen, 41–76. Durham, NC: Duke University Press, 2019.

Sands, Rosita, and Bertram Lyons. "A Working Model for Developing and Sustaining Collaborative Relationships between Archival Repositories in the Caribbean and the United States." *International Association of Sound and Audiovisual Archives*, no. 32 (January 2009): 26–39. https://www.iasa-web.org/sites/default/files/IASA_journal32_part6.pdf.

Santoy. "Brimstone Hill Tragedy." *Caribbean Voyage: Nevis and St. Kitts Tea Meetings, Christmas Sports and The Moonlight Night.* Various artists. Alan Lomax Collection: The 1962 Recordings. Rounder Records 82161-1731-2, 2002. CD.

Sebastian, J. M., ed. "Marcus Garvey Visited St. Kitts." *Union Messenger*, November 3, 1937.

Sethares, William Arthur. *Rhythm and Transforms.* London: Springer Science & Business Media, 2007.

Sharma, Sarah. *In the Meantime: Temporality and Cultural Politics.* Durham, NC: Duke University Press, 2014.

Shaw, Andrea. "The Other Side of the Looking Glass: The Marginalization of Fatness and Blackness in the Construction of Gender Identity." *Social Semiotics* 15, no. 2 (2005): 143–52. https://doi.org/10.1080/10350330500154725.

SKNVibes. "De Sugar Band Lashes Out against Violence Stigma." July 9, 2013. http://m.sknvibes .com/news/newsdetails.cfm/68125.

———. "Friends of Labour—Toronto—Gala Awards Dinner, Dance: Remarks by Dr. the Hon. Timothy Harris, Minister of Foreign Affairs, International Trade, Industry, Commerce and Consumer Affairs at the Friends of Labour-Toronto 7th Gala Awards Dinner and Dance on Saturday, April 26, 2008." April 29, 2008. https://www.sknvibes.com/news/newsdetails .cfm/18613.

———. "Toon Center—Is This What We Encourage?" January 3, 2014. https://www.sknvibes.com /toons/details.cfm?Idz=98.

———. "Toon Center—Parenting Standards out the Window." December 11, 2013. https://www .sknvibes.com/toons/details.cfm?Idz=86.

———. "Where Are They Now? Sundar Popo—the First National Carnival Road March Champ." February 26, 2014. https://www.sknvibes.com/news/newsdetails.cfm/85799.

Small, Christopher. *Musicking: The Meanings of Performing and Listening*. Middletown, CT: Wesleyan University Press, 1998.

Snead, James A. "On Repetition in Black Culture." *Black American Literature Forum* 15, no. 4 (1981): 146–54. https://doi.org/10.2307/2904326.

Steinberg, Philip. *The Social Construction of the Ocean*. Cambridge: Cambridge University Press, 2001.

Stephens, Michelle, and Yolanda Martínez-San Miguel, eds. *Contemporary Archipelagic Thinking: Towards New Comparative Methodologies and Disciplinary Formations*. New York: Rowman & Littlefield, 2020.

Sterne, Jonathan. *The Audible Past: Cultural Origins of Sound Reproduction*. Durham, NC: Duke University Press, 2003.

St. Kitts Nevis Carnival. "Judging Criteria for Road March." http://www.stkittsneviscarnival .com/press-single.asp?conid=4.

St. Kitts and Nevis Nat Com for UNESCO. "Video Documentary on History of SKN Music— UNESCO." September 2014. https://unesco.edu.kn/programme/video-documentary-on-his tory-of-skn-music/.

Stoever, Jennifer Lynn. *The Sonic Color Line: Race and the Cultural Politics of Listening*. New York: NYU Press, 2016.

Streicker, Joel. "Sexuality, Power, and Social Order in Cartagena, Colombia." *Ethnology* 32, no. 4 (1993): 359–74. https://doi.org/10.2307/3773458.

Sutton, Constance R., and Elsa M. Chaney. *Caribbean Life in New York City: Sociocultural Dimensions*. Staten Island, NY: Center for Migration Studies, 1987.

Taylor, Timothy D. *Global Pop: World Music, World Markets*. New York: Routledge, 2014.

Thomas, Deborah A. *Exceptional Violence: Embodied Citizenship in Transnational Jamaica*. Durham, NC: Duke University Press, 2011.

———. *Modern Blackness: Nationalism, Globalization, and the Politics of Culture in Jamaica*. Durham, NC: Duke University Press, 2004.

———. "Time and the Otherwise: Plantations, Garrisons, and Being Human in the Caribbean." *Anthropological Theory* 13, nos. 2–3 (2016): 177–200.

Thompson, Dave. *Reggae & Caribbean Music*. Milwaukee: Hal Leonard Corp., 2002.

Thorndike, Tony. "The Politics of Inadequacy: A Study of the Associated Statehood Negotiations and Constitutional Arrangements for the Eastern Caribbean, 1965–67." *Social and Economic Studies* 28, no. 3 (1979): 597–617.

Tlostanova, Madina Vladimirovna. "Transcultural Tricksters beyond Times and Spaces: Deco-
    lonial Chronotopes and Border Selves." *Language, Philology, Culture* 2, no. 3 (2013): 9–31.
    https://doi.org/http://publishing-vak.ru/file/archive-philology-2013-2/1-tlostanova.pdf.
Treaster, Joseph B. "What's New under the Sun; the Caribbean: In Shape for the Season." *New
    York Times*, November 17, 1985. https://www.nytimes.com/1985/11/17/travel/what-s-new-under
    -the-sun-the-caribbean-in-shape-for-the-season.html.
Vargas, Wilfrido. "El sambunango teleño." *Mas que un loco*. Opa-locka, FL: Sonotone Latin
    Records LP SO-1423, 1988. LP. https://www.discogs.com/release/6128557-Wilfrido-Vargas
    -Mas-Que-Un-Loco.
Vazquez, Alexandra T. *Listening in Detail: Performances of Cuban Music*. Durham, NC: Duke
    University Press, 2013.
Walcott, Derek. "Isla Incognita." 1973. In *Caribbean Literature and the Environment: Between
    Nature and Culture*, edited by Elizabeth M. DeLoughrey, Renée K. Gosson, and George B.
    Handley, 51–57. Charlottesville: University of Virginia Press, 2005.
Walser, Robert. *Out of Notes: Signification, Interpretation, and the Problem of Miles Davis. Musi-
    cal Quarterly* 77, no. 2 (1993): 343–65. https://doi.org/10.1093/mq/77.2.343.
WCK. "Culture Shock." *Culture Shock*. Dominica: Charlo's Productions LP Home 002, 1990. LP.
    https://www.discogs.com/release/7766566-WCK-Culture-Shock.
Webster, Ronald. *Scrap Book of Anguilla's Revolution*. Anguilla: Seabreakers, 1987.
Weintraub, Andrew N. *Dangdut Stories: A Social and Musical History of Indonesia's Most Popular
    Music*. New York: Oxford University Press, 2010.
Whittaker, Steve. "Climate Change Adaptation, Ambient Air Quality and Health in the Eastern
    Caribbean." PhD diss., Yale University, 2018.
Wiedorn, Michael. *Think Like an Archipelago: Paradox in the Work of Édouard Glissant*. Albany:
    State University of New York Press, 2018.
Williams, Brackette F. *Stains on My Name, War in My Veins: Guyana and the Politics of Cultural
    Struggle*. Durham, NC: Duke University Press, 1991.
Williams, Raymond. *Keywords: A Vocabulary of Culture and Study*. New ed. New York: Oxford
    University Press, 2014.
Wilson, Peter J. *Crab Antics: A Caribbean Case Study of the Conflict between Reputation and
    Respectability*. Chicago: Waveland Press, 1995.
Zumaqué, Francisco. "Colombia Caribe." *Colombia Caribe*. Colombia: Discos Fonosema LP-
    714003, 1985. LP.

Index

Page numbers in italics refer to illustrations

www.ingramcontent.com/pod-product-compliance
Lightning Source LLC
Chambersburg PA
CBHW032136020426
42334CB00016B/1192